NOTES TO MY* DAUGHTERS

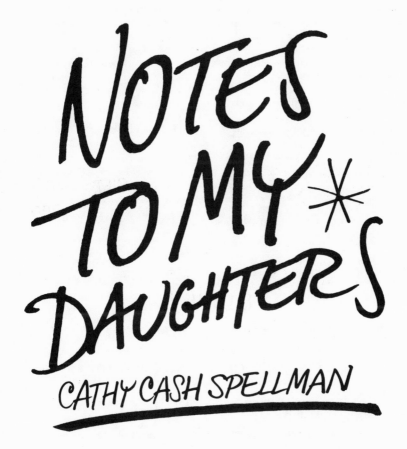

NOTES TO MY DAUGHTERS

CATHY CASH SPELLMAN

Crown Publishers, Inc.
New York

Inquiries should be addressed to Crown Publishers, Inc., One Park Avenue, New York, New York 10016

Printed in the United States of America

Published simultaneously in Canada by General Publishing Company Limited

Library of Congress Cataloging in Publication Data

Spellman, Cathy Cash
   Notes to my daughters.

   1. Mothers and daughters. I. Title.
HQ755.85.S66 1981   306.8'7   80-28465
ISBN: 0-517-543311

Design by Leonard Henderson

10 9 8 7 6 5 4 3 2 1

First Edition

The author gratefully acknowledges permission to use material from the following sources:

Edgar A. Guest, *Collected Verse of Edgar A. Guest.* Copyright 1934. With the permission of Contemporary Books, Inc., Chicago.

John Holt, *Instead of Education.* Copyright © 1976 by John Holt. Reprinted by permission of E.P. Dutton.

Dr. Karl Menninger, *Man Against Himself* by permission of Harcourt Brace Jovanovich.

Edna St. Vincent Millay, *Collected Poems,* Harper and Row. Copyright 1931, © 1958 by Edna St. Vincent Millay. Reprinted by permission of Norma Millay (Ellis), Literary Executor.

Cat Stevens, *"Home in the Sky in the Morning."* Copyright © 1974 Freshwater Music Ltd. All rights reserved. Used by permission of Warner Bros. Music.

To my daughters, Cee Cee and Bronwyn . . .

with infinite love and thanks for being exactly who you are.

"If any wisdom burn in the imperfect page, the praise be thine."

Robert Louis Stevenson

Contents

Acknowledgments   ix
Why This Book . . .   xi
To Begin With . . .   xv

1   THE MIND AND THE EMOTIONS

     Self-Esteem   2
     The Half-Full, Half-Empty Glass   8
     Anger   11
     Pleasure and Happiness   20
     Therapy   26

2   THE SPIRIT

     Religion and the Quest for the Spirit   32
     Death   39
     A Fighting Chance, or, Belief in Miracles   44
     The Will to Live   47

3   THE RELATIONSHIP BETWEEN MEN AND WOMEN

     The Man/Woman Equation   52
     In Defense of Men   57
     Sexuality   61
     Love   68
     Fidelity   74
     Marriage   78
     Divorce   83
     Living Together   89
     Expectations about Love   93

4   ON BEING A WOMAN

     Pregnancy   100
     Birth   105
     Motherhood   109
     What It's Like to Have Children   115

5   THE HEALTH OF THE BODY

     The Mind/Body Connection   122
     How to Help Yourself Be Healthy   131
     Weight   137
     Contraception   142

Abortion   156
Observations about Aging   162

6 HOMESPUN PHILOSOPHY

Generosity   168
Failure   171
Trust and Honor   175
Responsibilities in the Home   180
Graciousness and Good Manners   185
The Art of Being a Friend   188
Help When You Need It   194
Keep on Keepin' On   198
The Unexpected   201
The Task That Couldn't Be Done   206
Being Direct   210

7 LEARNING

Learning vs. Education   216
Poetry   223
Reading   226

8 CHOICES

Sex   230
Drugs   242
Alcohol   249
Peer Pressure   255

9 WORKING

Choosing Your Life's Work   261
On Being a Woman in Business   267

10 JUST MY OPINION

Patriotism   274
The Draft   283
What Is ERA and Do We Need It?   289

11 ENVOY

Looking Backward   300
Envoy   304

Acknowledgments

My grateful and loving thanks to:

Joseph Spellman, my husband, for being the last unicorn in the forest; Catherine and Harry Cash, my parents, for their extraordinary gifts of knowledge and of love; Conny Cash, for being the best and dearest sister the world has ever known; Johanna Lee, for a lifetime of perfect friendship and superb spelling; Patty Kerr, for young wisdom and a loving heart; Carole Baron, for incalculable common sense, inspired editing and encouragement; Connie Clausen, for believing; Helen Gurley Brown, for consummate generosity of spirit; Lenore Hershey, for sound and sage advice, graciously given; Dr. Herry Teltscher, for wisdom and rationality; Susan Dresing, for all the aid and laughter; Alexandra Penney, for enthusiastic encouragement; Suzanne Bersch, for kindhearted organization and fine suggestions; Dena Kaye, for perseverance and loving help; Susan Alfin, for always being willing to Xerox the manuscript "just one more time"; Robynne Froman, for maintaining everyone's sanity in the eye of the hurricane; Dianne Moriarity, for typing above and beyond the call of duty; and Edith Heal, for final typing and an overall eye.

My daughters, Cee Cee and Bronwyn Spellman, and their friends, Lola Goodroe, Gigi Nieves and Wanda Rodriquez, are the young people whose comments appear throughout this book. Their generosity, vision and diligent common sense make me believe that the future is in good and loving hands. For that fact and for their gracious help I am most truly grateful.

Why This Book . . .

When I was twenty-three years old I left a frightening and unhappy marriage, with my two infant daughters tucked resolutely under each arm, and began my epic struggle with the world.

I was hurt and frightened and felt like a failure (my life was obviously not going at all as I had planned), but I was convinced there was no turning back, and therefore forward was the only way to go. At twenty-three, anything seems possible.

Friends have often spoken of my courage in those early, terrible days. While I heartily welcome the compliment, truth is, there were few options. My love for my children, my wounded pride and sheer animal instinct made my choices easy. If we were to live and eat and have a roof over us, there was no choice but to fight back. I was determined we would survive, and so we did.

My relationship with my children was then, and is now, not run-of-the-mill. They had to become more independent than most, because I worked and wasn't always there to help. They grew to be inordinately responsible—they knew when there were housekeeper troubles to be solved, when money was scarce, when trauma loomed or illness threatened, and they tried to behave accordingly. I'm told it is often the case in single-parent homes that children are friends, as much as children, to their parent; this was the case with us. My daughters matured early and made every conceivable effort to help me keep our little ship afloat. As they were nine and ten when I married Joe Spellman, we had a lot of years in which it was just the three of us against the world.

During all of those awful early years of being poor and frightened and often seemingly hopeless, the goal I kept in the back of my harried brain was this: if I could ever get my daughters safely raised to fourteen or fifteen years of age, my battle would be won. Why fourteen or fifteen rather than eleven or seventeen or twenty? I haven't a clue; it really didn't matter. It just seemed to me that by those ages they would no longer be fragile, vulnerable children at the mercy of an uncertain world, but rather very nearly grown-ups, capable of choice and judgment. Safe at last, or well on the way to being so.

About a year and a half ago I realized that those momentous fourteenth and fifteenth birthdays would be coming soon. Bronwyn and Cee Cee were at a most critical moment in time, perched precariously between child and woman. Struggling to separate themselves out from me, to become independent beings, and yet I had so much more that I wanted to tell them. . . .

Not that we weren't talkers, they and I. But their ages seemed an inhibitor to what had always been an open and free dialogue. Suddenly there were uncomfortable subjects like drugs and sex, complicated ones like divorce and abortion. Anyone who has a twelve- or thirteen-year-old knows that most conversations take place as they are headed out the door, or when they are accompanied by a cast of thousands. There were also things that I wanted to pass on as experience, not advice— yet somehow at their ages "advice" is what it inevitably seemed. So I started to write what I really wanted to *say* . . . and a wonderful thing happened. I felt free to ramble as I couldn't do in conversation. And my daughters got into the act.

My notes to them would disappear for a week and turn up with margin notes. Taboo subjects would be digested in writing and then suddenly pop up in conversation. Chapters began being handed to friends, and lists of topics would appear on my desk in varied handwritings.

What I had hit on, it seems, was a means of communicating with youngsters at a tough, tough age for communication. A device to get thoughts across without their seeming to demand a one-to-one instant response. "It's really easier to talk about *anything* since you started writing notes," said one of my children, "because now I pretty much know where you stand on everything." Believe me, the process let me know where they and their friends stand, too. It's been a remarkable education for me.

A friend suggested I pull it all together—she knew I kept everything—and share it with others. I reorganized, expanded and eliminated, but basically what you will read is just as I wrote it for my daughters . . . the kids' comments in the margins are Bronwyn's and Cee Cee's and their friends'. As you'll see, some of the topics (like sex and contraception) evoked considerable response; others (like graciousness and good manners), very little. One way or the other, the very fact that the notes had been written seemed to provoke dialogue between us. I learned a great deal from these young people about communicating—and about everything else!

Because of the purpose for which it was written, this book is a very personal one—*my* thoughts and opinions, *my daughters'* ideas and questions, their friends', too. Unlike Mary Poppins, I am *not* a practically perfect person. I am a woman, a mother, a wife, a daughter, a business person—but most definitely not an expert; and although I'm well aware that my views (and theirs, for that matter) may be vastly different from those of other mothers and daughters whose life experiences have differed from ours, I would like to share them as a catalyst and a methodology. If these chapters do nothing more than provoke honest-to-goodness dialogue between other mothers and daughters, in which they, too, can find out for sure "where each one stands," I shall be elated. One of my friends gave a copy of the manuscript to her teen-ager with a note that said, "I don't agree with some of this material, but I'd really like to hear how *you* feel about it. . . ." Last I heard, they were still talking it all over.

For any mother who may read these pages, it is my earnest hope that even if you disagree violently with my philosophy, it will somehow help *you* to communicate *your own thoughts* and ideas to the daughter you love. For any daughters who may read this book, I hope with all my heart that you will find it a means to help you make this *the last generation* in which mothers and daughters find it hard to be honest friends.

To Bronwyn and Cee Cee from Mom:

To Begin With . . .

I made a list of things I'd like to talk to you about and ran out of paper. These days you are always on the run between school and social life, and slowing down long enough to talk things through, as we did when you were younger, is probably Number 67 on your priority list. So I have another idea.

Whenever anything comes into my head that I want to pass along, I'll write it down. If you feel like writing back or bringing up something on your own, I'll welcome it. If you'd rather wait until the notes are as long as *War and Peace,* that's fine, too. But before you begin reading, there is something I'd like to tell you about what is to come. I'm not setting out to write Cosmic Truths in these notes, or ideas to be engraved in cement. What I *will* try to write are the observations of a lifetime. Observations of one who has had more than her share of experiences and adventures. Experiences that in a way belong to you, too, since you have shared my entire adult life.

It seems to me that everyone knows the problems women face in society—second-class citizenship, lower pay, fewer opportunities to rule the world and so forth. But now that you are just on the brink of womanhood, I'd like to talk to you about some of the good parts, too . . . the reason that after three and a half decades of the experience I think being a woman has quite a lot going for it.

My list covers a good bit of random ground. I think we as women have the better part in sex, in integration of our self-image, in being able to give birth, in being willing to trust our own intuition, in our inherent flexibility, in our emotional makeup and in the one thousand little womanly pleasures that no one seems to be mentioning lately. I'd like to take the time to explore some of these possibilities with you.

I'm very much aware, my dear daughters, that you are inheriting a different world from mine. As all life and knowledge are accelerating at warp speed, you will fall heir to more complicated societal pressures, more complex dilemmas and simply more accumulated information to amass and cope with, than any generation in the world's long history.

You will need, I believe, a very strong sense of self to withstand the velocity of such change; a sturdy sense of what it means to be a woman, in a time when women will be expected to excel at everything, just to prove that they are equal. With all this in mind, some observations about the nitty-gritty parts of being a woman seemed a good place to begin my musings.

These are subjective thoughts, entirely mine. Some may, I hope, apply to your life and, of course, some may not—depending on how your path wends its way. I'll be overjoyed if some of these ramblings prove useful, informative or helpful; just read them with an open mind and make your own good judgments as to which are relevant to your life.

All my precepts needn't be yours, just as my lifetime has brought me different decisions, opportunities and experiences than yours will uncover. But I do very much want you to know what my precepts are, so you can evaluate them fairly. Times change, customs change; what was a basic code of honor in 1820 would be quaint today. Some things remain forever the same.

You judge. I trust you.

```
THE MIND
AND THE
EMOTIONS
```

How to guard your self-esteem, how to face failure, how to deal with anger, how to just keep on keeping on— these and other thoughts are the how-to's I would like, with all my heart, to pass along to you both.

Whatever wisdom I have took me half a lifetime to accumulate and I hold it very dear. It is my earnest hope that some of this hard-won knowledge may save you a bit of time in your own accumulation of what I believe to be essential wisdom.

> *If a man does not keep pace with his companions,*
> *perhaps it is because he hears a different drummer.*
> *Let him step to the music he hears,*
> *however measured or far away.*
>
> HENRY DAVID THOREAU

Self-Esteem

I had a sharp ego-blow this morning, and it has prompted me to write to you of such things. So much a part of living. So easy to be hurt by.

As I took my wounded ego into a taxi, on the way to my next meeting, I began to try to evaluate all such disconcerting experiences, and here is how I've netted out:

The world contrives, in great measure, to upset the applecart of our self-esteem all throughout life. As little children, we seldom do things well enough or grown-uppedly enough to meet with approval from our elders. In school we are constantly being corrected, reprimanded, exposed to how much we do *not know*. Once we are grown, we must make our way in a professional community with subordinates snapping at our heels, and those on top too often willing to put us down merely to keep us from snapping at *their* heels.

All tough stuff on the ego. All calculated to make us feel inadequate and insecure—as if we somehow never reach a plateau in life in which everything we do is acceptable or praiseworthy. So where does all that leave us?

I think the truth of it is that we must hoard our own self-esteem as if it were our greatest treasure. We must learn to evaluate what is said of us *dispassionately;* decide if any part of the criticism is valid, and act upon that. Then discard the rest, utterly, as excess baggage.

For one thing, criticism has too many highly suspect origins. People criticize us because they are jealous, because they dislike us, because they simply want to take us down a peg or because they have serious problems of their own. Do you remember, Cee Cee, when you were very small, there was a girl who ridiculed your sneakers and told you they were dumb and ugly? Then it turned out she had said that only because she wanted you to give her the sneakers, which she secretly envied? Often in life we are criticized by those who have ulterior motives for doing so. Only occasionally do people criticize us in an honest effort to help us improve ourselves. Therefore, we must be careful to judge the *motives* behind the criticism we receive, as well as the words themselves.

Having considered the source of our criticism, I think, we must sift carefully through what has been said of us to separate the wheat from the chaff. Kipling said it well: "If you can *trust* yourself when all men doubt you / But *make allowance* for their doubting too" (my italics). After all, even from a badly motivated crank we can sometimes cull a piece of useful observation. Bron, I seem to remember someone telling you that you looked like an unmade bed, a while ago. You were quite hurt by the statement, I know, but you retaliated by developing a fabulously well-honed sense of style, so I think you must have decided there was some tiny germ of useful truth in what had been said.

All through our lives we are molding ourselves, responding to changes around us, reworking our act, as new information comes our way. So it doesn't hurt to make use of criticism—if it has any validity to it—to help improve ourselves.

But regardless of what is said about us we must always hold our own good opinion of ourselves first and foremost, remembering there is more need for us to conform to our own good standards than to other people's arbitrary ones.

It sometimes helps to remember that everyone who had the chance criticized Mme. Curie, Socrates was given hemlock to drink and Modigliani was told he didn't know how to paint. All these innovative thinkers were criticized, all were ridiculed and ostracized, and in the final analysis all were terrific contributors to mankind.

If no one ever bucked the system, there would be very little progress ever made. Everyone would still be doing things the same way they'd always been done, and no new ground would ever be broken. Most visionary thinkers spend their lives being criticized by people of more narrow vision, yet without those people who could take criticism and still believe in themselves, there would have been no American Revolution, no civil rights and no sure knowledge that the world isn't flat.

Remember, Bron, when you were going through an especially glum time a few years ago, and Pop told you that every morning you should get up out of bed, look in the mirror and say, "I'm really terrific. There's nobody in this world who's just like me." He was suggesting a simplistic but very direct means of encouraging your self-esteem. You did it dutifully for about two weeks, telling me it was the dumbest thing you had ever heard of, and then one morning you said to me, "You know what? There really isn't anybody just like me, is there?" And, of course, we all laughed a lot about it— but something important had happened. While standing in front of that mirror, feeling foolish about talking to yourself, *you'd started look-*

ing at you. You'd begun to gain your own vision of yourself, and begun to discard the debris that was dragging you down.

Remember Rick Nelson's song of a few years ago called "Garden Party"? He had given a performance at Madison Square Garden and been booed from the stage, so he wrote a song that said, "You can't please everyone, so you gotta please yourself." He sold over a million copies of that record and I have to believe that none of the smart alecks in the audience who had booed him ended up with as constructive a result from that evening's adventure. It's pretty obvious his sense of self was strong enough to turn a defeat into a resounding victory.

All through your life, no matter how old you grow, you'll be open to criticism. The more you achieve, the more jealousy you'll engender; the more visible you are, the more probability there is of people taking potshots at you. Even if you wanted to, there's no way you could please everybody. But if you believe *in yourself,* judge your own motivations, trust your own instincts, follow your own dreams—you can achieve your goals and have peace of mind while achieving them.

My mother taught me a long time ago to question authority—not to buck it just for fun or mischief, but rather to make my own determination of its validity. "Be it parent or government," she said, "teacher or employer, priest or politician, you have an obligation to follow only that which you believe to be for the good of your soul, your health, your moral convictions, your own loved ones, or the world in general." Not bad advice.

To follow it, you must believe in yourself. Learn all you can. Become the best person you can be, given the wherewithal that nature has bestowed on you; then follow the dictates of your heart, mind and conscience. Listen to what people say about you, certainly. It can at times be helpful and informative. But if you believe yourself to be in the right, no matter what the world's position, then stick to your guns. Critics have more facility for tearing things down than for building them up, and in the final analysis, building is what life is all about.

It is difficult to accept criticism, but if it makes us aware of our weak areas, I guess it can help us make ourselves better and happier.

Gigi, age 15

I would really rather raise a kid to have a good sense of herself than to be the most civilized person that ever lived. A lot of mothers would rather have the most civilized kid. Their goal is to raise perfect people. But who would even want them? They'd probably just be really repressed. Who needs that?

Bronwyn, age 15

If a girl is pretty it's easy for her to have self-esteem.

Cee Cee, age 14

I think it's very important to have self-esteem, because if you don't respect and like yourself, then how can you respect and like others, or expect them to like you?

Cee Cee, age 14

You've got to be your own friend before you can be anybody else's friend. You've got to like yourself before you can like anybody else. You've got to be happy with the person you are. You have to have pride in yourself, and feel good about the characteristics that make up your own being. After all, if you don't like who you are, you can change!

Bronwyn, age 15

Self-esteem means having confidence in yourself and feeling that you can do whatever you plan each time. When you succeed at doing something well, it makes you feel the next time you can do even more.

Cee Cee, age 14

I think you need the help of other people to make yourself successful—nobody can accomplish everything in life alone, but if you really want to be successful, you can do it. No matter where you come from, or what the obstacles are, I think you can succeed if you believe in yourself.

Gigi, age 15

If someone is being happy in what they do and being totally honest with everybody while they're doing their own thing, then you admire a person like that and you feel they have a lot of self-esteem.

Wanda, age 15

The Half-Full,
Half-Empty Glass

Have you ever noticed how some people see a glass as half-full, and some see the same glass as half-empty? It's an immensely important distinction—far more philosophical than material—and the whole course of your life can be dependent upon which of these two outlooks you possess.

None of us inherits a perfect life. None is perfectly beautiful, perfectly smart, perfectly gifted, perfectly proportioned, perfectly financed or perfectly content. Everybody gets a smattering of the needed equipment, a little excess here, a little inadequacy there. I was standing behind an extraordinarily beautiful young woman in a store the other day—exquisite face, perfectly sculpted body. As I was musing on how nice it would be to look like that, the poor girl spoke in a voice that would shatter glass, and made it clear in seconds that she had a

8

single-digit I.Q. In other words, everybody gets a few of the necessary pieces of life's equipment, and it's up to each of us to figure out how to make the best of our assets and how to use them to compensate for our liabilities.

One of the assets or liabilities we bring to the party is our outlook on life. We can look at the equipment we've been given and give up on the spot, or we can assess what we've got to work with, go after what we're lacking, and jump willingly into the fray.

There's a poem called "Opportunity," which tells the story of a soldier whose sword breaks in battle. He's so disgusted by having to fight with an inferior weapon that he throws it away and runs from the field. A king's son happens on the broken sword, grabs it gratefully and uses it to vanquish his enemies, happy of the "opportunity" it gives him.

Point is, of course, that to a great degree we make our own opportunities. To do so, we mustn't get bogged down in the knowledge of what we *haven't got*. The truth is, only what we *have got* is relevant. There are times in life when all we've got right then and there is pluck and the determination to win. Amazingly, that is often enough.

Lincoln taught himself to read and write by candlelight. Edison became an inventor because he didn't have the education to get a real job. If either had accepted the evidence of what *they didn't have* going for them, they would have been defeated before they began to achieve.

In other words, if you can train yourself to see beyond the shortcomings of life (and, believe me, everybody's life has them), to see that what equipment you have been given is quite usable, you will be way ahead of the game. Like the king's son in the poem, by utilizing what is at hand to your own advantage, you can sometimes accomplish wonders. Beyond that you can feel confident in your ability to cope, and secure in your own natural resources of strength, intelligence, womanliness and instinct. At different times in life, each of those special assets (and all the others you possess) will prove its own indispensable worth to you.

Cee Cee, your heavenly, articulate gift of gab, your wily, analytical mind, your earthy humor and your sensitive soul make you a rare and remarkably complex treasure. Bronwyn, your overwhelming life-force, your bubbling, effervescent stage presence in everyday life, and your bountiful nature make you light up a room like a Roman candle. You've each been given wonderfully individual characteristics and gifts. Very special attributes—each quite different from the other's. I'm really looking forward to seeing how you use your gifts and resources to fill your life with experience and with personal goodies.

I believe that finally your opportunities will be bounded only by your vision of what those boundaries are. Seeing the glass as half-full rather than half-empty is like knowing you have hidden oil reserves in the midst of a gas crisis.

I mostly look at things as the half-empty glass. That's bad. I know you should always be optimistic and not look at the bad point of view of everything—try to look at the good points—but sometimes it's hard for me.

Cee Cee,   age 14

If you always look on the bad side of things I think you stray away from the good things. I've noticed that people who always look on the gloomy side of things have pretty miserable lives.

Bronwyn,   age 15

> *I was angry with my friend:*
> *I told my wrath, my wrath did end.*
> *I was angry with my foe:*
> *I told it not, my wrath did grow.*
>
> WILLIAM BLAKE

Anger

Anger is something I learned of only as a grown-up. For years I honestly thought I didn't have any anger. When things happened that hurt me, I never got angry. I just got sad or sick. I knew the sad part was connected to the hurt, but it took me a long while to realize that the getting sick part was, too.

It seems to me we are all programmed from the minute we're born not to show anger. When you're a little child and someone takes away your toy, you're not supposed to punch him, even though you'd love to. When your parents do something thoughtless or arbitrary or mean, you're not allowed to say, "Hey, don't do that—it hurts me," and so on through life. Unfortunately, many people grow up believing they can't get angry at a friend or a parent or a child without doing irreparable damage to their relationship. But, of course, the anger must go somewhere. So where does it go?

11

Well, probably the most usual thing that people do to un-
leash their anger is cunningly to "pay back" whoever hurt
them. To do this we hold on to the grudge—the remembered
hurt—and wait till an opportune moment comes when we can
do something "back" to the one who hurt us. It may be a word,
or an ill turn, or any number of sneaky pay-backs, depending
on what we can get away with.

The perfect example of this kind of delayed-reaction pay-
back was your relationship with each other when you were
little children. You, Bronwyn, being the older and larger, always fought sibling battles with your superior strength. You,
Cee Cee, being the younger and smaller, always fought with
your articulate tongue. Remember how it worked? Let's say
Bronwyn would take away some toy by force. Three days later
Cee Cee would tell some outrageously embarrassing story about
you to retaliate. Right? Nothing was ever really forgotten; instead, a lot of anger was just put on hold for future reference.
Until I learned to do differently, I'm afraid I, too, handled
anger in just that roundabout fashion.

The problem with this method of dealing with anger is that
it can take a long time to come to fruition. You may have to
walk around with that anger festering in your mind and body
for days, weeks, even years, before you get a chance to pay it
back. It's as if you have to carry around a big sackful of grievances and hurts, just waiting for the chance to get even. This
method is very burdensome, but a lot of people like it because
they never have to confront the person who hurt them. In other
words, it's sneaky.

Another thing people do is to sulk. They mope around and
make it obvious to everyone that they are unhappy or dis-
pleased. When someone asks what's wrong, they just say, "Oh,
nothing," in the best martyred fashion. Needless to say, these
mopers are paying back by making the atmosphere around
them dreary, negative and tense. Again, they choose misery
rather than confrontation.

There are countless other very human, very typical methods we all use at times to deal with the anger that wells up daily over the injustices, annoyances, cruelties, vagaries and stupidities that are part of daily life, but I really only want to talk about the constructive means I've learned to combat the problem. A plain and simple means of fighting back. It goes like this:

Express what you feel, the moment you feel it. If your friend says your hair looks like a robin's nest and it hurts you to hear it, say, "Hey, that's a creepy thing to say, you hurt my feelings." Tell her you are mad that she would dare say something so mean and uncalled-for, and put the ball in her court. If your husband "forgets" to tell you he's bringing home eleven people for dinner and it upsets your applecart, tell him it was a thoughtless, inconsiderate thing to do and that you're angry because he didn't give you the same courtesy he'd extend to a relative stranger. If your boyfriend tells you you're getting fat, tell him he's getting rude.

See what I mean? Get it off your chest. Don't let it fester. Don't turn the other cheek. Don't be a martyr. If you do, you'll only suffer in the meanwhile and eventually pay back that other person in some sneaky, unsuspected way that may damage your relationship and confuse you both.

I know. I know. I can hear you saying, "Sure, sure, I can just see what would happen to me if I told my teacher I was mad at her because she plays favorites in school. She'd throw me out the window."

Let me try to explain something. I'm not suggesting for a moment that by this straightforward method of unloading your anger you can control the reaction of the person you are angry with. That person may respond to your anger very unconstructively. What I'm suggesting is that despite the possibility of provoking an explosion, you will have done several very constructive things by expressing your anger. You will have gotten a potentially destructive energy out of your system so that you feel some relief. You will have been *honest* with the person you are angry at so that he will have a fair chance of responding correctly. You will have dealt with whatever caused the problem *immediately* so that it needn't be carried around as a burden by you or the other person.

Don't just believe me because I say so. Try the method a couple of times. You may be very surprised about how often this straightforward approach clears the air and makes it possible for you to proceed with your relationship with less tension, less hostility and more genuine understanding.

Truth is, far more damage is done to a relationship by the dishonesty of never expressing what you feel, and by the pressure that is built up by suppressing anger. It is *normal* to get angry sometimes at someone you are close to; annoyances big and little are inevitable in a long-term, close relationship between people. It's just human for us and those we love to be imperfect. We can't always do what's right for each other. Sometimes we're thoughtless, sometimes we misunderstand. But whatever the problem that arises, if we can let it out— express the anger we feel about it—and then go on from there, we avert enormous problems.

The explosiveness of suppressing anger is a far more dangerous threat to any relationship than the expression of anger. By letting off steam we can actually protect our relationships from potential volcanic eruptions, but to do so we must know how to handle arguments constructively.

Why People Argue

People argue for a lot of reasons. Sometimes they argue for very different reasons from what they think. Let me give you a for-instance:

Someone at school (we'll call him Charlie) cheats from your test paper and passes a test he didn't study for, all because of your efforts. You can't yell at him because the teacher would go

berserk and your friends would get mad. So you don't do anything. Two days later, Charlie starts a conversation with you
and you bite his head off. *In other words, you start to argue
with him about whatever's handy, because you are really mad
at him about what happened on the test.*

The same thing happens in families: current fights may hark
back to things that happened years ago. Let's say your mother
went to work when you were a little girl, so that you were left
with a housekeeper who frightened you and made you angry.
You were too small and scared to express that anger, so you
tucked it away. Ten years later something triggers a remembrance of that experience, and the first thing you know, you're
having an argument with your mother. The argument may
seem to be about housework or money or something else that's
current, but deep down inside, you're really still angry about
what happened a long, long time ago.

Long story short, the first thing to do when it comes to arguing is to figure out what you are really angry about. If you're
mad about something current (someone at the disco said you
have two left feet), express your anger immediately and directly ("I'm angry that you said such a mean, stupid thing. You
dance like a pregnant buffalo, so who are you to throw
stones?"). If it seems to be leftover anger that's causing the
trouble, try to think it out—maybe even write it down just to
get it out of your system. Then tell the person you are angry
with that you have some old gripes against him that you need
to unload.

One clue to recognizing old gripes is the constantness of your
arguing. If you find yourself having continual arguments with
one person—maybe a parent, a sibling or a friend—chances are
two things are happening:

1. You haven't touched on what's really bugging you.

2. You aren't expressing your anger right, so you can *feel
relieved.*

The Difference between Angry and Nasty

Unexpressed anger has a tendency to turn into chronic nastiness. It's like a constant irritation—a stone in your shoe—that makes you grumpy and out-of-sorts. You may be a really nice person most of the time and to most of the world, but when that one person toward whom you hold unexpressed anger comes into view, you turn into the Incredible Hulk.

How to Do It Right

Believe it or not, there is a right way. It goes like this: say what you are angry at, as briefly and directly as possible. Blurt it out! Don't intellectualize it, or embroider it with wasted words. Say how you feel, rather than what you *think!* "*I feel hurt* by your getting divorced." "*I feel angry* that you never really listen to what I say." "*I feel angry* that you didn't understand me when I was little." *These are feelings being expressed.* When you get a feeling out in the open, *you feel relieved, and the person you're arguing with has something real to respond to,* so there's more possibility of his being able to respond well. If he does not, at least you've got something burdensome off your back.

Here's where the problem sets in: if you don't find a way to dump these angers, you may subvert them into perpetual nastiness. When you express anger, you get relief. When you express just plain nastiness (often the offshoot of unexpressed anger), you don't feel any better when it's over. You get no relief and the recipient of the nastiness doesn't know what hit him.

How to Let Everybody Win

There is a way. It takes courage and a willingness to let things get fixed. Sometimes, you see, we cling to our angers in order to get attention, to be in control, to punish others who have hurt us, or because we're simply *afraid* to live without angers.

To get things straightened out, you must evaluate grievances honestly and fully. Make a list. Make it complete. Next, you must express your feelings as best you can. Sometimes the easiest way to do it is in writing, so you can collect your thoughts properly and in detail. Then you must try to express your anger, and let the chips fall where they may. Once you've got your anger out of your system (by whatever means is practical) *you'll feel relieved no matter what the other party does or says.* If you don't feel relieved, you've fooled yourself by expressing something other than real anger. Try again, till you get it right. The results will be well worth it.

Forgive and Forget

Chronic unforgivers are the most unfortunate people. The grievance junkies, who never let themselves or others have the pleasure and relief of forgiving and forgetting, are doomed to misery. Generally, they seem to be the ones who have never developed the ability to express their *real* feelings. They may rant and rave and excel at nastiness, of course, but they never allow themselves or others the relief of getting it all out and over with, once and for all. Sadly, such people stay crippled with the weight of their angers sometimes for a lifetime, when all it would take to free them is an honest expression of their feelings, and an honest desire to *feel better.*

What it comes down to is this: a person must feel, deep down inside, that he deserves to feel good and to feel relieved. There is pleasure and good feeling in allowing yourself relief from anger, strain and mistery. If you feel that you don't really *de-*

serve to be happy, you are up the creek. But more about that later.

Arguing can sometimes be helpful, but only if it helps prevent a fight. Fighting doesn't solve anything. Trouble is, people don't realize that until after *the fight. Talking things out with a person can solve everything, provided the other person is also willing to talk honestly.*

Gigi,   age 15

You've said some really good stuff about getting out your angers—that's important. The trouble is it's harder to get out your angers honestly with grown-ups than with kids. With kids, I don't care—I'll tell anybody what I feel. It's only with grown-ups that it gets hard. And with teachers, it's impossible!

Cee Cee,   age 14

I think that people shouldn't take out their angers on others. By taking out your angers on someone else it only makes matters worse. I believe you must learn to deal with situations and control your anger.

Gigi,   age 15

I think that controlling anger is a sign of maturity.

Gigi,   age 15

Arguments *are necessary to any relationship . . . they happen . . . and I guess they can't really be avoided. But of course you always wish they could be—it seems like sitting down and having a nice friendly discussion or even a debate would be a lot better than a fight.*

Lola,   age 15

It's not healthy to walk around with your emotions all tied up inside of you . . . with no way to let your feelings or emotions out. Pretty soon it all comes out anyway, and that may not be at the time you'd like it to! If you're mad at somebody, I think you should tell them right then. If you can't do that, I think you should hit a wall . . . or throw a teddy bear across the room . . . or get an "encounter bat," or a big pillow you can sock! You've got to let your angers out or it's just not healthy. If you keep it all in, eventually you'll burst. Or maybe even get sick.

Lola,   age 15

I really like the idea that people don't always agree, but they can still survive each other and love each other, and talk about it.

Bronwyn,   age 15

I used to be very quiet. I never used to let anyone know why I was so angry and upset. Until one day I realized I'm *the one who's getting the worst of it. Now I try to get the angers out of my system.*

Lola,   age 15

You should get your angers out and you should tell people how you feel, because if you keep them inside, you are going to just build up more and more angers, and one day you are just going to burst.

Cee Cee,   age 14

*There is no duty we underrate so much
as the duty of being happy.*
                    ROBERT LOUIS STEVENSON

Pleasure and Happiness

There is an extraordinary book called *Man Against Himself,*
by Karl Menninger, which I hope you will someday read. It will
explain to you, in infinite detail, the reasons that people don't
allow themselves pleasure and happiness. What I'd like to do,
for the moment, is give you a small idea of the ways by which
we sometimes short-circuit our own joy and a few of the reasons that we do it.

From infancy on (and before, while still in the womb, by the
way), we are recording everything that ever happens to us. It's
all there: the color of the wallpaper in our nursery, the first
step we ever took, the least important moments and the most.
We are also recording all the messages we ever received from
those around us . . . and that is where the problems start.

Think of this: from babyhood on we are being told and
shown that we aren't "okay." We do things wrong: we have
trouble tying our shoelaces, we wet our pants, we can't cut our

food right, we don't know how to read or write, we stumble over words, we make mistakes. Hard as we try, we fail a lot; not because we mean to, but just because we're too little and too inexperienced to be able to do better. You can't cut meat until your motor development is sufficient to the task. You can't put the pieces into a puzzle until your perceptions are keen enough to sense where they go.

See what I mean? Just by nature of being a little child, we have a lot of flops. And we get yelled at. Exasperated mothers, fathers, teachers and other assorted adults reinforce how bad we feel about our failures and inadequacies. "You did it again!" "Can't you ever learn to do that right!" "Oh, boy, look at Clumsy!" You've heard all these terrible negative inputs, I'm sure.

Okay. Now let's look at *what* these negative recorded messages say to us: They tell us we're not so hot, that we're not as good as the next fellow, that we deserve to be punished, that we deserve to feel guilty, that we deserve to get caught being inadequate. In other words, they tell us we don't deserve happiness, we don't deserve peace and plenty, we don't deserve pleasure, we don't deserve joy.

Because these destructive messages were programmed in a long time ago, we don't even remember they are there. Just as you don't remember learning to add two and two, you just know it's four—so you don't remember learning to say, "I don't deserve happiness." You just know that's the way it is.

An amazing amount of self-defeat and self-destructiveness can emerge as a result of this kind of negative programming. Some of it is fairly obvious and recognizable (like alcoholism or drug addiction), but what about the subtler forms of self-defeat? What about the man who works his fingers to the bone for a new account and then does something stupid at the last minute, to ensure his *not* getting it? Or the athlete who practices eight hours a day for years and then comes down with the flu the night before the finals? Or the college kid who studies for a whole semester and then freezes during the exam and can't remember a thing? These seemingly "accidental" self-defeats have a lot in common. They mess you up at the eleventh hour, they effectively block your victory, yet they are done in a way that seems accidental and therefore blameless.

Do you get the drift, my darlings? The name of the game is self-defeat. A means by which our minds or bodies (or both) can work against us, without our knowledge or conscious consent. Generally, to fulfill some ancient, stupid program from our past, like "We didn't deserve to win," or "We don't deserve so much happiness," or "If we get that account, life will be too good." Whatever the trigger point, the result is the same: in minor cases, self-defeat; in more major ones, self-destruction.

One of the most subtle aspects of the problem is *not allowing yourself to feel pleasure because, way down deep inside, you feel you don't deserve it.*

Remember now, this is quite subtle stuff, so you must try to understand that it all happens on a subconscious level of the mind, not right out in the open where you can recognize it immediately!

Yet subtle or not, it can affect us adversely in many ways. It can affect us in school—consider the student who gets 95 on a test, then frets that it wasn't 100; or does superbly at math, then frets that he or she does only average work in English. It can affect us in business—consider the man who no matter how much he achieves, desperately needs more and never feels satisfied. It can affect us most often in love—consider the person who loves greatly, but always picks someone who returns misery instead of happiness. In other words, this antipleasure programming can manifest itself in every area of a person's life. Unfortunately, this inability to accept happiness frequently masquerades as something other than what it is. For example: the student who does badly can blame it on his teacher; the businessman can blame his workaholism on his wife's expensive tastes; the disappointed lover can blame the inadequacies of love—yet in truth the blame lies within their own negative programming.

How do you combat something so insidious?

Take a good hard look at yourself. Are you enjoying life? Do you get a kick out of school or work or whatever you spend your time at, or is it simply a never-ending series of traumas and tensions?

Do you derive pleasure from little things around you . . . the beauty of nature, the fun of a new dress, the satisfaction of a good mark on a test? You know the items that apply to you. The point is, are you getting a lot of pleasure and joy from life, or are you short-circuiting yourself, so that no matter what comes your way, you always end up unsatisfied, cranky, sad or empty?

Next: having tracked down the areas in which you are short-circuiting, try to figure out why it keeps happening. Is there a trigger point that always provokes misery? Do you get happy for a minute and then create some disturbance to mess it up? Can you handle happiness when it sneaks up on you? It may be that you can't allow yourself the pleasure of just plain *feeling good,* or it may be that you let yourself feel happy for a little while, but then start worrying that if things get too good, something awful will happen. In other words, do you always manage to allow some anxiety to creep in and mitigate your happiness?

Remind yourself that you deserve to be happy. You are not an ax murderer. You are not a terrible person. You are an ordinary, decent human being who tries her best to be civilized and lead a good life. You deserve joy, not misery; happiness, not sorrow. You have done nothing to be punished for. Your mistakes have been just that—mistakes. It is only human to make your share of them.

In other words, you should remind yourself frequently—in fact, every day, until it becomes ingrained—*that you deserve to be happy. You deserve peace and contentment. You deserve to be fulfilled and satisfied.* You will be absolutely amazed how such positive thoughts can lead to convictions, and those convictions can lead to a happier life.

Watch your own progress. Keep an eye on your own learning process. If you find yourself slipping back into old habits of tension, anxiety, pressure or other short circuits, *remind* yourself that you deserve to be happy.

Read what very competent psychologists have to say about how to dump old programming. I'd suggest *Man Against Himself* and *Love Against Hate* by Dr. Karl Menninger; *The Courage to Create, Love and Will,* and *Psychology and the Human Dilemma* by Rollo May; *I'm O.K., You're O.K.* by Thomas A. Harris, M.D., *The Neurotic Personality of Our Times* by Karen Horney, *Man's Search for Meaning* by Viktor Frankl. There are a great many works by truly gifted thinkers that are both accessible and very understandable. I would encourage you to explore the ones that seem to apply to you, and to read with an open mind. There is so much lucid, sound help to be gathered from such works that they are more than worth the effort of reading them.

If you find the old programming is really too ingrained to fight by yourself, seek a competent and compassionate counselor or therapist who can help you to understand better your own motivations and patterns. You owe it to yourself to be able to enjoy the fulfillment of a happy life. No effort or price is too great to expend toward achieving that goal.

I feel that pleasure and happiness are very important in life. Just because some of us don't have everything we want, doesn't mean we can't be happy. We should look for things that make us happy in our everyday life, and enjoy them as much as we can, instead of waiting for perfection.

Gigi,   age 15

There should be pleasure and happiness in everybody's life. I think three-quarters of your life should be pleasurable and happy.

                                        Cee Cee,   age 14

Pleasure and happiness—first of all don't forget there's a difference. Pleasure is just for the moment . . . pleasure is sort of a temporary thing. Happiness could last a lifetime.

                                        Lola,   age 15

I think you're either a happy person or you're not. Happiness has a lot to do with the way you look at things. I guess you have a responsibility to make yourself happy, and to do the best you can with what you've got. You should learn how to look on the bright side of everything, because there is a bright side of everything if you look hard enough, and if you have confidence in yourself, you can have a good life. If you are a crabby person and wait around for others to make you happy, you're in big trouble.

                                        Bronwyn,   age 15

I am larger, better than I thought,
I did not know I held so much goodness.
                    WALT WHITMAN,
            "Song of the Open Road"

Therapy

I suspect that you take a dim view of therapy at this point in your life. It is too tangled up with the stigma of mental illness and too open to peer-group criticism to be appealing at your age. Nonetheless, I would like to open the subject—if not for now, then for later.

Imagine being given the chance to learn all there is to know about yourself; to study yourself as if *you* were a subject being taught by a brilliant teacher. Imagine being able to unravel your toughest problems, understand your deepest motivations, remember all of the useful material stored on your mental "tape recorder"—and, beyond that, to understand better the needs, motivations and actions of everyone in your world. Wouldn't such knowledge be beyond price?

This, in a nutshell, is what therapy can give you: a knowledge of yourself and an insight into others. I'd like to talk to you about therapy now, despite your being so young, because I have found it to be such a positive force in my life, and I believe it may someday be so in yours. Whether it takes the form of serious self-exploration, or simply of family counseling to get past some specific day-to-day problem, therapy can provide a safe, sane, creative solution to questions that may seem too complex or cumbersome to tackle on your own.

If you think of a therapist as a great teacher—one who has spent a lifetime studying behavior patterns and the psychological makeup of the human condition—it becomes easier to accept the fact that he or she might have some useful information to impart to you. A good therapist can help with just about any area of life that's either complicated or troublesome. I've seen people helped through mental blocks that inhibited schoolwork, writer's blocks that inhibited earning a living. I've seen kids helped to cope with their parents' foibles, and vice versa. The trauma of death or illness, the hurtfulness of divorce, the tensions of a new stepparent, the confusions of early sexuality, the inequity of school life, the pressures of modern society—all these are potential problem areas that can discombobulate kids as well as grown-ups. You know, problems and confusions are simply part of the human condition; they are not confined exclusively to adults.

I firmly believe, by the way, that therapy is best for the sane and the intelligent. It would be a lot harder for the mad to be able to profit from it, or the stupid, for that matter. It seems to me that the amount of progress one can make depends on motivation, experience, time spent and, of course, the skill and intuitions of the therapist. Needless to say, you must be very careful at any time in your life about choosing the right therapist. The best way I know is word of mouth—listening to other people talk about their therapists and evaluating how commonsensible they sound, and, for that matter, how sane you think they are. Rapport with and trust in a therapist are absolutely crucial to the process of therapy.

Now to the questions of who needs therapy and when. I believe utterly that any intelligent, self-interested human being can benefit from the wisdom and guidance of a good therapist. Therapy can open new frontiers, vistas of self-investigation you might never touch otherwise, and it can teach you necessary information that might take years or a lifetime to learn in the ordinary way.

We have all been shaped by our early experiences. By understanding how and why we have been so shaped, we can save ourselves the trauma of repeating ingrained mistakes. We can learn better role models than the ones we inherited by chance and birth. We can undo the masochism we all are heir to. We can learn that we deserve to be guilt-free and happy.

Unfortunately, because of the stigma and cost attached to therapy, its remarkable gifts are seldom tasted until after one's life is in serious disarray. Generally we seek help only when all else fails, and our burdens become unendurable or our questions too unanswerable.

It would be my wish for you that you might have the good fortune to seek such self-enlightenment *before* you find yourself in any serious pickles. If young people spent two years in college and two years in therapy before being shipped out to face the slings and arrows of the world, I believe they would be far better equipped for the tests life brings.

The money I've spent on therapy was the best and most rewarding money I've ever expended. An investment in me. In my future. In your well-being. In the future of all whose lives ever touch my heart or mind. My mother used to tell me that to educate a woman was to educate an entire family. That's precisely how I feel about therapy. It is an education in the complex art of living. An investment in the future.

When Socrates said "Know thyself" he said a mouthful. The wisdom of the advice hasn't changed with the centuries, just the methodology of following it. It is an enormous gift that a method exists that can shorten your learning period, cut down on your trial-and-error factor, and increase the joy you take from life. I hope you may someday have the good fortune to take advantage of it.

Therapy has had a use in my life, but it doesn't seem like the biggest thing to me, because I have pretty much the same thoughts as the shrink does. I just talked to him . . . got everything off my chest, and it made me feel better. That's it. But I think I could have done that with anybody else! He never told me what to do about life. I had to come up with that all by myself. Of course, I guess that's what they're there to do, help you come up with your own answers.

Bronwyn, age 15

It helps to have an objective person who doesn't know anything about any of the people you're talking about, until you tell him. A therapist listens to your point of view and helps you figure things out for yourself. Of course, I sort of wonder if you couldn't do the same thing with a bartender!

Lola, age 15

My experience is that therapy is definitely a good thing. But it can also be a bad thing! Some people won't say anything unless it's okay with their therapist. It's as if they stop thinking for themselves, and start thinking only what their therapist thinks. They let their therapist run their lives and that's really scary.

Bronwyn, age 15

I think therapy is a good thing because it helps you talk out your problems and sort out what you really are after. Sometimes it's not as easy to know what you want or need in life.

Lola, age 15

2

THE SPIRIT

I have a firm conviction that religion is about to stage a comeback. Not orthodoxy—for the world is becoming a bit too complex for pat answers to profound questions—but rather a serious return to the search for meaning in life; what other generations would have called the search for God. 815067

I believe a far more free-form style of communication with God will emerge in the rest of this century, a more personal connection with nature, a more relevant communion with spirit. Pierre Teilhard de Chardin, the gifted paleontologist and mystic who threw the Catholic Church into a tizzy with his unorthodox visionary teachings in the Twenties and Thirties, was convinced that man's next evolution would be of the spirit . . . perhaps the most important evolution of them all. There seem to me signs all around us to suggest that he was right.

The notes I have gathered in the following pages are offered simply to tell you how I *feel* about things spiritual, not to suggest that your religious explorations will lead you to the same place mine have. I was raised in the most orthodox of Catholic ritual, and grew to evolve my own peculiar but very satisfying amalgam of religious convictions. As Robert Louis Stevenson once said, "Every man is his own doctor of divinity, in the last resort." So, with the thought that you may wish to add my notions to the curriculum, when you are studying for your own personal spiritual doctorate, I offer you the following.

Religion and
the Quest for the Spirit

In the old days—the old days being my youth, and everything
that came before that—religion was a central part of living.
The churches were a spiritual and social hub of most commu-
nities, and everybody, when asked for a religious affiliation,
seemed to have one!

There were a number of very fine results of this system, it
seems to me, for even if people did not always measure up to
the standards of moral conduct set by their particular faith, at
least they were well aware of what those moral standards were.
Such obvious religious guideposts made morality a fairly un-
complicated business—there was good and bad, and they were
very different from each other. There was also sin, which,
while it seemed to differ from Presbyterian to Baptist to Catholic to Jew, at least was a concept that everyone understood in
some measure. There were, of course, also a number of not-so-

good results from this fairly simplistic system, like guilt and repression—but more about that later.

Curiously, when I was a little girl, people seemed to be discouraged from investigating other people's religions. Catholics were forbidden to read non-Catholic Bibles; Protestants were not supposed to go inside a Catholic church. My mother had a fabulously rich and replete book called *The Bible of the World*. It contained everybody's Scripture: Hindu, Buddhist, Catholic, Protestant, Jewish and a few esoteric sects thrown in for good measure. I can remember how furtively I watched that book on the shelf, thinking my mother extraordinarily courageous to own such a forbidden volume, yet fearful of looking inside it, until my curiosity finally got the better of me. What a glorious book! I've always been a pushover for poetic, archaic language, and this one several-thousand-page volume had it all. My guilt, of course, was nearly overwhelming, because the nun who taught me religion in school had said that reading forbidden books was a horrible sin with appropriately horrible punishment. I used to watch my mother and my aunt, both of whom I knew read *The Bible of the World* frequently, to see if lightning would strike them for their heresy. I know it sounds absurd and melodramatic, but in those days people tended to follow rules, and religions were superb rulemakers.

As the world became a bit more sophisticated, as people traveled to exotic places, saw new cultures and became more aware and tolerant of other peoples' customs, I think our somewhat parochial American attitudes toward religion began to change. World War II, Korea, Vietnam and all the travels they engendered exposed our young people to new ways of thinking, which eventually flowed over into the religious sphere as well. I also think that the sexual revolution of the sixties took its toll on organized religions. As people, male and female, began to explore their own sexuality in a less puritanical way, many left the religions of their childhood, because they felt the old constraints were incompatible with the new freedoms.

All of which brings me to religion *now*. It seems to me that young people are seeking something to replace the religions of the past. Perhaps that's why so many curious cults have sprung up and gained followers. I truly believe that the need for belief in a Power greater than ourselves is a basic human one. People need some kind of understanding of their own connection with the universe and with eternity, some meaning for their lives beyond the here and now. In an age like ours, the search for that connection can be a confusing one.

That is why I would like to encourage you to explore other peoples' spiritual thought. You might begin by trying to learn as much as you can of your parents' religion. It may have a great deal to offer you. After all, you don't necessarily have to switch from the faith you were born into to find spiritual fulfillment. If you feel the need to go further, you might go to a Sabbath service or two with friends of a different faith. If that doesn't completely satisfy you, try investigating some less well-known possibilities, like Metaphysics, Unity or the Eastern religions, like Zen. You may be surprised, as I was, to find that there is great similarity in the basic spiritual teachings of the world's great faiths, although they are generally draped in different rhetoric and trappings.

I would encourage you to do these things because I believe that religion, at its best, is both a strengthener and a comfort. Belief in a Power beyond ourselves, understanding of our own connection with the universe, and knowledge of a morality based on the brotherhood of man under the parenthood of God are all very important and valid reinforcements in a less-than-stable world.

Whether you find spiritual fulfillment in an orthodox form of religion or in a connection to God that you forge for yourself, I believe you will be strengthened and uplifted, both by the seeking and the finding of such spiritual enlightenment.

Cults and Mind-Controlling "Religions"

Because so many kids have been taken in by the mind-controlling influences of cults and cult leaders, I'd like to add a word of caution about your spiritual explorations. From what I've been able to gather, the kids who are most vulnerable to such groups are those who are alienated from their families and seeking what seems to be a safe haven in the bosom of a community. Many ruthless people have exploited that vulnerability in the name of religion, which is one reason that so many cults have been able to gain a foothold among our youth in the last ten years.

I think it's wise to be very careful of anyone or any group that wants to do your thinking for you. One of the reasons for exploring religious ideas beyond the orthodox is to gain freedom of thought; anyone who seeks to dictate to you what you *must* think or believe about God, or anything else, is surely suspect. Any group that insists that you *must* live with them and lose contact with the outside world is suspect. Any religion that excludes all others and says "I'm the only valid spiritual path" is suspect. Any leader who demands that you abandon your own thoughts and accept *his* is suspect. Any leader who demands that you *worship* him is suspect. Any body of religious thought that goes against your own instincts or your own sense of safety and well-being is suspect. Any "religious" group that insists that you turn over all your money and property to it is suspect. Any leader or group that seeks to *control your mind for you* is suspect. It just takes an extra heavy helping of common sense to sort out for yourself what's safe and what's not, and, of course, it takes confidence in your own instincts.

I have high hopes that your generation and your children's generation will be able to evolve a more spiritual brand of religion for yourselves than the current ones. Not so temporal and involved in the politics and finances of the world, but more of a spiritual strengthener, a help to people in developing a genuine feeling about God. Not fear of His punishments or damnation, as my generation and all before me had, but belief in His goodness, the beauty of His universe and His desire "to give you the Kingdom."

I once knew a wonderful Metaphysician named Eleanor Wrench, a student of Emmet Fox, who told me repeatedly that "It is the Father's own pleasure to give you the Kingdom." I didn't at that time have the foggiest notion of what she meant, as such thinking was directly in opposition to what my Catholic upbringing had taught me. (As any good Irish Catholic knows, misery, pain, suffering and self-sacrifice are the passports to our heaven, and who ever heard of a God who was standing around giving out goodies!)

I have since learned that the lady was right: that much of the misery we are hurt by is man-made, not God-given, and that the world is indeed filled with glories that are within our reach, if we believe that they are there for us to share in.

There is so much of God in each of us, if we are able to see, feel and touch it. If our souls are immortal, as so many faiths teach, then we, too, are kin to God, and could operate in harmony with the limitless universe if we had the key.

I hope your generation finds the key, sought so long, by so many. Perhaps science will help in the quest. Perhaps the open-mindedness that your generation seems equipped with will make the way easier. I wish you great good fortune, my dear daughters, on what I hope will be a joyous spiritual quest.

There are so many different types of religions, and so many different people telling you what's right. They all have different morals and standards and they're each telling you they're the only right one! It makes the whole business pretty suspicious. You just don't know which to pick. But I really think you should have the right to pick your own religion if you want one.

Lola,   age 15

I think today kids are pretty confused about religion. They're pretty turned off by people who are overreligious—you want to run screaming from the room when somebody really pushes something on you that you're not sure of. Maybe it would be good for you, but maybe it's not something you can understand or respond to, so you feel like a hypocrite saying "I believe," if you really don't.

Cee Cee, age 14

Kids today are so confused about religion, I think that's why cults have started. All these famous cults are really frightening. Any kind of mind control, where someone else does your thinking for you, is not for me. It's scary though, because cults are attracting a lot of confused kids who are looking for something to believe in, or looking for a home and a family.

Lola, age 15

Sometimes I feel Jewish and sometimes I feel Catholic, and sometimes I feel something else. I like parts of a lot of religions, I guess. Gee, God, I'm sorry. I don't mean to be sacrilegious, if that's what I'm being!

Bronwyn, age 15

Maybe it's just that we all have too many choices. But everybody needs something to believe in, and it's getting harder and harder to find something you can be sure of.

Lola, age 15

I believe in the Force!

Bronwyn, age 15

I think maybe that they should cut it down into two types of religion . . . like Jewish and Catholic, or Protestant and Buddhist. That would make life easy. Or maybe they should just pick out all the important ideas and morality and make it into one big religion, so we wouldn't have to feel so confused.

Bronwyn,   age 15

I know a lot of kids from the U.N., and I've learned a lot about different religions from knowing kids from different cultures. The trouble is, I've heard some pretty weird stuff that people believe in. My friends from Nepal even believe in a little kid who's a goddess, and they think that if you look in her window, you die. It's pretty silly and that kind of thing makes you suspicious of all religions. How can you know which to choose, if everybody thinks their beliefs are the only ones, and if you know it's all just stuff that gets programmed into you, depending on where you live?

Cee Cee,   age 14

I go to Catholic school, though religion is not the most important thing in my life. I believe in God. But sometimes I ask Him for things, and He doesn't make them happen, so I don't really know if He is there.

Cee Cee,   age 14

My mom is Catholic, so I'm a Catholic. I believe in God, and I get angry sometimes because I say to myself, "If there's a God up there, why does He let all these horrible things happen to people? Girls get raped and people get killed." I don't understand why He lets that happen.

Wanda,   age 15

Come the morning, I'll be far from here.
Slowly rising in the atmosphere.
Oh, sweet earth, good-bye,
'Cause I'll be home in the sky in the
morning, bye-bye.

CAT STEVENS

Death

My father's father died when I was six and I had loved him very much. It was decided that going to his wake or funeral would be too sad for so small a child, and I was left behind. To this day, so many decades later, I regret bitterly not having had the chance to say good-bye.

I have a very old-fashioned conviction when it comes to funerals. I believe we must be there to help our friends and loved ones bury their dead. I believe there is not only a respect due to those who have died, but a duty to help those who grieve, and that the presence of friends at the funeral home or graveside is, without question, a comfort to the ones left behind.

I know the American way of death has been called barbaric by many. Wakes and their counterparts in other religions are, God knows, among the most difficult of life's duty calls—no one ever knows what to say or how to behave. But customs like the Jewish tradition of sitting shiva for a week with the family of

39

the deceased do, after all, give far-flung relatives a chance to pay their last respects, and they do give those closest to the one who has died a chance to be comforted by the loving memories held by others who have known their loved ones.

I have been to the funerals of those so old that they had outlived most of their friends and therefore needed company to see them on their way. I have been to the funerals of the young, perhaps the saddest of all, where there are many mourners, but still the need for people to say their last farewells. It seems to me that we should lend our strength and courage to those who are grieving and should help in whatever way we can with their sad loss.

I have a peculiar attitude toward death in general. Having read much, and having had some unique experiences in hypnosis and in meditation that reinforce my conviction, I feel most comfortable with the idea of a continuance of life after death.

The explorations of Dr. Elisabeth Kübler-Ross into the experiences of people who have been clinically dead for a period of time, the experiences of the great mystics and religious thinkers and my own belief in a benevolent God-Force in the universe, among other things, lead me to believe that the life-force which animates us continues through more than one lifetime in its quest for enlightenment.

I don't suggest for a moment that you subscribe to my belief. Such thoughts are immensely personal and private, and you must find your own way. I simply tell you my feelings, so that you can add them to the volume of data otherwise available to you.

I have absolutely no fear of dying because I seem to remember what it was like from the past. For some reason, I can reach other levels of consciousness with ease, and I believe death to be simply that. It is also the last frontier—the last great adventure, and as my life has grown continuously better as I grow older, I somehow feel that death will be the last, and perhaps the most important, experience for this lifetime.

And so I, for whatever reasons, have been spared the fear that others feel toward death. That is not to say that I look forward to its coming too soon. Death should be the culmination of a life, not a short circuit happening at the wrong and unexpected time. Robert Browning said it best:

> Grow old along with me!
> The best is yet to be,
> The last of life, for which the first was made.

One of the reasons I do not fear death is that I believe dying will be a reunion of sorts. That theme is expressed in the following excerpt from a poem by Robert Louis Stevenson:

> He is not dead, this friend—not dead,
> But in the path we mortals tread
> Got some few trifling steps ahead
>   and nearer to the end;
> So that you too, once past the bend,
> Shall meet again, as face to face, this friend
> You fancy dead.

That's how I feel about it, you see. That somewhere, in an eternal place, the souls of those who have gone before await us. The souls who have loved us and who have passed the last great barrier will be there to take us by the hand. My grandfather will be there, to whom I never said good-bye . . . my grandmother, whom I never knew (she died before I was born) but whose facial contours I seem to have inherited. All will be there, waiting for me. For I do not believe that love dies, it being the strongest force in the universe—I think it continues, like the soul, forever.

So there you have it, my dear children, my own peculiar vision of death. It needn't be yours, of course, but perhaps when the time comes for you to bid me farewell, it will help you to know that for me death holds no terrors and no finality. I expect I'll just be going home.

Death is a very natural thing. I'm not scared to die. I would like to die a natural death, without pain and suffering though.

Lola,   age 15

I, for one, am scared to die. I know the time has to come for everyone, but I wish I could live forever and ever. I know that in the future, they'll find medicines to cure most diseases, so that's why I would like my body to be preserved when I die—so that eventually they can revive me.

Gigi,   age 15

I'm scared of death, because I know that I'm going to hell— maybe that's just because I go to Catholic school.

Cee Cee,   age 14

No one close to me ever died, except for Uncle Joe, but he was a priest and I really didn't know him because he spent most of his life in the Church, so I don't know much about death, but it doesn't sound too good to me.

Cee Cee,   age 14

I think death isn't such a bad thing. I'm not going to go out and kill myself or anything! I'm going to live my life, every minute. But when death comes to my door, I won't worry about going. It's going to happen sooner or later, so why not go at it enthusiastically and experience some new thing. By the way, I want Peter Frampton to sing at my funeral!

Lola,   age 15

I'd just say life is a cycle, and sooner or later you'll die. And you figure that if you go to hell and your friends go to heaven, well, let's hope there's a telephone!

Bronwyn,   age 15

I'm not looking forward to death, but when it happens I'm going to be ready. You know how people say that they want to experience everything at least once? Well, you're going to experience death at least once. Right? I don't think death is something to fear, just a new experience.

Lola,   age 15

I know it sounds weird, but I love this subject. I used to wake up when I was a kid and I would cry and cry because I was so scared of dying. But now I'm not. I used to think, "Oh, wow, all this good stuff has to end." But now I just sort of think of death as a continuation of life. In a way it's like a beginning, you know? It's like another part of living. Everybody has to die sooner or later, right? I think that death might turn out to be wonderful. Death is something new and unexplored. The last frontier, as they say on "Star Trek."

Bronwyn,   age 15

I don't know why, but I'm very scared of death. I know I have to die because everyone does, so I wish I could feel the way you do, but as much as I try not to be afraid of dying, it doesn't work. I had a close friend who died, and when I do think about that I get terrified.

Wanda,   age 15

A Fighting Chance,
or, Belief in Miracles

Apropos of the sick rabbit we were nursing the other day, I remembered a phrase of my father's that I've always loved: "Give him a fighting chance." He used it when looking at seemingly hopeless cases, generally, but it was really a cornerstone of his philosophy. For example, if there was a choice between sending an animal to the pound or trying to find a home for him, he'd "give him a fighting chance," and call everyone in the neighborhood to find him an adoptive family. If a pet was sick, and the vet suggested putting him to sleep rather than attempting to nurse him back to health, he'd opt for giving him a fighting chance by nursing him against all odds. No matter what the hopelessness of the case, he always opted to try, not to give up. It was not only a belief in all creatures' indomitable will to survive, but a belief in miracles.

My mother had an inordinately well-developed sensitivity

for the underdog. She had a capacity for attracting the waifs and tempest-tossed that rivaled the Statue of Liberty's. Having collected the needy, be they handicapped youngsters, starving Indians or the children of people temporarily unable to cope for their own, she would then set about giving them a fighting chance by whatever means were at her disposal—money, effort and the power of her own overwhelming life-force were all brought into action. Looking back, I think many people were miraculously prodded into survival by the sheer force of her willing them to do so. It was as if her own indomitable spirit made *them* believe that they could do battle with fate and perhaps emerge victorious.

Once, when I was grown, I told my parents of a friend of mine who was dying of spinal cancer. The man was in terrible pain and I said it would seem much kinder if the doctors would put him out of his misery. They said, "As long as he's alive he's got a fighting chance." Sometime later I was having lunch with that erstwhile dying man, who had recovered from the disease and was hale and healthy. It was an extraordinary case, written of in medical journals, and I asked my friend how the miracle had happened. He said one night, while lying in bed in absolute agony (the doctors having given him up for lost), he was suddenly infuriated by the unfairness of it all, and decided to "fight." It's now fifteen years later and he's a healthy man with a spine that regenerated itself. A miracle. A fighting chance.

I love three things about my parents' belief in "the fighting chance": the compassion, the faith and the common sense of it. *Compassion* because it means that no matter what the odds, you demand for everyone and everything an opportunity to live. *Faith* because your belief in miracles must be very strong to continue unabated against great odds, and against the cynicism of a world that doesn't believe in them. *Common sense* because it is obvious that if you give up and don't fight, you have no possibility of victory at all—if you hold the line, there is always a spark of hope.

In your devotion to the rabbit, Bronwyn, by sitting and nursing, feeding and loving that little creature, you were giving him a fighting chance. You are heartbroken now, because he didn't make it. But I know that you filled his last hours with love and compassion, and that one day someone or something in your life will *survive* because you'll give it a fighting chance.

I've seen many miracles in my lifetime: not only people cured of hopeless illness, but people cured of hopelessness. I've seen people win against impossible odds, because they believed in themselves, or because they just plain decided to fight.

The point of all this is, I think, twofold. I hope with all my heart that you will always have compassion enough to give others a fighting chance, and courage enough to give yourself one. Whatever the odds, there is always a hope of victory if you believe in the possibility (not always easy to do, by the way) and if you are willing to fight like hell for it.

I do believe in miracles. My brother was in a terrible accident not too long ago, and he almost died, but didn't. I think you should never give up hope, faith and prayer. I think they may be what kept my brother alive.

                                                            Gigi,   age 15

The Will to Live

Thirteen years ago I went to the doctor for a routine Pap smear and discovered that I was in the very early stages of cervical cancer. The news was more shocking than perhaps you can imagine just reading about it; more shocking than even I can connect with from the vantage point of all these intervening years. There is a dreadful feeling of invasion, of violation, in knowing you carry within you some insidious horror that could kill you. I felt an irrational urge to tear it out, whatever it was; an overwhelming sense of fear, frustration and failure.

You were two and three years old. I was quite literally struggling for survival—yours and mine. There was a ghastly recurrent nightmare that had been haunting my sleep since my divorce. You and I were on a ferryboat that was sinking fast. I was desperately trying to keep us from drowning. First one of you would slip away and I'd grab hold of you, then the other would go under, then both would slip out of my fingers,

47

numbed from the icy waters. All through the dream I knew that there was no way to keep us all above water, that the struggle was clearly hopeless, and yet I would fight so desperately that by morning I'd be too exhausted to get out of bed. At night I was afraid to go to sleep for fear of dreaming.

We had very little money. I hated myself for having failed at marriage and I couldn't imagine the future. I worked all day, came home to two insecure, terrified and demanding babies, played with you till you fell into a fitful sleep and then did free-lance work until two or three in the morning. I was stretched so thin from loneliness that I felt I might shatter like glass. And I feared everything—most especially myself. Unquestionably, this was the most self-destructive moment in my life.

When I hung up the phone after hearing the doctor tell me what he'd found, I sat dazedly looking at a wall, thinking, I'm going to die and my children won't have anybody. The unfairness of it seemed unspeakable, beyond my grasp.

I went into the hospital, still numb, still terrified. I had a portion of my cervix removed. An artery in my uterus was cut accidentally, and badly repaired. I left the hospital and nearly bled to death when the artery opened. Back into the hospital. Another accident caused my cervix to heal shut, so that I had to return a third time two months later for that mistake to be repaired. I started hemorrhaging violently. The doctor suggested a hysterectomy. I stared at him with the intense hatred of a trapped animal in my heart. I was terribly sick, very weak and very close to despair.

That night, as a particularly sadistic nurse was digging with a syringe into the back of my hand, searching ineptly for a vein she never found, I started to scream—for the first time in all those months of pain and fear and resignation. I screamed to remind myself that I was alive. To summon myself back from a very dark place. To stop being a victim.

Quite simply, I had decided not to die. The realization that I had been unwittingly destroying myself from within was grotesquely clear to me. I knew, by a single brilliant flash of light in absolute darkness, that *I* was the reason for the changing tissues. *I* was the reason for the hemorrhaging. *I* was the reason I was a victim. *I was being done in by my own consummate sorrow.*

All these years later, science is just beginning to make the connection between cancer and loss, between cancer and sadness, between cancer and self-destructiveness. Thirteen years ago on a dismal night in a dismal hospital, I knew the connection.

Since then I've read reams on the mind/body connection; I've studied hypnosis and metaphysics in an effort to learn more; I've talked to people who've had similar experiences. While all these data have supported my belief in the role played by the mind in illness, still it is the "natural knowing" of that long-ago moment which stands out neonlike in my memory.

The will to live is, I believe, the key to life. Some people embody it in health foods and jogging, some in sheer feistiness, some in love. What it really boils down to, I think, is that if you believe strongly enough in life and are determined to survive, odds are you will do so. Just as people have survived the Nazi death camps, the horrors of Siberia, war, pestilence, famine and holocaust, because they willed their survival against all nightmare odds, so do I believe we can will our survival against the buffets of life.

Karl Menninger, in his book on the war between self-interest and self-destructiveness, *Man Against Himself,* put it this way:

We must not forget that there is also a will-to-live. In spite of the death-instinct, we see life all about us. Indeed, the recognition of self-destructiveness has as its object the combatting of self-destruction, and the encouragement and support of the life-instincts in their battle against it.

My reason for telling you this history of the gloomiest episode in my life is not to burden you with the sadness of it, but to pass along to you the hard-won knowledge that I gained: the knowledge that the will to live must be strengthened and fortified and believed in.

A year or two ago, when it was all the rage among gynecologists to show women what their cervices looked like, my doctor showed me mine. It was disfigured and battered and scarred; and I was momentarily saddened to see this ravaged bit of me; as if my injured cervix was a visceral symbol of all the injuries I have ever allowed to be inflicted on my heart or body or mind. And then, quite subtly at first, I began to feel proud of myself; proud of my survival. Perhaps it's the way an old soldier feels about his war wounds. I was proud of the self-protective knowledge I had battled for and won.

You, my dear children, are full to bursting with life-force. What I would like to pass on to you as a result of this experience of mine is the knowledge that the better you know yourselves, the more intelligently you will be able to understand whatever self-destructive urges you, like the rest of the human race, may harbor; the more sturdily you will be able to strengthen your will to live, and with it ensure the future of your minds and bodies and spirits.

Everyone should have a will to live. If you don't have a will to live, then you belong in Bellevue! If you don't have a will to live, I don't think you'll last very long.

Cee Cee,   age 14

3

THE RELATIONSHIP BETWEEN MEN AND WOMEN

Your relationship with a man can be the most rewarding, fulfilling, joyous experience of your life—or the most miserable. As a matter of fact, the same relationship will probably bring you both ends of the emotional spectrum and everything in between!

The relationship between men and women is, of course, changing just as radically these days as is everything else. Boys and girls seem to be developing *real* friendships, men and women are striving for more honesties, people are trying to put sex in a proper perspective—all very hopeful signs.

Yet I have to believe that the accumulated experience of ten thousand generations of male/female relationships will not become obsolete in a single decade, so perhaps what I and the many generations of women before me have learned can still have validity for you. Thus, in the grand tradition of older women passing on to younger ones their knowledge and observations on the heady subject of men, I pass on some of mine.

The Man/Woman Equation

The question of which sex is superior to the other one has been under scrutiny for a million generations. Men traditionally have thought themselves the A–Number 1 best, and we, even if we've been a trifle quieter about it, have every bit as firm a conviction of our own superiority.

Truth is, I suspect that we are each superior in some things and inferior in others. Men can lift heavier weights, but women have a more enduring strength. They can run a three-and-a-half minute mile, we can better stand the cold. They were mighty hunters, but we as gatherers provided 80 percent of the food of the tribe. They have, up until now, enjoyed far more worldly successes, but on the other hand, we outlive them—a very major point in our favor!

Did you know that once upon a time goddesses had it all over gods? There were centuries in which all worshiped a mother goddess and revered woman because she was the author of life,

the procreator of the species. Unfortunately for our suprema-
cist ambitions, as soon as man realized that his sperm was
necessary for impregnation, the goddess's days were numbered,
and we, for a variety of reasons, have spent several thousand
generations as Number 2.

The how and why of that happening are, as you might imagine, a very complicated business . . . based upon religion, biology, sociology and a host of other forces too numerous to name.
It seems to me, however, that one overwhelming biological fact
has most slowed women down over the millennia: the fact of
pregnancy.

Since the result of woman's sexuality from time immemorial
has been pregnancy (a quite incapacitating condition in olden
times) and birth (a great hazard up to the last century), we
were pretty effectively kept out of the more energetic, demanding and overt areas of life. Not that there weren't exceptions—
the Eleanors of Aquitaine, the Boadiceas, Diane de Poitiers, the
Xenobias and the George Sands. There were a few iconoclastic
women in every age. But they were not, by any means, the run
of the mill.

There are lots of theories about why we have contented ourselves with being Number 2 over the centuries, but frankly I
think the practical long and short of it was simply that we
didn't have much choice. We'd been programmed into subser-
vience, religioned into suppression, romanced onto pedestals
and ignored into unimportance for eons. Women weren't educated, exposed to worldliness or encouraged to be anything but
helpers to men. And, of course, as we were the bearers and
rearers of the young, we pretty much had our hands full in
minding home and hearth. Any woman with eleven children, a
not unusual circumstance in days of yore, didn't have much
time left over for writing symphonies.

But don't think for a minute that all these years of being
Number 2 have been for naught. It seems to me, my daughters,
we have learned many useful things during this time. We have

learned to work hard, to be enduring, to be conscientious, to be patient, to bear burdens steadfastly, to be unselfish and still to love the other half of the human race, despite their often underestimating us.

We have learned to make do, and to improvise—and we have learned to rely upon ourselves to make the decisions of everyday life. Child-rearing is an enormously practical undertaking. It teaches a continuing efficiency and a minute-to-minute common sense and ability to cope with crisis. All of these attributes are, of course, very useful in business as well as life.

Why then have we been so willing to be second-best until now? you might ask. Could it be that our own feelings of superiority have made us complacent—that we have felt little *need* to do deeds we felt quite capable of doing? Could it be that we have taken a back seat for the sake of our men, thinking it cruel to let them know of our conviction in our own strength when they were involved with pride in their own? Could it merely have been self-serving for us to remain in second place? Deposed kings are probably woeful bedfellows, so we may have been protecting our own interests by keeping their egos in high gear all these years. Could it be that we've been afraid? Afraid to tackle the problems, and content just to complain about how badly men are doing everything? Probably a little of each, I expect.

We have not written the operas, painted the immortal works, invented the skyships or run the governments. Of course, we have borne and trained the ones who have done these things, but nonetheless it seems to me we've remained amazingly steadfast in our feeling of superiority against incredible odds! Yet you have only to listen to a gaggle of coffee-klatching housewives or three women executives at lunch, talking about their husbands, to know that despite it all we have maintained our confidence in our own strengths.

Our belief in our own equality springs, I believe, from some quite pedestrian sources. We know our own resourcefulness, conscientiousness, capacity for hard work and practicality, and we have learned *to know* men very well. We are their mothers and sisters, their daughters, their lovers and their friends. We know their weaknesses as *they* know their strengths. We see their tantrums as well as their triumphs. We see the giant of the boardroom in his Jockey shorts, unable to remember where he put his socks. We see his humanness and we provide the support that helps him carry on.

So what is to happen? you might wonder. Now that women are entering the arena fully armed and that the whole order of things may well be changed in the not too distant future, as Number 2 gives Number 1 a run for the money?

Wouldn't it be wonderful if we as women were able to engender a gentle revolution? A reaching out for each of us to try not only to understand the other sex, but to accept it? Accept its hopes, its fears, its dreams, its strengths, its weaknesses? Blended together, male and female seem to form a perfect whole. Yin/yang—force fields of mind, heart, spirit—all talk of superiority lost in the perfect fit of puzzle pieces.

Maybe your generation will do better, more lovingly, more compassionately, more honestly, than all the rest have done. Maybe for once each sex will love the strengths of the other and support the weaknesses. Maybe jealousies will dwindle and unity will form a force so strong that only the mad would not wish to partake of it. Then the marriage of true hearts will quite conceivably beget a better world; a world where 50 percent of the human race won't be expected to lie fallow to show its love for the other half. A world where children can draw strength from both sexes at their best, and where the intense pleasure that comes of union with another soul can at last be realized.

Maybe it will take a little longer than just one generation, but it will certainly be worth the wait, and there's no time like the present to get started on helping the future do better.

We all know it's better to light one candle than to curse the darkness. Perhaps yours is a generation with the opportunity to strike the first match.

We all know that women are superior to men—because I am a girl and I think so! Haha! But really, there are good points and bad points to each sex, so you can't say one is superior. People long ago seemed to think that men were better, but these days women are getting all their rights, too, so things are evening up. I think that's good.

Cee Cee,   age 14

In Defense of Men

Very often we women do a great disservice to ourselves and to men by perpetuating myths about them. "They never grow up," "Isn't that just like a man," "Men's toys are just more expensive than boy's toys," and on and on and on. I'm sure you've heard all the slurs. It occurs to me that in the interest of simple fairness someone should come to the defense of men, since generalizations are usually as unfair as they are inaccurate.

Men are different from us, after all. They have different needs, different turn-ons, different potentials and a different ego. Because of our own female chauvinism, I believe we often allow these natural differences to become unbridgeable gaps between us, and the older I grow, the sorrier I am that this should be so.

I cannot in a few words or pages put this whole vast problem in perspective for you—of course, that isn't even my aim. What

57

I would like to do is to offer some observations and attempt, at least, to define some of the questions for you as I see them. The answers must come from your own experience. What's important, it seems to me, is that you don't underestimate or misunderstand half the human race; that you get to understand men as much as possible so that you can live with them, love them and be honest with them throughout your lifetime, to the ultimate betterment of your life and theirs.

Some of the Problems

One of the differences between men and women that seems to cause us both a lot of trouble is that *men are bred in our society with one goal—success.* They are trained, I believe, to place the eggs of their self-worth in that one basket, so that if they succeed in their profession, they consider themselves successful in living; and if not, they see themselves as failures. This is a lopsided state of affairs since it not only pressures them into a one-track vision, but it also puts all the premiums on success by any means—not on successful living, on development of character or morality, and certainly not on emotional happiness or fulfillment.

The goal of becoming a success is not in itself such a bad thing—it tends to keep everybody busy and eating—but pursuing such a goal relentlessly often precludes other valuable life experiences. And it sets the scene for extraordinary tensions and anxiety, as time goes on and ambition escalates.

Because this success orientation is inculcated early and intensifies as the man progresses, it takes up a lot of his time and energy. It is not nearly so easy to reach fame and fortune as we all think it will be when we start out, and as one progresses in any profession the demands become greater, not smaller. It is very understandable that between society's success orientation and man's own built-in ambitions, men often succumb to the unidimensionality of having nothing at all in their lives but their profession. And this very success drive that they've been led to believe we find attractive very often becomes a major stumbling block for us in trying to achieve a well-balanced relationship.

The second programming that seems to discombobulate men and women's relationship with each other has to do with the fact that *men are systematically trained never to show emotions.* Little boys shouldn't cry. Little boys should be brave little men. Stoicism is mannish. Emotions are for sissies. Men who express their emotions are an uncomfortable embarrassment for their less communicative brothers. What a repressive and unfair cross for them to bear!

This one particular piece of programming probably does more damage to them and to us than all the others put together. For one thing, such programming puts an inordinate strain on them. Just imagine never being able to cry, never being able to explode with anger or fear or horror or just plain glee. Imagine being told you are sexually inadequate if you feel deep emotion or show it. Imagine never being able to hug or kiss your friends, or to seek advice by talking over intimate questions with a chum. That's pretty much man's fate in our society.

So what happens when they fall in love? Suddenly, without any preparation and emotional training, they are supposed to be able to feel deep emotion and express it—to be openly affectionate, lovingly sensitive to their spouse's needs, and able to be open and honest in talking about feelings they weren't even supposed to have until a minute ago!

To be loving and open and communicative and committed is not exactly the macho image men are taught to covet and emulate. Machismo instead is tied into indiscriminate sex, lack of commitment, transitory ties and, of course, that ever-present success/power role that seems central to male programming.

And last but not least, *men are taught to mistrust the other half of the human race—us.* Men are taught (could it be by their mothers as well as society?) that we are out to get them— get them to marry us, to support us, to take care of us, to be our meal ticket. They are taught to fear our sexuality, our intelligence, our capabilities and our endurance. They are taught to attract us via money and power, not through love, devotion, intellect, sensitivity or common sense. And inasmuch as the system has lasted quite a long while, I'm afraid we must be responding to these stimuli.

Long story short, they haven't got the easiest row to hoe. So what can we do about it? you might well ask.

We can listen better and try to respond unstintingly. We can help them express emotion and feel good about it. We can help them feel loved because of who they are, not just because of what they achieve. We can learn to communicate in a more open and loving fashion. We can be honest in the way we treat them, and never fake anything. Despite whatever stupid old programming is left over from other, less enlightened times, we can try to be whole, healthy, sane people ourselves, and thereby help them strengthen their own realities. And finally, when the time comes, we can raise our sons with better role models, more sensitivity and a clearer vision of what it means to be a real man.

Then we can love them truly. That's not anything new, of course, but maybe in your generation it will be done with more openness, honesty, common sense and improved communication, and therefore with more *real love*, as love is meant to be.

I think men are the best thing that ever happened!

Lola,   age 15

I think boys and girls have much better communication now than in your generation. I have boyfriends who are really friends. We're more honest and open with each other these days.

Bronwyn,   age 15

> *Whenever you are sincerely pleased, you are nourished.*
> RALPH WALDO EMERSON

Sexuality

I used to think that Freud placed far too great an emphasis on sexuality as a motivating force, but I've now lived long enough to know that sex is so intrinsic a part of our being that it pervades everything. I have been aware of being enormously sexual all my life, so that it came as quite a shock to me recently when I realized that I had shut myself off from a certain segment of my own sexual being one fine day when I was fifteen, and didn't reattach myself until years later. It seems to me an important enough realization that I'd like to share it with you.

When I was very young I feared my own sexuality. It was unruly and always in evidence; it was powerful and threatened to overwhelm my control; it was dangerous for I could get pregnant. It was tricky and resilient; I hadn't expected it to be so persistent and rampant, but there it was.

61

When I was fourteen or fifteen, I was wildly, passionately attracted to a European boy. I mention his Europeanness because it played an important role in the ensuing dilemma. American boys I could handle. They played the same ritual game as I. They tried to "make out," as it was called; I reneged. Nice girls kissed and petted, no more than that. They acted disappointed, but they knew the ropes—they hadn't expected to go further!

Then there was this other young man from a different culture appearing on the scene, who expected to explore, to feel, to know. Him I couldn't handle. More than this, he had a mother who accepted his sexuality as a matter of course—she permitted him both privacy and discretion. While other parents were peeking into parked automobiles and flashing lights onto darkened porches, she was seemingly quite content with her son's need for both sex and privacy. I was devastated. I knew that if I were alone with him one more time I would relent and open myself to feeling, to wild abandonment, to God knew what.

But my mind prevailed over my body's urging; my mother's admonitions and society's pressures combined to make me opt for flight. In a way, it was just as well, I suppose, since I could never, in that age and with my structured programming and no knowledge of contraception, have handled the guilt, never mind the fear, such abandonment would have entailed. Yet I realize now, so many years later, that I did a terrible thing to myself in walking away. I shut myself off from my own sexuality; I *numbed* myself in order to keep control; I let my mother's apparition peer over my shoulder in sexual areas she had no place in, and by doing so, I surrendered a portion of my own unmitigated passion, so subtly that it took me many years to know what I had lost.

But to complete my saga: I grew up to a life of lusty sexuality. It frankly never dawned on me that no matter what the passion of the moment, in a curious way *fear* always re-

lentlessly intervened; that highly develoed antenna of mine,
which senses when something is going to get through my
guard, was always the sentinel. While this may not seem so
serious a sacrifice since I still enjoyed sex and indulged myself
as much as possible, in retrospect I think it covered up a terrible loss of sentience.

In a way, I was not in touch with my own passionate nature;
I was one step removed from my sensory self; a wall of fear
was interposed between me and my most pleasurable sensitivities of feeling, because something in the back of my brain
kept saying, "Be careful. Men can hurt you via sex." In a way,
I think this sentiment was the prevailing sexual attitude of my
generation. Sex, that most visceral of "feelings" was often, in
my day, layered over with wariness; feeling was replaced with
fearing. I wouldn't want you to make the same mistake.

What am I really trying to say to you? Am I suggesting that
sexual recklessness is sensible? That passion should overrule
common sense? That indiscriminate sex is the answer to being
in touch with yourself on a primal level? I think not.

What I am saying is that *nothing should be permitted to
interfere with your own sexuality, your own womanliness.* You
should not insulate yourself from it out of fear; you should not
have your mother looking over your shoulder. You *should* encourage yourself to take as many intensely pleasurable sexual
feelings into yourself as you possibly can.

The *taking in* of pleasure, by the way, is a very apt description, I think. Women are equipped by nature to experience
enormous pleasure from the *taking into themselves* of a man.
This is an important statement metaphysically, as well as physically, because in order *to take in,* you must *open up.* You must
open your legs and your most personal female parts, open your
most vulnerable self to exploration. If you've been conditioned
to fear this entry as an invasion rather than to welcome it as an
inordinate pleasure, you will steel yourself against it, thereby
cutting yourself off from your own intense pleasure and best

interest. If you mistrust men, or yourself, you will be wary and unopen; if you insulate yourself because of this wariness, it will be difficult to *feel* without mitigation.

In other words, the danger I think generations of women have succumbed to is that they have all been trained to fear, dislike or mistrust men, to fear pregnancy and to fear their own lustiness to the point that they have sealed off their own vulnerabilities and sexualities as a self-protective gesture—generally without ever knowing they've done so.

What can you do to stay in close touch with your own sexuality? you might wonder. I think you can remind yourself that you deserve to be happy, remind yourself of your own femininity, remember that no matter what the world says, your own sexuality is a treasure beyond price, a happiness so intrinsically part of you that *anything which threatens it, threatens you*. To feel intensely, to take a man into yourself openly and joyously, to enjoy limitless orgasms, to be filled deeply by a man's pleasure-giving body, these are your birthrights as a woman.

A New Kind of Safety

I realize fully, my darling daughters, that by taking the position I've just expressed, I am flying in the face of what ten thousand generations of mothers have told their daughters . . . ten thousand generations of mothers who have stressed safety, virginity, carefulness and tightly closed knees above all things! Perhaps a word of explanation would therefore be in order.

I believe that we as women and mothers must teach a new kind of safety to our daughters; a less insulating and more strengthening safety, one which protects with strength from within, rather than with outside insulation. Let me try to explain what I mean. If I constantly stress the danger of assaults from without (in the form of suggesting that men, by virtue of their sexuality, could do you damage physically or emotionally), I encourage the erecting of a shield wall around your feelings, based on fear. A by-product of this kind of safety is, I think, that it also insulates you from your own instinctive sexuality. Like Pavlov's dog, you begin to react to sexual stimulus with wariness. If, on the other hand, you are strengthened *from within yourself* by security of ego, strength of instinct, confidence in your own wholeness, then you needn't fear opening yourself physically or psychologically to sex, for you are not frail and vulnerable; you are strong and sturdy and quite able to *feel* without threat of danger.

By encouraging sexual experimentation I am not, by the way, encouraging sex without emotional ties. I believe that sexuality for the majority of women is deeply connected to the urge to love and be loved, a need which I imagine will not change in the foreseeable future, if at all. What I am strongly advocating is a freedom to feel intense sexual pleasure. To my mind, this neither precludes nor interferes with emotional commitment. If you wish to experiment with casual sexual encounters as part of the learning process, you can do so without attaching more significance to the encounter than it deserves, and without the kind of fear that incurs withdrawal from feeling. When the time comes that you find the person to whom you want to commit your love as well as your sexuality, you are free to do so with all the passion and feeling you are capable of. In other words, the same process takes place as would anyway, but with freedom from fear and guilt—and with increased intensity of pleasurable feeling.

Sexual responsiveness, joy and intensive pleasure are your heritage as women. You have been equipped by nature with the natural lustiness of the female. You have been given robustly healthy womanly bodies and spirited dispositions. All that remains for you to come into your own sexual birthright is that you know your own body, love it enough to listen to its urgings; that you be strong enough within yourself to be able to feel pleasure fearlessly; that you genuinely like men. If you remain true to your own best instincts, you can choose wisely and happily both your companions and your experience, so that in opening yourself up, you will be able to take in all that you need for happiness.

There are a lot of kids, and you've got to give people credit for it, who really care for somebody, and have sex with him because they want to do something special for this person. The worst is when it's only a one-sided feeling. And that can be painful as all hell. But I mean, what can you do? You can't have perfection every time.

Lola,   age 15

Sex is a very touchy subject these days. Casual sex is more accepted, and I guess people aren't really sure of what's okay and what's not. Kids today don't really have the moral values that their parents and grandparents had, where good girls "didn't," no matter what. The double standard is changing— but only a little. A girl is still considered "bad" if she loses her virginity and screws around (if you'll pardon the expression) a lot. But on the other hand, most girls think sex is a pretty wonderful thing and they're anxious to try it.

Lola,   age 15

Sex should be special between two people. But people worry too much about it. This person isn't going to like me if I don't, or maybe I won't do it right. Sex is a very natural thing, but it's like a learning process, you know. You aren't expected to be Almighty God, and know everything before you start. I know people are afraid to ask questions. Maybe afraid to find out the answers. I don't know. I was so scared to ask questions. You shouldn't be afraid to talk about it—everything would be less awkward if you could talk honestly about it to someone.

Lola,   age 15

I've never had sex, but I feel that sex is something people should do when they are in love. They say that sex can bring a relationship closer together, but I've seen some relationships get torn apart by it—I guess it depends on how mature the people are. Sex should not only be shared physically but also shared mentally and emotionally.

Gigi,   age 15

I think girls are just as sexual as boys. I mean, it's only tradition, really, that has allowed boys to be the ones to be the experimenters, while girls were expected to be virgins. Things are changing some, but it's slow.

Bronwyn,   age 15

Kids worry a lot about what their friends will think when it comes to sex. It's getting harder these days, too, because all the boys expect that any girl is willing to go to bed with them. They don't even feel they have to know you well. It's pretty discouraging. You don't want to feel like the only one who's not doing it, but you don't want to be pressured either.

Bronwyn,   age 15

I don't know why but I don't agree with you on this topic. I guess it's because I've seen what some of my friends have gone through about sex. I think I'm really afraid of sex because I've seen a lot of girls get hurt by it.

Wanda,   age 15

*The only thing that worries me
is that parents talk to their kids about sex,
but they don't talk to their kids about love.*
                                   LOLA GOODROE,
                                   Age 15

Love

I would like to talk to you of *love,* my dear daughters, because I truly believe it to be the single most powerful force in the universe. In fact, I believe love to be the most profound experience we humans can fall heir to. Love is an intensely active force for good—it can expand our vision, prompt kindness and generosity, help us believe in miracles, sometimes even help us to achieve them. I've seen love last beyond human limits of endurance, I have seen it defend itself against impossible odds, I have seen the steely strength it gives to those who truly possess it. I'd like to share with you some thoughts on the subject.

The most difficult aspect of love when one is young, I think, is figuring out how to separate it from just plain sexual attraction and from infatuation. There may be many men you are sexually attracted to in life—sexuality is so ready a part of a woman's being that it doesn't take much to trigger its response mechanism. Love, on the other hand, is rare. Its feelings are elusive and hard to describe. Its raptures aren't quite like anything else.

Infatuation can feel very much like the real thing. I suppose you might say it's an intense attraction that doesn't stand the test of time. It's a definite tingle of the body and emotions easy to confuse with real love, but it fades and disappears, rather than growing and enduring. Perhaps the best way to distinguish an infatuation from a real love is, as it has always been, to give it time. The old adage "Marry in haste and repent at leisure" has a lot of practical advice in it. The only true way to test a relationship is to see where it goes; see if it progresses and prospers, or begins to fray around the edges.

The problem with real love, annoyingly enough, is that you haven't any firsthand experience of it till it happens. You may *think* you are in love many times; you may genuinely care for people without "being in love" with them. Until you really are, there's no easy way to tell the difference. There are, however, some clues, some absolutely essential ingredients you might look for in a relationship before you consider it "being in love." Perhaps it would be helpful to list the ones I can think of.

Honesty

How really honest can you be? Must you play pretend games to keep your lover's interest and affection? Does he know *you* or a "you" you've manufactured to attract him? Unfortunately, we've all been trained for generations to be dishonest about our feelings when dealing with men, and this can be a terrible trap for all concerned. Are you able to be comfortably honest—sexually, emotionally and intellectually? Can you trust him to allow you the luxury of this honesty, without his threatening to disappear? You'd be amazed how the ability to be honest and open contributes to security and to continuing love.

Give-and-Take

Do you give equally to each other? Does he provide as much love and fulfillment for you as you do for him, or is one of you working overtime while the other is on an emotional vacation?

I'm not suggesting that you must have everything 50/50 all the time, dividing up acts and thoughts like jelly beans, but rather that each of you gives what the other wants and needs—and with the same generosity of intent. The big and little givings and takings in a loving relationship are like the bricks that pile up into a strong and sturdy fortification for your love, and I truly believe that honesty is the mortar that holds them together.

Growth

Is your relationship fertile, growing, changing for the better? True love generates an enormously fertile energy, so that one plus one equals the strength of ten, not two. A relationship that's static hasn't much future potential, after all.

There is a subtle bond that links true lovers. It persists through their ups and downs, through wealth and poverty, sickness and health, better and worse times. If that kind of bond is genuinely existent, you will surely know it and feel its strong potential for growth and endurance.

How Important Is That Other Person to You?

It may seem a curious question to ask, but would your instinct be to guard and protect the one you love against all odds? Would his instinct be to so take care of you? You might learn a lot from the honest answer to so naïve a question, mightn't you? The real point is, just how important is the one you love to your life, and you to his?

Comfort

There is a tender comfort, very difficult to explain, that accompanies love. It engenders the ability to communicate without speaking, to feel strengthened by your lover's presence, to feel profoundly touched by his existence in this world. It is a comfort which transcends sex, although in truth it adds a dazzling dimension to lovemaking, which is both mating and communion.

I have frequently heard women say, when they finally find the right man, "I never knew life could feel so peaceful and comfortable." What this translates to, I think, is that in the wrong relationship there is so much tension and aggravation, and so much compromise, that it is terribly wearing; while in a good and loving relationship, the compatibility and communion of thought and feeling provide a sense of utter contentment which is both loving and restful.

Love Lasts

Love endures, grows, progresses, blossoms, and happily, it lasts. Finally, I think perhaps the surest test of love is time and devotion. There is a wonderful poem written by the Irish poet Thomas Moore that says it perfectly. He wrote the poem as a letter to his wife, who had left him because she feared that the tuberculosis she had contracted would waste her beauty and therefore erode his love for her. He reassured her in this loving way:

> Believe me, if all those endearing young charms,
>   Which I gaze on so fondly today,
> Were to change by tomorrow, and fleet in my arms,
>   Like fairy-gifts fading away,
> Thou wouldst still be adored, as this moment thou art,
>   Let thy loveliness fade as it will,
> And around the dear ruin each wish of my heart
>   Would entwine itself verdantly still.

It is not while beauty and youth are thine own,
  And thy cheeks unprofaned by a tear,
That the fervour and faith of a soul can be known,
  To which time will but make thee more dear;
No, the heart that has truly loved never forgets,
  But as truly loves on to the close,
As the sun-flower turns on her god, when he sets,
  The same look which she turned when he rose.

The language may be flowery and archaic, but the sentiment is, I think, as valid today as it was when the poem was written.

I think that perhaps the soaring divorce rate these days is a tribute to the fact that people have a pretty shaky vision of what lasting love is all about. The best safeguard you have in making a wise choice in love, commonplace as it may sound, is your own self-knowledge, self-esteem and common sense. If you are in close touch with your own instincts and your own loving nature, I believe you will gravitate toward a healthy union.

I believe it helps, too, to give yourself *time*—time to grow, to experience, to live and learn. Time to grow close to someone you think you may be in love with—time to wait and see.

Love in books, movies, songs and stories is so overwhelming a rapture that heroes and heroines spot each other instantaneously. In real life, love at first sight is pretty rare. Most times, love grows out of friendship. It's easy to be attracted to someone instantaneously, but after that first blissful flush, there can be quite a few surprises in the "getting to know you" stage.

Nobody, if the truth be known, is very analytical where love is concerned. Most people just follow their hearts around for a while, before common sense sets in. But eventually, if love is to continue and prosper, friendship—real honest-to-goodness friendship—must be established. Imagine trying to live a lifetime with someone who was not your friend!

The best advice I can give you is to see how the relationship makes you feel. It's quite normal for love to have you topsy-turvy at first, but after a while a good loving relationship should make you feel pretty solid: strengthened by being two instead of one; fulfilled and nourished by your communion of spirit; closely bonded, despite life's ups and downs.

If it all sounds complicated—it is, a bit. But it's also a wonderful learning process. Perhaps the most joyous one life provides. You will experience all the nuances of love in the years to come, I expect; the adventure, the passion, the mystery, the uncertainty, the pain, the pleasure, the completion. I hope you will do so with a robust strength, a sense of your own womanliness and with the sure knowledge that to the best of your ability you've chosen to love someone who is capable of loving you deeply and enduringly in return.

I think that love is very good for people. Love should mean togetherness—and being with a man you are "in love" with, and trusting him, and caring about him, and being together as much as possible.

Cee Cee,   age 14

Everybody wants to be in love, but nobody knows what it will feel like.

Lola,   age 15

A lot of people get very infatuated. The worst thing in learning about love is that it's hard to tell it from everything else. It's hard to tell love from just wanting to go to bed with somebody, from really being infatuated with him. How are you supposed to know the difference?

Bronwyn,   age 15

There's no set definition for love. Different people have different opinions—you accept that maybe there are some very different ideas on the subject. The trouble is we use the word love too indiscriminately. "I love ice cream" and "I love you" are very different but the word is the same! Maybe there should be some kind of defining what 'love' really means in a long-range relationship.

Bronwyn,   age 15

When we that wore the myrtle wear the dust,
And years of darkness cover up our eyes,
And all our arrogant laughter and sweet lust
Keep counsel with the scruples of the wise;
When boys and girls that now are in the loins
Of croaking lads, dip oar into the sea—
And who are these that dive for copper coins?
No longer we, my love, no longer we—
Then let the fortunate breathers of the air,
When we lie speechless in the muffling mould,
Tease not our ghosts with slander, pause not there
To say that love is false and soon grows cold,
But pass in silence the mute grave of two
Who lived and died believing love was true.
EDNA ST. VINCENT MILLAY,
"XXXI," in Fatal Interview

Fidelity

I had lunch with two women today and their conversation prompts me to talk to you about fidelity in marriage. They said there's no such thing. I said there certainly is. They said I was naïve. I decided I was talking to the wrong two women.

This is a jaded time sexually, and New York is a jaded city, but inasmuch as fidelity is something I feel strongly about, I'd like to tell you what I think.

Is fidelity necessary, desirable or realistic in marriage? Fidelity is desirable and necessary, if it is important to *you.* I believe that in this age of open marriages and new moralities, the thing that is important in marriage is that two people agree on what is right for them. If both believe in fidelity, or both believe in playing around, or both think it doesn't matter one way or the other, I think it's probably all right. Unfortunately, what seems to me to happen most often is that each partner pretends to be faithful and then one or the other isn't. Or, one partner goes along with agreeing to the infidelity of the other but hates every minute of it! Such action seems to me unconscionable; not only dishonest and shoddy but confusing and degrading to the one who is fooled. I'm terribly suspicious of all the men who have told me that their wives sanction their extramarital activities (or at least turn a blind eye toward them). I suspect what really happens is that they throw such a smoke screen over their activities that their wives are simply fooled into a false sense of security. After all, it is only human to want to trust the person you love.

Does fidelity exist? It absolutely does, and I think perhaps in greater measure than a single woman living in New York might imagine. There are men who commit themselves to women with utter loyalty, devotion and fidelity—just as there are women who so commit themselves to men. There are men and women who take their marriage vows with great serious-ness and who strive to live up to them for a lifetime.

I personally believe wholeheartedly in such faithfulness in marriage. I would not consider sleeping with another man, nor do I believe that my husband would consider being unfaithful. We have committed ourselves to each other for better or worse, richer or poorer, in sickness or health, to love and to cherish, till death do us part. That's just how I feel about it. To sleep with a man other than my husband would be the ultimate betrayal of that very serious and well-considered commitment. I can't conceive of our ever repairing the damage that would be done by such a betrayal, although I know that some people's marriages do survive such problems.

There is an extraordinary completion that two people feel within the bond of such a loving commitment. I cannot imag-ine that those who love casually ever feel such heights of emo-tional fulfillment. There is a strength that comes from such a bonding. A strength that can survive hardships, battles, ups and downs and still be cosmically, passionately loving and complete—and probably stronger for having been tested.

What I'm saying, I think, is that the decision to espouse fidelity or not is just that . . . a decision. You must not be jaded into believing there's no such thing anymore; nor must you accept other peoples' visions of what the proper marital relationship is—including mine! So many people settle for an unsatisfactory situation simply because they can't conceive of a better one.

Perhaps it has to do with your sense of self and the standard of behavior you set for yourself, and for those who touch your life closely. I'd opt for the best, if I were you. I'd hope to find someone who will love you honestly and committedly. Life is complicated enough without the burden of having to mistrust the person with whom you've chosen to spend your future.

People talk of fidelity as if it were old-fashioned, naïve, unrealistic and unrewarding. I'd like to write the brief for the other side. It seems to me that faithfulness in marriage is loving, responsive, stalwart, loyal, mature and as realistic as you'd like it to be. It is a way to build toward the future with trust, loyalty and commitment as your bulwarks. It is a touch of passionate permanence in an uncertain world. It is a way to live and die "believing love is true."

Whatever you decide your needs are in this regard, I hope you'll find a man who shares your convictions—and in my heart of hearts, I hope he chooses to share them, and himself, with you alone.

I think fidelity is the most important thing ever. Well, there are different kinds of being faithful . . . you can be faithful to your husband or your boyfriend, or you can be faithful to your best friend, or to somebody's memory, or you can be faithful to your parents, or to an ideal. I think fidelity is a good thing, in general, and especially in love. If you've made a commitment to somebody—whether it's just friendship or marriage or living together or boyfriend/girl friend, whatever the relationship—

being faithful is a very important part of that relationship. It has to do with trust. If someone trusts you to be faithful to him, then that's what you should be. It would be a terrible disappointment to find out someone you loved wasn't as faithful as you.

Bronwyn,   age 15

To love and to cherish from this day forward. For better for worse, for richer for poorer, in sickness and in health till death do us part.
I do.

Marriage

In my day, when sex was untalked-of and surrounded by much mystery, many, many young women married the wrong person simply because they wanted to try sex, and, having done so, had to sanction the act by calling it love. Others married to escape bad homes, or to have a chance to be grown-up. Others married because it was the expected thing to do, because their family wanted grandchildren, or because they didn't have the skills or profession to earn a living on their own. Before that, for most of history, people married because their parents had made a match for them or to better their prospects. In other words, more people than you can imagine married for the wrong reasons and were left "repenting at leisure," or divorcing, or enduring—most times, with children to complicate the issue.

Your generation, it seems to me, is the first in history with the opportunity to marry for all the right reasons. What a glorious prospect! Because I believe firmly that marriage as an institution has existed and prospered through a million years of evolution because it has enormous merit as a way of life.

I'd like to tell you why I feel marriage has so much going for it, and why I think it is a possibility you ought to eventually consider, even if you choose to live with your partner before making a legal commitment.

Strength in union. There is a bond between husband and wife in a good union that is so tough and enduring it can weather troubles, fights and foibles, and remain intact, absolutely. The companionship of a good marriage is a fruitful and emotionally fulfilling experience, hard to explain. It is lovely to grow with another soul, to learn by living, to expand together; to know each other so well that words are hardly necessary. It is extraordinary to feel not bored but enriched by the continuity of it.

Sex in marriage. Sex with one you love deeply, spiritually and committedly is vastly more wonderful than a casual sexual encounter could ever be. You and your husband not only grow more knowledgeable as lovers as time goes on, so that you each know the other's needs and wants instinctively, but as the depth of your relationship increases, so does the sexual fulfillment of your union increase.

You've probably heard people say that sex changes with marriage. It most certainly does—I think for the better. The first blush of anxious excitement diminishes, but neither the desire nor the pleasure does. There are moments with a longtime lover when you are wildly passionate, tenderly loving, merely snuggly or any number of other possibilities. Far from boring, such a relationship allows for infinite variety—and all within the protected golden circle of commitment.

Commitment. The state of being committed to a man is philosophically, as well as practically, very interesting. A commitment is, after all, a *voluntary proposition—something you decided to do and believe in.* If you fear it, or don't want it, or don't feel comfortable with it, you probably simply shouldn't do it.

Having taken such a step enthusiastically, however, the commitment of marriage has myriad rewards. Because of its permanence, it allows you to build with surety. Commitment affords stability and reinforces trust; it means that you and your husband plan to build a life—physical, mental, emotional—together, so that you can make use of both your strengths, both your intellects, both your energies, both your visions, to create a very special future. You are not transients in each other's world; you are not passers-by.

Commitment of spirit in marriage can also take you over the bad or rocky times, because it is stronger than momentary misunderstanding. I remember once having a terrible argument with Joe. We each, both absolutely convinced we were right, stood glaring at each other, face to face, in the bedroom, having said all we had to say. Finally my husband said to me, "You know what the problem is now, don't you? Neither of us is willing to leave the room, because if someone walks out, it will seem final." He was absolutely right. Our commitment to, and love for, each other was stronger by far than our current distemper. In a way, these words have always seemed to me to be the essence of marital commitment: when push comes to shove, nobody is willing to leave the room, lest that injure the bond.

Growth. I've heard many, many people talk of the boredom they feel is inherent in marriage. "No one can remain interested in the same person for a lifetime. Eventually you must get bored" is how the story goes.

I don't believe that is so. We do not, any of us, remain the same for a lifetime. We grow, learn, expand, change, as life progresses and experience accumulates; but so does our mate change and grow. There is no reason why a relationship must remain static or become boring. It can take a lifetime to learn all the nuances of your partner, to say nothing of your own.

If you care to expend the effort, the depth of knowledge available in a long-range partnership is enormous; the closeness you can achieve has potentially vast depths of understanding and love inherent in it; the time spent can be an ally to growth, not a deterrent to excitement.

There is both trust and camaraderie that grows with time. We've all seen elderly couples, long married, who have picked up each other's characteristics and even look alike. They have chosen to grow into a strong and solid unit. It seems obvious to me that they have learned things about love and devotion that one can only learn with the passage of time.

Everyday intimacy. It is difficult to express the delicate yet profound beauty of the everyday intimacies shared in a good marriage. There is great comfort in knowing that your spouse is always there—to talk to, share with, laugh with, learn with, love. There is *delight* in the tiny loving gestures that abound . . . a field flower picked at random, a back rubbed when you're tired, a book picked out in a bookstore that is just the one you wanted. There is everyday wisdom to be had from someone who knows you well, and is willing to be honest. There is joy in knowing you have someone always in your corner, rooting for you when the chips are down, rallying your spirit when it falters, sorting out when you're confused, supporting when you're weary, cheering when you win. There is exquisite strength in the kind of communication that doesn't always need words, that makes you happier at home together than out in the world in the most scintillating company.

I suppose what I really want to say to you about marriage is that it can work well. There are husbands and wives who are faithful to each other, who are exquisitely happy with their choice and with their love. Too often, I think, the loudest, most cynical voices are the easiest to hear, so when people tell you that "All those faithful old couples are just sexually naïve, and don't know what they're missing," I'd like you to know that there is another side to the story.

My husband once told me (long before we were married) that I was a unicorn, and as such I must never consider marrying a horse. He was quite right about the principle involved, I think. Like must find like in order to be happy. Then and only then can marriage be good and true, and closer to magic than anything else this world has to offer.

Marriage is wonderful. Marriage is fantastic. Marriage is the greatest thing they ever invented—because you fall in love with somebody and then you get to spend the rest of your life with that person, and it's a wonderful experience. Even if it's not exactly as wonderful as it's all cracked up to be, it still seems to me the best thing that can happen to you.

Lola,   age 15

You can't just go into marriage expecting perfection and expecting everything to be wonderful just because you're in love, but that's what everybody does. They're pretty stupid about it, I think. But I really like the idea of marriage. I think it's pretty wonderful.

Bronwyn,   age 15

I want to get married and have children. I don't mind committing myself to a man as long as he loves me and I love him.

Gigi,   age 15

Divorce

This is a tough subject to tackle. You have both been wounded by my divorcing and you have also, perhaps, been saved by it. The same could be said of me. As you know, my early life didn't go as I had planned it. My intention was to grow up, marry, have children and lead an orderly, comfortable, secure and quite ordinary existence, growing up and growing old within one marriage.

As it happened, I didn't choose a lifetime partner. You've sometimes asked me how I feel about having married your father. Truth is, because you are the progeny of that marriage, I'm glad I did it. Despite the fact that it wasn't a good union in other ways, had I never married him I would not have you—exactly *you* with all your heredity and all your nuances—so needless to say I'm very thankful that I made that choice.

Nonetheless, my having divorced when you were babies has not only caused me problems aplenty, but also has caused you insecurity, anguish, anger and fear, and that's a heavy burden

83

for you to have carried from infancy on. Therefore, it seems to me you deserve to have me tell you as best I can how I feel about the whole subject of divorce.

Frankly, I hate the whole idea of divorce, but I believe it to be an essential option. I believe one should try hard to make a wise choice of spouse, and having made that choice, try hard to grow creatively within the marriage. Yet one must surely be free to remedy a mistake, if marriage turns out to be one.

In bygone days, people married for life, for better or for worse, and I'm inclined to believe that a good part of the time it was mostly for worse where the woman was concerned: she had no rights, no escape hatch and no latitude to reinvent her role. However, those "forever" marriages did have one good thing going for them—their very continuity and permanency made it necessary that the parties try to work things out *together* over a long period of time. I'm by no means suggesting that we go back to the permanent bondage these marriages implied, but rather that we apply modern know-how to working within an oldtime commitment. It stands to reason that if you believe strongly enough in the concept of marriage and in the possibility of its permanence, you will have a better shot at growing together instead of separately, and of working your way through difficult situations rather than running away from them.

Without question, the best bulwark against a bad union is preventive medicine—making an educated choice of a partner in the first place. Taking the time to get to know someone after the first wild flush of attraction settles down; perhaps living with him if that seems sensible; trying to be as open and honest and as much yourself within the relationship as possible—all these are positive "protections" against later trouble. Yet I've lived long enough now to know that even having done all these things is not necessarily a guarantee of eternal happiness. People change with time and with the added pressures of children, responsibility and upward mobility.

A recent survey suggests that the biggest source of marital dispute is neither sex nor money nor in-laws, as most of us might think it would be, but rather unresolved angers . . . grievances collected to the point of unbearable burden . . . angers percolating into a Vesuvius of hostile emotion. I love Joe very much and I am as confident of his love for me as I am of the likelihood of the sun rising tomorrow morning—yet we sometimes are so angry with each other that steam comes out of our ears. I'm certain that in such moments we are saved by the fact that we believe so strongly in our commitment to each other, we care enough to fight out loud instead of holding silent grudges; and when the chips are down we are always allies of the soul. What might have happened to us in an age when fighting wasn't allowed and when women lived as silent servants—I don't like to imagine. But just as *we* are fortunate enough to live in a time that allows for open and vigorous communication, so are *you* fortunate to be growing into adulthood with the knowledge that such openness is desirable and within reach. I don't think any other generation has been so blessed, and in a way, this honesty and vigor will probably give your generation the best chance of all for living happily ever after.

Finding the right marriage partner is a tricky proposition. I remember a horrified friend, tearfully telling me she had met the man of her dreams but had found he was a disappointing lover; conversely, I've heard countless stories of wonderful lovers who were far from dream men! In looking for someone to share a lifetime, we are looking for a great many compatibilities. We want a man who will make us happy in bed and out, who will feel as we do about children, who will share our dreams and fantasies, and help provide a fairly stable financial and emotional environment through all the changes and growth of fifty years or so. And men, I daresay, want that and more from us! So it's not easy for any of us to make forever choices.

Bottom line: that I believe in marriage, and I wish you the fulfillment such a long-term relationship with a man can bring; that despite the odds, and the times, I believe you can achieve such a relationship; that in a curious way I also believe your generation is capable of raising marriage to a true loving partnership. But I also believe in divorce—as a last resort, of course, not as a precipitous decision. If it is the only way to remedy an incorrect coupling and to go on from there, I believe divorce to be the right act. I also hope with all my mother's heart you'll never have to go through one.

Single-parent households are pretty wild. Parents think they have to make something up to you because there's only one parent in the house. But that's ridiculous. Because having one parent—I guess it's different from having two—but that's not all that bad.

Lola, age 15

If the parents weren't so worried about what is going to happen to their kids in a divorce, and could relax about it, I think it would all be okay in a single-parent household. If the parents weren't so scared that the kids are going to grow up mentally deformed because of having one parent, everyone could have a good time. You've got to figure that a kid is going to grow up much stronger in a single-parent home. I think that when parents get divorced the kid is either going to crack under the strain or he's going to be the sanest kid you'll ever meet, because he's gone through so much.

Bronwyn, age 15

I don't think the relationship between a mom and kids is typical, when you had only Mom for a long time. Because being alone, and being a single parent and raising kids that way, is a different deal—for the parent and for the kids. I think kids develop a much more adult-to-adult relationship with their mom than child-to-mother relationship. Kids are not treated as much like kids as they are like friends and part of the family. In a lot of ways, I think it's good, because you mature much faster and you feel you are an important part of what goes on in life.

Bronwyn,   age 15

I think it's sensible, if people don't get along, to get divorced. Because if they don't get divorced, then they just have to lead a terrible life for years and that's just crazy. Of course, if you don't get married, you don't have to worry about going through all that.

Cee Cee,   age 14

I never want to get married. I want to be a swinging single, because I don't want to be tied down to one certain person, and if it doesn't work with that person, then I'd have to get a divorce. I don't want to have to go through all of that divorce misery, and I don't want to have to worry about any of those divorce problems, so I think I'll just stay single.

Cee Cee,   age 14

Most kids are pretty adaptable and they can handle most things that happen. Adults don't seem to realize that even if things like divorce are traumatic, they can put some starch in your backbone!

Lola,   age 15

There are maybe ten cases out of a million where a kid would fall apart about her parents getting divorced. The first couple of weeks or the first couple of months are pretty awful, but you get used to it and it's not that bad. We're a pretty adaptable bunch, us kids, let me tell you. We manage to live through most things. I think divorce is harder on the parents, because they have so much worrying. They worry about you and they worry about each other and they worry about themselves.

Bronwyn,   age 15

Divorce is a heavy subject. A lot of us kids have been through it. I think divorce is a terrific thing, actually. Because you shouldn't be stuck with a person who's wrong for you, for the rest of your life, and have no other options.

Gigi,   age 15

The trouble is, I think that people are giving up too easily on marriage. They seem to think divorce is the only way out, which it's not, of course. But it's a good thing to have the option of changing things just in case it's needed. And divorce usually is a sad thing, but it ends up much better in the long run.

Lola,   age 15

Before my parents were divorced, they were fighting all the time. And that was terrible. I mean, you'd come home, and you'd hear them screaming at each other and it was really hard on the nerves! I guess after they separated things got better. It was like I had two homes. My father lived in the big city, and I'd get to come visit him. I even saw more of him that way, because before the divorce he used to just come home at night and read, and not pay any attention to us.

Lola,   age 15

If you have kids and a creepy husband who's impossible to live with you shouldn't stay with him. Divorce is a bad thing for kids, I think, but they get over it. It's a big thing for kids to get over, but they do. What bugs me is when people choose divorce really fast, without having given things a real try. I think it's not a decision that you should come to in three days. People have to learn to give marriage its time, because I guess the first year is always the hardest—everybody has to adjust to living with the other one. If you make it through the first year, you might be okay.

Lola,   age 15

I thank God there is divorce because if there wasn't, my mom would be unhappy right now. I'm sure there are others who feel the same way.

Wanda,   age 15

Chastity is the most unnatural of the sexual perversions.
ALDOUS HUXLEY

Living Together

I believe it can make a great deal of sense to live with someone before you decide to marry, provided, of course, that you wish to do so. And provided you feel there is enough of a commitment between you both so that marriage is a good possibility. Just in case you are surprised that I would suggest this, here are a few of my reasons.

Living, not courting. Courtship, with all its romance and ritual, has very little to do with real life. During courtship you and the man in your life are on your best behavior. The first flush of love not only colors your rosy glasses, but it colors your actions and reactions as well. In order to know someone, you must live with him, day by day and night by night. You must see him when he's spiffy and when he's a wreck, when he's cheerful and surly, well and ill, tired and cranky as well as riding the crest of the wave. And he must see you in all these conditions before you really begin to know each other.

Learning intimacy. The ability to share intimacy takes some learning. Day-to-day living with a man affords the opportunity to learn how to share yourself far better than all the dating in the world ever could. Such intimate learning simply can't be done satisfactorily in sporadic meetings, under the circumstances of dating.

Practice. Living together lets you try your hand at being grown-up, independent beings. It gives you the opportunity to practice many important elements of growth: sex, love, sharing, dependence, independence, friendship. It allows you to do this practicing without the pressure of having to remain together forever. There are no children to bind or inhibit the relationship, or cause it to continue longer than it should. There is time and privacy to practice sex, not just as immediate stolen pleasure, but as a continuous shared experience. This is a very different experience from the more casual sex of dating.

Mistakes. Living together allows that if you do enter into a mistaken relationship, you can just walk away from it. No children, no encumbrances; just some lessons learned and some experience gained. In other words, it allows you mistakes, with positive, rather than negative, consequences.

Growth. It's pretty tough to make permanent decisions when you are very young. You haven't a lot of experience, you are still learning who *you* are—never mind trying to figure out who anybody else is! Although you may greatly desire love and a permanent relationship, it is quite difficult to choose the right one at twenty. For one thing, you still have some growing and evolving to do. For another, you still have limited experience to draw upon.

When you believe you are in love, living with someone rather than immediately marrying allows you to find out for *sure* before committing to marriage. If it turns out to be the right coupling, you can proceed toward making it permanent with knowledge and surety on your side. If not, you can continue your own growth, so that with a bit more experience to help, you can make a better choice next time.

I don't, by the way, suggest that you live with just *anyone*, or that you be in any way indiscriminate in your choice of living partner. After all, the giving of yourself, body and mind, is a very substantial gift to give someone. That person should be a worthy recipient. For that matter, the taking of someone is a large responsibility, too! Beyond that, there are practical considerations. Moving in lock, stock and barrel, or having someone move in with you, is a big logistical feat, and you'd hardly want to take it on lightly.

But let's assume that you have found someone you care about deeply, someone who seems to fit into your future as well as your present. I believe that because of your sense of your own worth, your intrinsic good taste and your ability to follow your own instincts, you would choose as wisely as possible. Living together to explore the relationship to its fullest before committing to marriage could make all the sense in the world.

I think living together is perfectly sensible. First of all, it gives you a chance to learn about another person and have a really close relationship, without making such a heavy commitment as marriage. You get time to share everything, to see how well you do get along and to see if the relationship is right, for both of you. It's like a trial marriage, and I think that's a good idea. With the divorce rate so high these days, the more you know about someone before marrying them, the better. But I don't think you should just go off and live with anybody. *You should have a real commitment before you live together. It isn't just like playing house!*

Lola, age 15

I think that living together with a man is a very good idea because that's what I'm planning to do—I'm not planning to get married at all.

Cee Cee, age 14

I think living together is fine as long as both of you have some kind of commitment to each other. But how about a man who really just wants to live with you because he doesn't want to be married to you? One who says, "Let's just live together and see how it works out." I'd feel really weird about that, because why should I give up my apartment and my life, and live with a man if he's really that uncommitted to me?

Bronwyn,   age 15

Expectations about Love

I had breakfast with a very wise young woman yesterday who said something I thought wonderfully well worth writing to you about. We were discussing the fact that there are a lot of terrific women around and few worthwhile men for them to date (remember my telling you that women, when they get together, tend to feel female chauvinistic!) when she suggested that perhaps these women's expectations were somewhat out of sync with reality. "Perhaps no one has told them," she said, "that if you want to be loved by a poet you can't expect him to be a ruthless titan of industry, too." I was absolutely riveted by the thought, so succinct and sensible. It started me thinking that our expectations of men and our perceptions of our own needs where they are concerned have a lot to do with the success of our final choices.

What does a woman have a right to expect in a man she likes or loves? It's a difficult question to contemplate, but I've taken a crack at putting together a list based on my own experience of some essentials of character (not all, by any means, confined to male rather than female) all of which I believe to be really significant to the potential of a long-term relationship. You'll think of additions to the list, I'm sure. But here's a beginning:

Strength. I think it realistic to seek strength in a man. Strength you can rely on, lean on if need be. Strength of character, which means that he be rooted in reality and in touch with his own good instincts. Not strength to be pushy and powerful, necessarily, but strength to be solid and responsible and honest.

Sexuality/masculinity. It is very important that the man you love have a well-integrated male sexuality. By that I mean that he is robustly, healthily male. Not showily macho, or flamboyantly boastful of his sexual prowess—two sure signs of sexual insecurity—but simply sure of his own maleness, comfortable with his own sexual being.

Many men make a big show of maleness. They talk about their escapades, make a point of having a beautiful woman on their arm, are proud of the number of women they've been to bed with. It's almost as if they spend their whole lives following their penises wherever they lead. Such men, I think, have not integrated their sexualilty with their whole selves . . . it's almost as if their penises have a separate life of their own, rather than being part of the whole man. It seems they must experience vast numbers of sexual encounters because they can't sustain a relationship with one woman. The integration of self and sexuality is terribly important to the future potential of any relationship. If a man is confident of his manliness he can feel genuinely comfortable with your womanliness; if not, you'll both be in trouble.

Sense of self. In order to be able to relate to you, a man must have a decent sense of his own worth. If he has this, he needn't be threatened by your confidence, or your strength, or your womanliness, or your talent. If he lacks this sense of himself, he may feel threatened enough by your wholeness to try to whittle away at it; he may mistrust you, and otherwise seek to bring you down to his size.

On the other hand, if his sense of self is strong and confident, he can relate comfortably to you on all levels; can cheer you on in your triumphs, help shore you up in your disappointments; in short, he can be a strong and positive force for good in your future life.

Integrity. Without assurance of a man's integrity, it's pretty hard to build a life. If you can't trust the person you love, you are building a house on a foundation of shifting sands. Integrity, honesty, trustworthiness are solid, forceful, real virtues. A man *must* have them to be worthy of being loved by you.

Sensitivity. I think men have been trained to notice different things from what we have; they have not been bred to cater to a woman's whims, as we in our traditional role of helpmate have been bred to notice their needs and fulfill them. Nonetheless, there is a wonderful sensitivity of spirit which the best of men seem to possess, which lets them tune in to your needs because of a genuine interest in *you.* It is this special antenna that helps you both bridge whatever gaps of understanding exist between man and woman, and that makes it possible to touch each other on an intuitive level that is very special.

Protectiveness. I'm sure most feminists would be incensed by this thought, but I believe that deep down inside, most women feel a desire to be protected by the man they love. For a million years the males of the tribe have protected the females and the young; to tell the truth, I can't see any reason why civilization should alter such a basic state of affairs.

Fairness. I frankly believe that fairness is an enormously important quality for a man to possess, as it is the one quality that can help to guarantee all the others. Whatever the issue that arises between you, if you can rely on his approaching all situations fairly (or at least trying to!) you are way ahead of the game.

Similarity of goals. While opposites may attract, they don't wear well. There is a great deal to be said for similarity of goals, of needs, of desires, of dreams. Often similarity of background contributes to such shared interests, yet people of very different heritage can be soul mates, too. The important thing is, unless you are both walking the same path, headed in the same direction, one of you will constantly have to compromise. Traditionally, it generally falls to the lot of women to do so— not much to look forward to long range.

Courage. You should, I think, seek courage in a man. Not courage to go out and rule the world, but courage of convictions, courage to prevail, courage to stand against the crowd. A man must have courage to face life squarely and directly, to follow his own inner voice and to create according to his ability to do so. Life is a game for the hearty, and your own courage can be bolstered when need be by the confidence you feel in the courage of your mate.

The ability to love. We as women, over the years, have had a terrible tendency to make excuses for men where the simple ability to love is concerned. We've told ourselves that we need too much affection as a species, that there aren't any men out there who love as truly as we do. We've compromised and often settled for those who give less love and affection than we really crave. And then, of course, we've carped at them for not giving enough to fill our needs!

I believe with all my heart, my daughters, that the ability to love—to give generously of self, to care truly about another human being—must be considered as essential in a mature man as it is in a mature woman. No compromises, no two ways about it. If a man can't love you freely and genuinely and passionately he is less than you deserve.

Responsibility. You have an obligation to yourself to look for a man who is totally responsible. Irresponsibility has no staying power, no building potential, and no solidity. A man, to be a man and not a boy, must take responsibility for his own life, for who he is, what he becomes and how he gets there. Only if he is fully responsible for himself can he consider taking on responsibility for you or for your children. Life demands responsibility of us at every turn in the road. A boy is not equipped for the job; a man must be.

Passion. This is, of course, part and parcel of sexuality, but I've set it apart to make a point. What I was talking about earlier was generic male sexuality—an integrated sense that a man has of himself as a male. What I mean by passion is a bit more than that. I think a man should be capable of great depth of feeling; the ability to love fully and deeply. He should have the same passion for living as he does for loving. A robust breasting of tempests, and having the courage to prevail, has a wonderfully virile strength about it. Passion to be, to do, to see clearly; passion to expand, to express, to achieve. While these are not exclusively male traits, they're wonderfully important ones.

And there you have it. The list is, of course, only a fairly personal set of guidelines. Ultimately, the choice is yours. I have no doubt that you will meet and know many different kinds of men. You must exercise your own good judgment in determining which of them is the right kind of man for you. Perhaps if you keep in mind the simple question, What do I really want? when getting to know them, you will be less tempted to compromise your needs, or make the wrong choices.

Let me give you an example of what I mean. Let's imagine a girl named Sally. Sally loves poetry, she is quiet and introspective, and her idea of a terrific afternoon is to curl up with the collected works of W. B. Yeats and watch the rain pitter-patter on the library windows. However, Sally secretly pines for Lance, the muscle-bound captain of the football team who thinks Yeats maybe played for the Dallas Cowboys. And she totally ignores Herbert, who can recite "Sailing to Byzantium" from memory, and is known on a first-name basis by librarians in three counties. So guess what would happen if Sally and Lance really got together? Boredom and frustration, mostly. Neither one would come anywhere near fulfilling the other's dreams. Even if they both bent over backward to compromise, I can't imagine their living happily ever after, can you?

In other words, you must know your own needs pretty clearly in order to gravitate toward the kind of man who can help you fulfill them. If you seek an artist, don't look for him in the corridors of power; if you seek a Board Chairman, don't expect him to have the soul of a poet. It is not only unfair but doomed to failure to seek the one and try to turn him into the other. And, of course, if you seek a very rare combination of the two, you must be patient in your quest for such a mate.

What it all boils down to, I think, is this: the better you know *yourself,* the better chance you will have of seeking and finding your soul mate. While you may experiment with and experience many men in the process of learning about life, the one you'll ultimately choose for a husband will be as much the result of your own self-knowledge and self-esteem as of fate or destiny.

I don't expect fire rockets, or even firecrackers, when I fall in love. But I do expect that I'll be happy, and just so overwhelmed that I'll be feeling wonderful about the person I love and nothing else will really matter. I guess love is being able to overlook the other person's faults, or his opinions that you don't agree with. Mostly, I just expect love to be wonderful— expect it to make me and the person I love happy.

Lola,   age 15

4

ON BEING A WOMAN

Despite the fact that the media keep telling me that your generation isn't particularly interested in having children, I decided to write to you about pregnancy, birth and motherhood because these experiences seem to me a primal part of your birthright as women. Your births, in truth, began my life as a woman; your children's births, should you decide to have children, will be profound landmarks in your own development.

Besides all this, of course, pregnancy and birth are where you and I began our collective odyssey, so it seems only natural in our verbal journey, for me to tell you what it's been like since the very beginning—not only for my sake and yours, my dear daughters, but in anticipating your children, yet to be.

Where did you come from, baby dear?
Out of the everywhere into the here.
GEORGE MACDONALD

Pregnancy

Nobody really prepares a woman for the process of bearing another life. Perhaps the connection between birth and sexuality makes it taboo, or perhaps the intimacy of the physical and emotional sensations of the experience makes it a tough subject for verbalization. Whatever the reason, it seems to me deplorable that we women have done such an inadequate job of sharing the *reality* of the experience of pregnancy and birth with each other and with our children. After all, giving birth is the one earthly process almost every woman knows intimately.

I'd like to tell you what I remember of the process—what I thought, what I felt, what I needed—because to be truly prepared is to be better able to enjoy, and to be unafraid. Because, too, you should have as much information at your disposal as possible when you get ready to decide if you *wish* to have children. Yours is the first generation in a position to make motherhood an intelligently planned choice, rather than an inevitable fate, so it seems to me you'll want to garner as much information about that choice as possible.

First of all, believe me, pregnancy and birth are a major miracle. The first time you feel your own child wiggle inside you, something primal and immeasurably important happens in your innermost self. Corny as it sounds, you are one with the universe, with all women, with all time. You are utterly and irrevocably female.

I remember many feelings. Some confused, some startling. Why hadn't anyone ever mentioned the strange sense of invasion? Coming to terms with another living being, who is temporarily inhabiting your body with you, isn't necessarily automatic. Wouldn't you feel odd if someone told you there was a person growing in your foot? Just because a person is growing in your uterus, which was meant for such growing, doesn't change the strangeness of the sensation. I had never heard another woman speak of this reaction until after I had shared the experience, yet I'm sure it is something felt by many.

I was frightened of the unknown, unsettled by the strange new physical sensations. Could the ankles I'd prided myself on ("You can tell thoroughbred horses and thoroughbred women by their ankles," my grandfather had told me) really be twice their normal size? Were those stretch marks to be mine forever? Could those strange road-map lines be varicose veins in my twenty-one-year-old legs? Was it possible that I could be this nauseated and still live?

All this turmoil was going on, of course, at the same time I was growing smugly proud of myself for being a grown-up woman at last. I was convinced I had somehow magically inherited the accumulated wisdom of the ages with my insemination, so that I, as a mother (remarkably, that word seemed suddenly cleansed of any impatience I'd felt with my own), would know *everything* necessary to raise my children to perfection. You should know, by the way, that I imagined you both as clean white blotters, ready to soak up all the love and knowledge I would impart. I also think I pictured you in my mind's eye as neat and tidy, in organdy pinafores, with long blonde hair—but that's another story.

I remember the ongoing and intensely personal communication I had with you growing within me. I talked to you all the time. I even knew what you would look like and did portraits of you as you would be. Curiously, they were accurate. I knew quite clearly that you would be girls. I wonder how I knew.

The physicality of being pregnant is as amazing as life on another planet. Morning sickness at first, nausea even at the smell of water, then a robust strength in the middle months that makes you feel mighty and very beautiful. The last two months, the prevailing need is for the suspense and discomfort to be over. God made pregnancy a month and a half too long; if there was ever any question in my mind about His being female, it was dispelled by the interminable ninth month of pregnancy!

Emotional hills and valleys are a typical complaint all during pregnancy, as your body organizes its hormones for a whole new task. I can remember feeling I could rule the world one day and wanting to pull the covers up over my head permanently the next.

It's normal to feel fabulously sexy and beautiful during the middle months, and just as normal to feel terminally lumpy during the last. It's also normal to feel out of control, as if some other life-form had suddenly taken charge of your being and you were just going along for the ride. In short, it's normal to feel a whole range of peculiar ups and downs, for pregnancy is a nine-month odyssey through new emotions, new physical sensations and new self-awareness. As such, I think, it can be viewed either as a cosmic seesaw or an amazing opportunity for growth and self-exploration.

The other day I heard a young woman say that she would never consider becoming pregnant because it would ruin her figure. She spoke of stretch marks, imperfect breasts and less-than-superb muscles as if they were the ravages of some loathsome disease. I was torn between amusement at the silliness of her remarks and sadness that she didn't even know what an extraordinary experience she would be missing.

The ability to have children is, it seems to me, a remarkable birthright we women possess. Should you choose to exercise that birthright, I believe the opportunities for love and growth and happiness that will accrue to you will more than make up for any small deficiencies you might encounter in muscle tone! I wonder, by the way, if the person I overheard had any idea that a woman who has had a child is far less likely to have breast or uterine cancer than one who has not. In other words, there are some very positive physical effects of pregnancy, as well as the few negative ones we sometimes hear about.

There's no denying that the last months of pregnancy are uncomfortable, even painful. Back aches with the strain, bladder gets squashed under Baby, breathing is a conscious effort, and waddling around is only worsened by sitting down and trying to get up again. Truth. All that.

But it is also astonishingly, wonderfully magical. The last two months, your baby is so very with you—wiggling, turning, touching, kicking, punching, moving viscerally into your awareness with increasing vigor. And you want so much finally to see it. Hold it. Touch its fingers, hear its sounds. I also think you fear most for your baby's safety toward the end. You want it to be born, so you can hold it and protect it and make it safe.

Dearest, dearest daughters, it is a miracle to carry a life you love inside you. Afterward you can never again be a child yourself. Not even in those rare moments when you long to be. Maybe you can never be absolutely private again, maybe you can never be wholly selfish again; but then, never again in your whole life will you ever be alone or unloved.

———————————

I think it would be wonderful to be pregnant, to know you're bringing a human being into this world.

Wanda,   age 15

I've never been pregnant, *I've never given* birth *and I've never been a* mother! *But in my opinion, I don't want to have children until I am at least forty, because I don't want to ruin my life with being tied down.*

Cee Cee,   age 14

I'm not planning to have children because I'm not going to spend my life devoted to kids. I'm spending my life devoted to me.

Cee Cee,   age 14

A baby is God's opinion that
the world should go on.
CARL SANDBURG

Birth

I saw both of you the moment you were born, a miraculous remembrance I wouldn't trade for anything. So is the holding of your own child for the first time. That is so extraordinary a feeling—of holding what was inside, on the outside—I don't think you ever quite get over it.

I'm sure birth is utterly, individually different for every woman. When I went into labor, my mother said to me, "It's the hardest work you'll ever do in your life." It is, of course. But it's so much more than that . . . so extraordinary an experience that I want to tell you as best I can what to expect. Most of us are simply too young, too frightened and too inexperienced to appreciate being party to a miracle; yet now, after all these years, when I look back, that's the best description I can find to fit the experience.

What I remember with most amusement was the unexpectedness of labor. Your generation, of course, never comes on anything unexpected; not after seeing everything on TV. But just in case nobody thinks to tell you of the unexpected: nothing about birth was precisely as I'd imagined it to be. The books I'd read (there weren't nearly as many available then as now) had been clinical and detached. The women I'd talked to had been vague and evasive, or downright terrifying. None of these less-than-perfect sources had told me that labor contractions could start in the lower back. Lord, did I feel inept! I was sure I would be the only woman in the world who wouldn't get it right.

My first delivery was frightening and, in retrospect, far more painful than was necessary. My ignorance of what was going on and the callousness of the people around me combined to make what should have been a wonderful experience into a miserable one. My second delivery, only twelve months later, was so different from the first that I couldn't believe the same process and the same body were involved. I felt minded and cared for throughout by a remarkable doctor, who was supportive, kindly, compassionate and smart. I breezed through your birth, Cee Cee, in record time, with minimal fuss and maximal comfort. Needless to say, as a result of my two contrasting experiences, I believe it is vitally important to find a doctor who genuinely likes women and babies, and who takes joy in being part of the remarkable experience of birthing.

The best way I know to find a doctor who likes women and babies is to talk to friends about their experiences. By the time you are in need of an obstetrician, I hope you will already have found a responsive and knowledgeable gynecologist or internist who may fill the bill. If not, or if you should be in a new community, as I was, I hope you'll feel free to ask friends and acquaintances for recommendations, and listen carefully to what they say about the doctor's compassion and responsiveness.

Once you've chosen your doctor, I'd encourage you to consider very carefully with him or her the method of birthing you choose.There are many possibilities available now. Some are very esoteric, like a birthing stool, which uses the help of gravity to get your baby into the world as effortlessly as possible. Some are old-fashioned, like birth at home, where you and Baby may be spared the clinical impersonality of a hospital, and the need to schedule everything at an institution's convenience, rather than yours and Baby's. You may want to find out about the new Leboyer method, which tenderly takes your baby, as it emerges from the warmth and security of your body, and places it in a warm, gentle bath so that its first moments in this world are not harsh and alien.

If you can arrange things so that you can *hold your baby to your body immediately after birth,* try to do so. It must be cold and frightening on the outside for a newborn infant, and the bonding that you will feel with your baby is so intense from this first moment, I truly believe you will both profit greatly.

I hope you'll have the good fortune of sharing the birth experience with your husband, to the fullest measure. You'll need him to understand all you are feeling; he'll need you to share an adventure he can't possibly comprehend without your help. Your baby will need both of you to be as close to each other, and as loving with each other, as possible, to help him or her get the best start in life.

Fear is surely the worst enemy a woman has when she is giving birth. Fear of the unknown, fear of pain, fear of old wives' tales, fear of inadequacy, fear for your baby. To help eliminate these fears, there are many positive steps you can take. Some wonderful books are available now to tell you the nitty-gritty details of the process of birth, both physical and emotional. You might try reading *Special Delivery* by Rahima Baldwin, or *A Shared Journey: The Birth of a Child* by Donni Betts, or *Loving Hands* by Frédérick Leboyer, or *The Gentle Birth Book* by Nancy Berezin, when the time comes. Your generation seems very determined to learn the how-to of everything, so I'm sure you'll make it your business to learn as much as possible about birth, doctors, anesthesia, etc. I'd like to encourage you *to learn all you can* about the process, via books, films, conversations—whatever's available. The more you know your body, and the more you are in touch with your body's needs, the less you'll have to be frightened of. You might find it useful to seek out a Lamaze teacher and learn about natural childbirth. Even if you should decide against using the technique for delivery, the physiological and psychological knowledge such Lamaze training can impart would be invaluable.

Inasmuch as you are both as garrulous as I am, I probably won't even have to remind you to *talk* to as many women as you can about birthing. Doctors and books can't really tell you about the feelings, the pitfalls, the important stuff; only women can. Try to sift it all out for yourself, plumb all your sources and then go to it. The birth of your children is something you will remember till your dying day. It is momentous. It is a turning point. It is a landmark in your growth as a woman.

Make it as fulfilling, as memorable, as love-filled, as comfortable, as wonderful as possible—after all, you have nine months in which to plan the event to perfection.

I think you're absolutely right about having a doctor who likes women and babies. If I were ever going to have a baby I would want to have a doctor who would help me understand everything and who would answer all my questions. I'd want to know all I could about what's going to happen to me when I give birth.

Wanda, age 15

I have never experienced birth, but they say that birth is a very beautiful thing. I don't know whether I would like to have natural childbirth, but I'd like to learn more about it so that when I have my first child, it will be a beautiful experience for me and my husband.

Gigi, age 15

Motherhood

When I was your age, everyone expected to grow up to be a wife and mother. Even if a girl worked after finishing school or college, she generally did so as an interim measure, marking time until her "real" career as wife and mother would begin.

These days, becoming a mother is a choice, not an inevitable event. Not only does such conscious choice-making allow women a more self-determined destiny, but, I hope, it will also mean that most of the babies who come into the world from now on will be truly *wanted* by their mothers. Both these results seem to be big steps forward.

The reason I'm writing to you about motherhood, despite the fact that you are years away from it, is simple. There are things I wish I'd known when you were little, as clearly as I know them now, that I'd like to share with you in the interest of you *and* your future children. I believe that the knowledge gleaned in motherhood is something that should be passed from one generation to the next, in a sort of loving continuum. Whatever I've learned from you both, I'd like to recycle to you, in safe-keeping for the future.

Basic Mothering

No matter how the world changes, some very primal needs seem always to remain the same. I'm convinced that the basic need of the young to be nurtured, hugged and loved is so intrinsic a part of human nature that we must use all our intelligence and common sense to find a way of fulfilling this need in our children.

Inasmuch as women of your generation are more likely to have jobs outside the home—whether because of your own ambition or economic necessity—you are going to have to find creative ways to assure your children of their proper nurturing quotient. Possibly taking six months to a year off from business for each child's birth would be the solution (in this age of small families, one or two such sabbaticals could hardly keep you from fame and fortune, if that is your goal). Taking special care to be physically demonstrative with your children would certainly help. Inasmuch as you are both very huggy by nature, I don't imagine that would be a problem for either of you!

There are a growing number of doctors and psychologists who believe that the feeding process is far more than caloric nourishment. It is emotional nourishment as well. Holding a baby in your arms close to your body while it is feeding (whether by breast or bottle) goes a long, long way toward building that baby's security system for a lifetime. Warmth, comfort, love, sensuality, cuddliness, caring: it's a bulwark against the terrors of life—a stability no one can ever take away from your child.

Most important of all is that you *follow your own instincts*. Not the admonitions of society, the leftovers of your own childhood or the advice of well-meaning friends. I believe the act of mothering would come as easily to us as it does to mice and tigers if we would only listen to our own good instincts. Looking back, I believe that if I had listened sooner to what *you* were telling *me* you needed in order to be happy (be it time, or toys, or explanations, or understanding) and had listened less to the rules and regulations I thought necessary to raise children properly, we both would have been far better off.

Psychologists tell us that we all have a tendency to replay scripts from our own childhoods. In other words, we simply recycle our parents' attitudes and actions, and, in so doing, perpetuate mistakes from generation to generation. Haven't you sometimes seen a young mother or father react in such an old-fashioned, uptight way to a child's behavior that it's apparent she or he isn't acting out of personal experience? I'm hopeful that if and when you have children of your own, you will sort through whatever you remember of my child-rearing methods and toss out the bad ones with never a backward glance; I'm hopeful you'll do the same with anything society, too, has to say about raising children.

I was in the elevator of a large New York hospital the other day and I heard an elderly doctor admonishing a younger, rather officious-looking resident. "Don't you ever let me hear you make short shrift of what a mother is telling you about the child's condition. You may have a medical degree, but the good Lord gave her the instinct." I wanted to hug the old gentleman, because that's precisely where it's at, I think. Nature would hardly have equipped elephants and zebras and kangaroos to nurture their young properly and have left us out.

Bronwyn, I often watch you with Alexis, your constant babysitting charge, with consummate glee. You handle her with such natural mothering, it's like watching a cat with her kittens. You play with her, talk to her, fuss at her and sometimes toss her around like a sack of potatoes, and she worships the ground you walk on. You've never, to my knowledge, read a book on child psychology, yet I've seen you painstakingly explain *why* she should or shouldn't do something, in two-and-a-half-year-old lingo that would thrill the Gesell Institute. No arbitrary "Do this or do that"—sweet reasonableness, good sense and respect for Alexis as a person are the tools you use.

Which brings me to my final thought on mothering. The key to successful child nurturing, it seems to me, is thinking of your children as *people*—not as children. *People* have rights to privacy, to love, to security, to explanations, to protection from cruelty, to ownership of possessions, to courtesy, to kindness and so on and on and on. Children seem not to be granted these rights by most parents. They are punished cruelly and arbitrarily, they are left in the dark, they have their toys and animals taken from them without a court of appeal. They are yelled at, ordered around and sent to the store a lot, without very much consideration of how battered they feel as a result. It seems axiomatic to me that the kids learn from this parental behavior that they are second- or third-class citizens, whose opinions matter nothing and whose personal well-being is of little consequence. It's no wonder so many people go a lifetime without ever really reestablishing the sense of self they were probably born with. If you think of your child as a person, with all the same rights you have and many more needs, you won't go wrong in helping him or her establish self-respect.

There are some gloriously open-minded books available now, like *What Every Child Would Like His Parents to Know* by Lee Salk; *The Self-Respecting Child* by Alison Stallibrass; *The First Three Years of Life* by Burton L. White; and *The First Five Years of Life, The Child from Five to Ten,* and *Youth: The Years from Ten to Sixteen* by Arnold Gesell, M.D., Frances L. Ilg, M.D., and Louise B. Ames, Ph.D.; and *Escape from Childhood: The Needs and Rights of Children* by John Holt, that would be well worth reading when the time comes, just to see the scope of vision available in the world about the "proper" way to raise children. But best of all would be to plumb the

depths of your own good natures, so you can respond instinctively to your child's needs with love and kindness.

Motherhood is a privilege, an awesome responsibility and a
wondrous joy. The bad news is that no one does it perfectly.
The good news is that it probably doesn't matter. I sometimes
wonder if perhaps the things we do wrong for our children
contribute nearly as much to their knowledge of coping with
an imperfect world as the things we do right.

If you let them, your children will teach you every bit as
much as you'll teach them. And happily, the learning they will
impart to you will be open-ended, for their generation will pro-
pel you into the future, just as yours connects them to the past.

_____

*From what I see, it's very hard to be a mother. Sometimes when
I do something wrong, and I see how upset my mother feels
because of it, I feel terrible. My mother has gone through a lot
for us kids.*

Wanda,   age 15

*I really want to be a mother and I babysit a lot to practice. The
one thing that drives me crazy is that I see a lot of mothers who
only want to be mothers when it's convenient. I think that if
anyone is mature enough to have a child, then she should be
mature enough to handle it, and to stay home and to love that
child and take care of it. A lot of mothers just buy their children presents from time to time, to remind them that they're
around.*

Bronwyn,   age 15

*You don't have to stay with a child twenty-four hours a day, of
course, but going out twenty-four hours a day, and seeing your
child only when she wakes up in the morning and before she
goes to bed at night, is just not right.*

Bronwyn,   age 15

Motherhood is a serious job, it's not to be taken lightly—but I think a lot of women do that. It just doesn't seem right to me. It's not fair to the child. It's not fair to the mother either, because she's missing seeing her child grow up and learn.

Lola,   age 15

Motherhood has got to be the single hardest job in the world. You're forming people and you're giving them their values, and their morals, and their expectations about life. It's like being a sculptor with a piece of clay, and you get the chance to mold it into something spectacular. I don't envy mothers, that's for sure. But I'd like to be one someday.

Bronwyn,   age 15

As long as you've tried your hardest to be a good mother, and to show your children that you love them, that's all that's needed, because your children know when you're trying. You can sense when your parents love you, and you can sense when they're just keeping you around because they have to. Kids can always tell the difference.

Lola,   age 15

If I do all the things I want to do for myself before having children, then when I do have them, I can make it a good experience, because I'll have a better understanding of myself to bring to motherhood.

Gigi,   age 14

I think parents boss kids around too much without thinking of kids as people. They treat them more as slaves. "Go to the store." "Clean the room." "You have to do what I say, because I"m your parent." "Do what I say, not what I do." That's annoying—because it makes you feel like a second-class citizen.

Lola,   age 15

> *Little girl, just half-past three*
> *This is what you mean to me,*
> *More than all that money buys,*
> *More than any selfish prize,*
> *More than fortune, more than fame,*
> *And I learned this when you came.*
> *Other parents know it, too.*
> *Nothing matters more than you.*
>   EDGAR A. GUEST

What It's Like
to Have Children

Inasmuch as no one ever tries to give you a realistic view of what it's like to have children—to live with them day by day and night by night—it isn't any wonder that most of us come to the task of parenthood naïve, ill prepared, with incorrect expectations and with the wrong training.

Having babies sounds like fun. They will be pretty and playful and pink or blue, and will live in a beautiful nursery surrounded by unbroken toys, uneaten books and an immensity of parental love and guidance. We see ourselves as mothers, never, never making the mistakes our mothers made—never yelling, never angry or frustrated, never, never instilling guilt or causing pain. So much for the fantasy.

The reality, like most of life, is a bit more complicated. For children are with you twenty-four hours a day, seven days a week, when you are tired and when you are ill and when you are distracted and when you are weak—just as inexorably as when you are whole and strong and up to coping. They are utterly needy and demanding. They need your love, your nurturing, your body, your mind and your emotions, as symbiotically as they did when they were inside you. Only, having been born, they are harder to handle, more unruly, more unpredictable. Finally, they are *themselves.* Not clean white blotters, waiting to absorb your teachings—but feisty, fully formed human beings, with talents and shortcomings, strengths, weaknesses and awarenesses all their own from the minute they plop into your world.

So there you are—having prepared yourself for an idyllic love-feast—finding yourself in the midst of a life-and-death struggle with a tough, strong, intelligent being who can tax you to your limits, and who needs and loves you very much.

I can remember holding a nauseous Cee Cee in my arms, cleaning Bronwyn's soiled diaper and throwing up in the process, when the three of us, all alone in the world, had a terrible case of the flu. I can remember my frustrated tears on realizing that I had to do it all, no matter how sick I felt—it was up to *me* to take care of *you.* I remember, too, my desperate desire to help you, knowing you were as sick as I, and in much tinier and frailer bodies. I remember my terror that I might faint or die and leave you unprotected.

I can remember sitting up all through the night, holding you, Cee Cee, when you had the croup—fearing you would stop breathing if I put you down for a minute. (Remembrances, too, of a time when I was three or four and, having bronchitis, was afraid to go to sleep, lest I forget to continue the painful process of breathing. My father said he'd watch me all night long and remind me to breathe if I forgot. And he did.) I can remember you, Bronwyn, in my arms, teething painfully, crying pitifully, as I walked back and forth, back and forth, endlessly, singing lullabies and Irish freedom songs—the only ones I knew with sufficient verses to keep me going!—all night long. Only to fall asleep at dawn and be awakened minutes later by your hungry morning cry, Cee Cee. How can you ever explain

those moments (and there are many, many of them in a childhood) to a child, when later she stands defiantly before you and
flings back all your love and courage with a single well-aimed
"I hate you—you don't love me at all"? As every child, at some
point, does.

The first five years with a child are, I think, a total labor of
love. Babies and toddlers are messy and mischievous. They
stick beans in their noses, and their tongues into light sockets;
they ask ten million questions, tug at your skirts and heart-
strings, chatter incessantly, cry at the drop of a hat and absorb
every bit of love and energy you can feed in, like infinite
sponges.

Now for the good news. There are also, during this time, a
phenomenal number of rewards. Your little ones love you
wildly and indiscriminately. They drink in all that you can
give them; they love you *despite your failings* and they trust
you absolutely, whether you deserve it or not. They laugh with
you, play with you, cuddle with you, love you and try to be like
you.

Children are not, of course, born civilized. They scream
when they want something, piddle in their panties, pour oat-
meal over their heads and eat peas with a knife (if they can
catch them) and they take much longer than you think they
should to succumb to civilization.

They also run into traffic, stick their fingers into fires and do
other horribly dangerous, odd things that scare you half to
death. And this is why one of the biggest parental pitfalls happens, it seems to me. For these dangers precipitate Mother into
becoming policeman; the one who always admonishes, always
keeps you from what you'd rather do, always says No to what's
fun, the one who makes you toe the mark relentlessly. It's a
terrible state of affairs for both—awful for the harried child,
terrible for the harassed and worried mother. That dread policeman role seems to me the one thing it's hardest for the
child to forgive, or the mother to forget. I believe it's the reason
that most people for a lifetime rebel against, and feel guilty

toward, their mothers; while most mothers for a lifetime forget to trust their sons' and daughters' ability to do what's right and competent.

In the second five years, all that love, time and effort begin to be paid back in a very full measure. The fruits of your labors become evident. Your children take on form and dignity; they are easily recognized as individuals; they are "full of wonders, like a cup." They are people, not babies, and they are making surer gains on being civilized. They are learning things of great moment in school. (Oh, the joy of the first page in a book that your child reads to you, all by herself!)

A mother is able to see her children's strengths, their weaknesses and their needs very clearly in these years. They are still little enough to come to you with their troubles and triumphs—you can still kiss things and make them better—and you can still garden them gracefully, tugging at a weed here, fixing a tattered blossom there. You are still in charge, in a way, although daily they are grasping to take the rake and hoe from your hands. These are wonderful years if you are fortunate enough to recognize them, and if you are lucky enough to have the time to pay attention.

When both of you were very young, older women would frequently cluck their tongues and tell me that you wouldn't be little long enough, so I should enjoy every minute of your childhood. As it happens, I've lived to see that they were right.

One of my worst and most profound moments as a mother came one day when I put my arms around you, Bronwyn, and I realized I was hugging a woman, not a child any longer. In an instant, like life before a drowning man, a thousand images flashed through my mind. It suddenly was clear to me that you were both nearly grown. That I would never be able to hold you in my arms and soothe away your pains again, never take you on my knee and make you laugh when you were crying, never be able to surround your world with my protective embrace, to keep you safe. Suddenly, I was mostly out of control, and you were mostly in.

It wasn't that I didn't trust you to take care of yourselves. I did. But I knew so much better than you the dangers and the pitfalls that somehow it had never occurred to me that a day would come when I could no longer protect you from them with my maternity. To this minute, when you are troubled or besieged, in my heart of hearts I feel that I could fix it all if I could simply take you on my lap and hold you in my arms once again.

One of the hardest parental trials comes with teenagerhood—where you are now. Teenagerhood is something like the ritual of passage in a primitive tribe, but it takes a lot longer and the pitfalls are more manifold. Inasmuch as I happen to think that being a teen-ager is possibly the most difficult thing you'll ever have to go through, I am particularly pulling for you now.

These days it's even harder to be a teen-ager than ever before. The protective guardrails of other generations have been thrown over; and by dint of all the information at your disposal, the terrible responsibility of sophistication is yours. Yet despite all this information and exposure, egos still get hurt. Feelings still get injured if you don't look like the group looks, or you don't do what the group does. New emotions still have to be coped with, new physical sensations still must be brought under control; you still have to find a way to net out of it all, as someone you'd like to be. *All these things are just as hard to cope with as they ever were, despite your superior knowledge and sophistication.*

Teenagerhood is probably the toughest time for parenting. You youngsters are trying hard to separate yourselves from us parents in order to be independent beings on your way to adulthood. While this is a good and healthy process, it also complicates things, because just at the moment when you children seem in most danger and we feel we have most useful information to impart, you no longer want to listen. So we parents are left on the sidelines, rooting for you kids, hoping we've instilled enough common sense to see you through, wanting to trust in your judgment, and scared to death of all the horrors that you must sidestep.

Yet it's glorious to see you both, children no longer. To see not only the fruits of my own labors, but the flowering of your selves—to see you as healthy, whole, sane and functioning beings, almost ready to take on the world—full of talents, data, insights, strengths and foibles all your own. I feel I'm particularly lucky that you treat me as a friend—perhaps not a confidante at this stage of the game, but nevertheless a friend. Maybe I can't take you in my arms and fix your ills anymore, but I think you know that I would do the emotional or physical equivalent, if you needed help.

So, you might ask me, how does it all net out in the real world? Are there more goods than bads to parenting? Should you be wary of it, or run out to meet the opportunity head on?

I can only tell you how I feel. To me the good and beauty of your children more than outweigh all of what I've just recounted. So much so that most of the time, once your children are through these difficult stages, you never even remember the hard parts. Mother-daughter love (I don't know anything about mother-son love firsthand, so I can't comment, but I imagine it is the same) is so pervasive, so overwhelming that just to see you—grown and whole and warm and vital and brimming over with life and your own specialness—makes my heart sing.

I would not trade being your mother for all the riches in the world. I love you endlessly, I'm proud of you. I like who you've turned out to be. You have taught me things so singular, and so important to my own evolution, that I can only be grateful. You have been my friends, my companions (my mother, too, at times), and you have been my dear daughters . . . a unique and meaningful adventure for me and one that is still unfolding.

I, plainly, cannot imagine life without you. You are inextricably part of me—of my heart's fiber, of my mind's recesses, of my body's blood and bone. Life, had you not been born to me, might have been considerably easier, but not anywhere near as good, or as filled with love and learning.

5

THE HEALTH OF THE BODY

For a number of years, when you were quite young, I was plagued by a rash of serious illnesses that went from bad to worse, regardless of my attempts to get well. Certain of my experiences during that time led me into explorations of medicine and healing that I might otherwise never have pursued. They also inevitably led me to some firm convictions about the link between mind and body that is, I believe, the key to health.

If there were just one concept I could be assured of bringing to you—aside, of course, from the perception of how much I love you and believe in you—it would be the idea that mental, emotional and physical health are not only inextricably intertwined, but are in great measure within your own conscious control. That statement is, I know, not only radical, but enormous in scope, for in essence it places both the potential and the *responsibility* for healthy living in your own grasp.

Our bodies are so much a part of what we are and what we can become that they probably deserve a good bit more investigation and effort than most of us give them. With that in mind, I offer the following thoughts, in the hope that they may contribute in some measure to your essential health and happiness.

*This Being of mine, whatever it really is,
consists of a little flesh,
a little breath and the part which governs.*
MARCUS AURELIUS ANTONINUS

The Mind/Body Connection

In the Orient, the mind/body connection has been understood for centuries. A yogi can control his heartbeat, change his blood pressure, eliminate pain, even control bleeding—all by using the power of his mind; yet Western medicine has taken a very long time to admit that this extraordinary connection exists at all.

Instead of learning that our mind and body are both interconnected and under our own control, we are trained to see our mind and body as two very separate entities (needing separate specialists to keep them in tune, I might add) which are curiously divorced from each other. We are also trained to be rather suspicious of our own bodies—as if they were somewhat unreliable machines which might contrive to do us in, if we're not careful. Because of this peculiar programming, "I just can't get my body to do what I want it to do" becomes a more easily understood concept than "I *am* my body—of course, it will do what I want it to do."

I believe that such divorcing of mind and body leads to the strangest state of affairs, in which a person may feel quite at the mercy of his own body: "I'm forever getting sick, so I can't have fun!" Or at the mercy of his own mind: "I can't get myself to concentrate. I'll never learn this stuff!" This kind of thinking is as bizarre as it is widespread, for when you stop to think it through, *you, your mind* and *your body* are all quite synonymous.

I firmly believe that my mind and my body are one continuous entity—me! And I'm in charge. As such, I most certainly can get *myself* to concentrate. I most certainly can keep myself from getting sick. And what's more, I'm quite *responsible* for my own mental and physical well-being—responsible for doing everything in my power to stay healthy. By keeping my mind and body working in harmony, not discord, I believe I go a long way toward fulfilling that responsibility.

This does not imply that knowledge of the body/mind link is the *only* means at our disposal of keeping ourselves in a state of heathful well-being. I believe firmly in our doing every sensible thing we know of to get healthy and to stay that way—but more about that later. What it does mean is that a sure knowledge that the mind/body connection exists can contribute greatly to our leading a healthy, happy life.

There is an ability to heal ourselves that we all possess. Everyone uses it to a greater or lesser degree. I'm certain that even the most orthodox doctors would be willing to tell you how important the will to get well is in the healing process. My experience has shown me that we are quite capable of healing even severe illnesses by the power of our own minds. I believe we can help *keep* ourselves well and whole in the same way; can protect ourselves from outside aggressions; can live longer by the very creative effort of making the power of our own mind/body work for us. I'd like to tell you some of the experiences that have led me to this conclusion.

Pursuing the Mind/Body Connection

Years ago, when I first began looking for answers about my-self, I was fortunate enough to meet a most insightful therapist who told me that he believed the colds and sore throats that were plaguing me were simply a trick my mind was playing on my body—a way for me to escape from something I couldn't face, through illness. I, of course, said that was the silliest thing I'd ever heard, so he offered to show me that I could control this "cold-prone" tendency, via hypnosis.

He taught me how to relax myself sufficiently to achieve the altered state of consciousness called hypnosis and suggested to me that the next time this "critical situation" occurred (in other words, the situation that was triggering the illnesses) in-stead of manufacturing a cold, I might manufacture an itch-ing left palm. I left his office thinking he was dreaming! Sure enough, the next time the situation I couldn't cope with popped up, much to my amazement my palm began itching outrageously, and no sore throat appeared. This was the begin-ning of my realization that my mind had something to say about what happened to my body.

I decided to find out what other revelations hypnosis might offer. I discovered first of all it is nothing like what it looks like on TV and in the movies. Hypnosis is not a means by which you can be made to look or feel silly; it doesn't make you do things you don't want to do. *It is not an experience in which you are out of control of yourself.*

Hypnosis is merely a different state of consciousness from the one we live in all the time. As I'm sure you know, other states of consciousness can be reached by many means—by meditation, by religious ecstasy, by self-induced trance, by drugs, etc. Science is increasingly aware of the variety of states of consciousness which exist, potentially, for each of us. *The particular state of consciousness* I have reached through hyp-nosis has been inordinately beneficial, which is why I'd like to try to explain it to you in detail. One word of caution before we begin, though: your teacher must be an experienced psychologist or psychiatrist, who has added hypnotic procedures to his armory of therapeutic tools. It is essential that you avoid so-called hypnotherapists who are not legitimate, should you decide to explore this area of learning.

The first thing you must do in inducing a hypnotic state is to relax yourself, all over your body. You (with the help of a trained professional hypnotist, not merely a dabbler) consciously relax your whole being. Relax your hair, relax your scalp, relax your eyes, relax your nose and on and on and on to your toes, in a conscious effort to thrust away the tensions that surround you—and as a means of establishing, strongly, the mind/body link that is the key to the process.

Having relaxed yourself thoroughly, you will find that there is a portion of your brain that acts as a monitor of what's happening to you. This monitor remains in touch with your immediate surroundings, so that you are not ever out of control of yourself, but rather you have a sort of dual-level consciousness: one part in touch with the world around you, and one part able to delve far into your own psyche. In this state it is possible to reach a deeply perceptive level of your mind, where there resides an endless repository of sensory information, old "tape recordings" of your entire life experience, and an enormous well of creative mind-power, which can be harnessed to your benefit.

In this deep level of consciousness, the garbage you have collected throughout life (the societal admonitions, the bad programming, the debris of guilts, masochism and neurosis that you've picked up or been force-fed) is swept away. You are in touch once more with your own good instincts, your own memories, your own best and most intuitive self.

In this condition of hyperconsciousness, remarkable things can happen. A complex dream you couldn't interpret in a normally conscious state is seen with utter clarity. Symbology becomes an easy translation . . . the mind speaking in the mind's own universal language. A baffling problem may seem quite simple. A totally forgotten moment may be reenacted in utter detail. The genesis of an illness may be understood with such perception that the means of healing it becomes apparent.

You can use the creative power you are thus in touch with to help heal yourself of illness. You can use it to strengthen your waking perceptions. You can use it to help clearly understand your own motivations, needs, desires. You can use it to help you learn.

In other words, in this "other" consciousness, you are in total touch with *you*. Not "you" as you have been shaped by environment or trauma. But you at your best and brightest. You at your strongest and freest.

My early experience of hypnosis was my first serious contact with the interwoven capacities of my mind/body connection—it was palpable enough to motivate me to learn more. So, true to my lifelong pattern, I betook myself to the bookstore and the library. I found a plethora of information, but it took a considerable amount of ferreting to do so, for all those years ago there was no mind/body section in any book department, and holism wasn't even a gleam in anybody's eye.

Curiously, as I pursued this elusive mind/body connection, I was led into many esoteric areas of healing. I found that Eastern medicine accepted the mind's power over the body so profoundly that it no longer even questioned its existence. I found early biofeedback experimentation, whereby scientists were developing electronic brain-wave monitoring equipment to help a person follow on a screen the monitoring of his own mental and emotional ups and downs. I found various meditational disciplines which taught disciples to reach altered physical states via peaceful mental concentration. And as time wore on, and I began to practice my burgeoning knowledge of the body/mind connection, I began to grow healthier.

Norman Cousins' recent book *Anatomy of an Illness* outlines the part played by laughter and determination in his successful struggle against what was supposed to be an "incurable" disease. It's been a best seller. Suddenly book titles like *The Mind/Body Response* and *The Wisdom of the Body* are appearing with delightful frequency in bookstores. In short, the connection between the mind and the body is beginning to be explored, tested and proven by medical and psychological researchers, and I have every reason to believe that your generation will reap the rewards of such investigations. Hallelujah!

How Your Mind Can Make You Sick

Let's consider for a moment the other side of the mind/body link—the dark side of the Force, you might call it. In other words, let's consider how our minds can contribute to making us ill rather than making us well—for I firmly believe that the creative energies of the mind/body connection can work both positively and negatively. Let me explain.

Illness

The mind can affect you physically, on a psychological level. This can work any number of ways. (1) Maybe you can't face a particular problem in your life, so you get sick and then the problem must settle itself without you. (2) Maybe you can't face the everyday tasks assigned to you in life, so your subconscious mind invents a long-term illness which takes you out of the running quite effectively. (3) You may even inadvertently create an illness because subconsciously you believe you deserve to be punished. So many people are programmed with horrible masochisms left over from a childhood in which they could never do anything well enough to satisfy their parents. Sadly, they really *expect* punishment of some kind as the natural order of things. This is often the case with abused children, who grow up convinced that they deserve punishment. If no one gives it they manufacture their own punishment in the form of chronic illness, without even knowing they are doing so. Illness, you see, has the added bonus of letting you manipulate the people around you with impunity. You can have everyone do your bidding and yet expect nothing of you in return.

In other words, a dilemma that starts in the mind may eventually manifest itself in the body as an illness.

Anger and Fear

The mind can affect the body on a very obvious physiological level. Unpleasant emotions produce very real physical symptoms. Anger or fear can cause the muscles at the outlet of your stomach to squeeze closed so forcefully that your digestive system becomes spastic. (When someone says, "That news hit me like a punch in the stomach," he can be quite accurate.) Your skeletal system and the muscles of your internal organs can become painfully tense, and if the problem persists long enough, you can develop muscular rheumatism or fibrositis as a result. Your heart rate can go up so radically, from the normal 80 or so to 200 or more, that a stroke can occur. During emotional sieges, the number of your blood cells increases and your blood clots more quickly than it normally does. Sometimes the coronary arteries of your heart can be squeezed hard enough by stress that angina pectoris or coronary occlusion can take place. Hyperventilation—breathing too fast or too deeply— can force too much carbon dioxide into your bloodstream, so fainting occurs.

In short, a problem that begins as an emotion may end in any number of physical disabilities. No one, to my knowledge, doubts the validity of this phase of the mind/body link. A quotation I once ran across from Charles H. Mayo of the famous Mayo Clinic explains it perfectly. "Worry affects the circulation, the heart, the glands, the whole nervous system. I have never known a man who died from overwork, but many who have died from doubt."

How to Explore Your Own Mind/Body Connection

If you'd like to explore your own mind/body connection, I'd suggest reading *The Healing Mind* by Dr. Irving Oyle, *The Wisdom of The Body* by Walter Cannon, M.S., and *Holistic Revolution* by Lillian Grant.

There are also several practical steps in the learning process that you might enjoy trying. It would certainly make things easier if you have a great teacher to guide you in this exploration, as I did, but basically here's how you might proceed if you'd like to try it on your own.

Talk to yourself. Not necessarily out loud. Practice communicating within yourself. Remind yourself daily to be healthy. Reassure yourself of your own strength. Learn to praise your own good body.

Visualize. Imagine yourself to be brimming with health and vitality. Imagine yourself looking as you want to look. Hold on to this visualization. A good trick is to picture yourself in your mind's eye looking into a mirror. Picture your image in that mirror, being as perfect-looking and as healthy as you can conjure. This visualization technique is being experimented with in many countries now. The results are most encouraging. People are being taught to use it to gain or lose weight, to change their mental attitudes, and to help heal themselves of illness. At the very worst, the technique can't hurt you in any way, and may help you to foster a more positive philosophy of life.

What it really comes down to is this: we walk into our own images, our own thought-forms. If we picture ourselves overweight or ill or bedraggled, we soon begin to project these tendencies outwardly. We've all known people who *look* like what they think of themselves. We're all known people who desperately fear a certain illness and end up getting just that illness; who fear a certain kind of accident and finally have it happen to them. I believe firmly that in each of these cases visualization is the key. Each person materializes the vision he holds of himself—for good or ill. If we could all train ourselves early to hold only positive, healthy self-images, our lives would change dramatically for the better.

There's no magic in this. Just the power of the mind harnessed to do good for us. Scientists claim that we use only 5 percent of our potential brainpower. I believe the remaining 95 percent is quite tappable if we know how. The mind's creative power is limitless, but we must understand how to use its potentials to our own benefit. The power of positive thinking has surfaced in many guises over the centuries. I really hope that your generation will be the one best to put it into practice.

————————————

I've never been hypnotized, but I would like to try it someday. I'm not scared. I think it would be a good experience to go through—it would certainly be interesting to know how it feels to remember things from childhood that I thought I'd forgotten.

Gigi,   age 15

I've never experienced hypnosis. I don't really know if I'd like to try it in the future, but right now I'm scared.

Wanda,   age 15

How to Help
Yourself Be Healthy

Medicine can do a great deal for all of us. From the instant we are born (and often before) modern medical science affords us as safe an odyssey through this life as it is able, and having an excellent doctor or two to rely on is a very important safeguard.

However, I would like to take the responsibility for being healthy a step or two beyond medicine . . . for the very word medicine suggests something curative to be done to us *after* we have become ill. I would like to talk to you about preventive health care; the science of staying as well as possible, as long as possible, by whatever means are at your disposal.

Get to Know Your Own Body

Most people are taught only the most rudimentary information about their bodies. I can't impress you enough with the importance of learning how *you* function; what each organ does, how your circulatory and nervous system work; what can be expected from every part of you. This is important knowledge so that you can stay healthy, and so that you may feel fully in touch with yourself, at every moment of your life. If you learn to understand exactly what each part of your body needs in order to be well and robust, it's easier to supply those needs.

For instance, do you remember when you were very tiny, Cee, you were absolutely terrified of getting cut and bleeding? Even an infinitesimal scratch would scare you to death. I was greatly puzzled by your overreaction untill I drew a picture for you of what *you* looked like on the *inside*. Your relief was overwhelming, and I realized you had been so terrified because you had hypothesized, in your three-year-old imagination, that all you had inside of you was blood, and your skin was keeping it in there, like the air in a balloon! Naturally, when you got cut, you were afraid everything would seep out through the puncture in the balloon. As soon as you understood how you worked, your fears were calmed.

In a way, I think knowledge of what goes on inside your body is as essential to your peace of mind as a grown-up as it was at age three. If you know how you function, you needn't fear, or be inept in handling those functions. If you know how your circulatory system works, I doubt that you'll overload it with an overabundance of artery-clogging saturated fats; if you know how your lungs function, it would seem foolhardy to injure them by smoking; if you know how your female organs function, there's no need to feel overly discombobulated by periods or pregnancy. And so on and on and on . . .

It wouldn't hurt to learn first aid, too, while you're figuring out how everything works. I once found myself with a girl who had fallen through a plate-glass window and cut an artery. Both she and I were glad I had taken a compulsory first-aid course in high school! You never know when an emergency could make you very grateful you made the effort to learn how to tie a tourniquet.

Learn about Nutrition

I was raised knowing about nutrition. My mother learned about kelp and wheat germ twenty-five years before it became chic. Unfortunately, as soon as I was on my own, I escaped into a Twinkie, and from that time on I went on the typical American woman's round of perennial diets, with their predictable weight gains and losses. Every regime from Stillman to Atkins to Scarsdale to Sanpaku has crossed my path. I mention this only to establish my credentials in discussing this with you, because my own experience has led me to some firm convictions. First: Americans are diet-conscious, not nutrition-aware. You would do yourselves a big favor by ferreting out some nutritional information beyond the calorie count for pizzas. You might try reading Adelle Davis and Carlton Fredericks for a start. Much of the food we eat these days is a sham and a delusion. Bread filled with fillers, turkeys plumped by hormones, flour bleached clean of its vitamins, artificial sweeteners and flavorers added to everything. I bought you a bottle of chocolate milk the other day and when I got home I discovered it had neither chocolate nor milk in it! You might consider reading labels to learn defensive food buying. And it really helps to learn what fuel your body needs in order to operate efficiently. There is also growing evidence that fresh food—fresh vegetables, fresh fruit, fresh chicken, fish—has more "life energy" to impart to you than the frozen, canned and supermarketed variety we often make do with. On my trip to Japan two years ago, I was startled by how much better I felt after two months of eating *only* fresh food. I also lost ten pounds while there, although I was never hungry for a minute.

Whenever possible, try to opt for real food as a fortification against the aggressions of pollutants and artificiality on your system. I think our bodies were constructed to assimilate more natural foods and to burn them up via more physical labor. In the absence of having to plow the back forty, you might just try to seek balance in your diet, with a smattering of fruit, vegetables, meat or fish, dairy foods, bread, along with whatever goodies you choose to treat yourself to. And it doesn't hurt to try a little extra exercising to burn up excess calories instead of constant dieting.

You might just read what nutritionists have to say, evaluate what advice they offer, and then experiment with their recommendations until you find the way of eating that satisfies you emotionally and physically. One month on a nutritious, balanced diet and I'm pretty sure you'll feel better, weigh less and have more energy. I hope it's enough to convince you.

Investigate Vitamins and Minerals

It doesn't seem hard to believe that in this age of synthetic foods, polluted environment and general lack of wholesomeness we need some fortifications in our diet. I think it's sensible to learn about vitamins and minerals whether you get them from food or from supplements. Do some reading about how to get the bulk of your daily vitamin and mineral needs from *eating* generously and variedly. You may be able to get most of what you need from food if you eat sensibly enough, and then you can simply supplement your diet with a vitamin or two where needed. I found a wonderful book called *Earl Mindell's Vitamin Bible,* which tells everything you might want to know about vitamins: which to take, when, what combinations are most helpful, what symptoms indicate deficiencies, and much, much more.

While you're reading, try Linus Pauling. He is, I believe, too brilliant a scientist to be dismissed as a quack, even though many doctors would have us think him one. Basically, Pauling believes there are voluminous data which suggest that vitamin

C is capable of helping our bodies' own defense systems repel outside aggressions. Again, don't take my word for it. Try it for yourself to see what's right for you.

Try Different Kinds of Exercise

Groan. This is a tough one for me. As you know, I consider exercise about as much fun as pestilence! However, you and I know that our hearts and our lungs need exercise to strengthen them; our circulatory systems need exercise; our complexions need exercise; and our stamina needs exercise. God knows *you* get enough of it now, so I suppose I needn't worry yet. But speaking from bitter experience, I can say that the key is not to let your enthusiasm for exercise get lost in the clutter of all the other things that fill your life as you get older. I suppose everyone can find some system of exercise that is pleasing and continuous. Ten minutes of exercise every day is better than an hour and a half, once a week, that can leave you stiff, pained and grouchy—and unlikely to keep it up for very long. It's sometimes better to plan a do-able mini-regimen than an un-do-able maxi one. I've solved the problem caused by my distaste for sports by becoming the world's fastest walker. I guess there's always some form of exercise that's appealing, no matter how silly it might seem to someone else.

The Most Important Part

Now that you've figured out what your kidneys do for a living, eaten some yogurt, taken your vitamin C and run the four-minute mile, I have one more small but multifaceted piece of advice on the subject of health, which I hope, with all my heart, you'll consider. *Take good care of yourself. Take time for yourself. Work at a job you like. Marry a man whom you love. Only be a parent if you really want to love a child. Give yourself time to realize some of your most cherished dreams.*

These are the elements that good health is made up of, just as much as food or exercise or any other possibility. Happiness and health are two pieces of the same puzzle and inasmuch as you deserve to have both, it's important to learn early on that they go hand in hand.

You should try to keep physically fit. Why do things that can be harmful to your body when you can just be healthy? It's easier that way. You live longer . . . and you have more fun doing it.

Lola,   age 15

I always feel good, so I never think about how to stay healthy. It just comes naturally to me.

Cee Cee,   Age 14

I think you can help yourself by doing exercises, eating right, getting out your angers, having fun, being serious when it is time to be serious, doing things you want to do and not always thinking of yourself.

Cee Cee,   age 14

> *Our body is not, in short, something we have,*
> *it is a large part of what we actually are.*
>
> JONATHAN MILLER

Weight

A heavy subject, yes? Speaking from a lifetime of dieting, I feel I speak if not with authority, at least with some rights of experience.

This may seem a peculiar topic to grace these already eclectic pages, but I think it's an important one because it has to do with how you feel about yourself, and self-image is crucial to your whole being, past, present and future.

I'd like to tell you about my own experiences. All my life (until recently) I thought I was too fat. Looking back at photos of myself, I realize that 99 percent of the time this was only in my own mind. I *perceived* myself to be fat and therefore I behaved as if I were. I dieted, I fought with food, I wore clothes two sizes too big. I struggled with my body and manipulated it, harassed it and abused it—and incidentally didn't change things much at all in the process.

My eternal struggle with my own weight continued unabated

until three things happened almost simultaneously. One was my annual checkup. After I had been examined and weighed, the doctor said to me quite cheerily, "You know, you are really to be congratulated, your weight hasn't changed a pound in six years." I almost fell off the examining table. During that six years' time, I had probably been on two hundred diets; sometimes miserable because of being fat, sometimes thrilled because I was finally getting skinny. The reality was that I was staying exactly, to the pound, the *same*. I was flabbergasted.

Could it be that all that effort and all those imagined ups and downs were really just mental gymnastics I was putting myself through? Could it be that my body had simply found a weight at which it was healthy and content? For all I knew, it might maintain that weight if I stopped manipulating it so relentlessly. The possibility was mind-boggling.

The second revelation was a more complicated one; it had to do with finally realizing that I had been insulating my fragile self against the buffets of a hostile world for a long, long time. I expect I'm not the first person to unwittingly pad my exterior in an effort to guard my interior!

The third piece in the puzzle was the discovery that through a series of circumstances, I had been *programmed* to think I was fat, so that in essence I had been walking into my own incorrect vision of myself for a lifetime.

The change in my attitude toward my own body, due to these three realizations, has been amusing and relaxing. I no longer struggle endlessly against food, I no longer *feel* fat, and—that's right, you guessed it—I still weigh exactly the same amount!

In looking back over what I've learned during my lifetime battle of the bulge (one which I think I share with most women, by the way), several lessons seem worth passing on.

First: where weight is concerned, try to evaluate yourself as accurately as possible. For years I measured myself against fashion models—a hopeless dream—and always felt enormous. I evaluated myself based on a dress size. If I was an 8, I was fine. If a 10, I was second only in size to the Goodyear blimp. In all those years, by the way, I was never once more than a 10, though to my mind I was often a fatty.

Second: evaluate yourself against what's right for *you,* not the rest of the world. Bronwyn, I've sometimes watched you when you were unaware and marveled at your stature. You are like a mighty oak; vast and full of life-force, like the Irish giants of legend. The weight that is right for your vivacious, effervescent 5 feet 10 inches of laughing, free-spirited young womanhood may not be the wraithlike stature of a fashion model. I hope you'll have the courage to decide for yourself what's right for you.

Cee Cee, my darling child, I look at you and see the most beautiful and female of women emerging. You move with a grace and fluidity of which you aren't even aware. You are a delicate and fragile flower—warm and soft and unutterably feminine. It is my earnest hope that you will always be able to see yourself clearly and decide what is right for you based on a gentle and generous vision of yourself.

Third: make your own judgments about weight—don't accept the world's view. I believe that this whole you-can't-ever-be-too-rich-or-too-thin syndrome of modern times is a passing fancy like the wasp waist, the bound foot and the farthingale. After all, what is plump in New York is emaciated in Milwaukee—and who knows if the skinny standards of the seventies will flip-flop into voluptuous eighties or nubile nineties. Such surprises have certainly happened before.

Women have long allowed themselves to be dreadfully manipulated in their desire to keep up with fashion. Maybe there is hope for your generation to learn to judge your own body by *your own* standard.

Fourth: train yourself to think of food as a healthy, pleasurable, nourishing ally—not an enemy. For years, with every bite I took, I pictured my hips automatically expanding. Curiously, now that I allow myself the pleasure of food, and envision that it introduces vitamins, minerals, nutrients and pleasure into my body instead of fat, I have become slender.

Fifth: if this weight business becomes a problem for you in life (as it has for so many women of our time), seek wise professional help. Overweight is, I believe, just the outer manifestation of other problems and insecurities that cause one to have to insulate oneself from a hostile world. Find out. Love yourself enough to get help.

I think that lately everybody's worried about her weight, and too much emphasis is placed on the importance of how much you weigh—being two pounds overweight makes you feel like you want to commit suicide! I know people like that; it's a lot of pressure, believe me. Because the person inside you is still you whether you weigh 150 or 250 or 90 pounds; but people treat you like a leper if you weigh too much.

Lola,   age 15

I don't worry about how much I weigh. I never had a really serious weight problem—maybe I'd feel differently about it if I had. I know I feel really good about myself when I lose weight and feel skinny, but I don't really try too hard, because it isn't all that important to me. I guess people are going to just have to accept me for my naturally chubby, adorable self. I guess that's really what I want. I don't want people to say, "Hey, I'll be your friend if you lose ten pounds." Who needs that kind of friend?

Bronwyn,   age 15

But you should understand it's hard sometimes, because some people don't like you if you're overweight. It's especially hard for a girl if she likes a boy and he doesn't like fat girls. But I think people like that are very narrow-minded.

Lola,   age 15

In this world there are just too many weight-conscious people, and I don't think that's right. It's a form of prejudice. It's worse than many forms of prejudice, come to think of it. It makes people feel terrible. I'm just saying that if people don't like you because of the way you look, forget about them. It's hard, but nobody said life was going to be easy.

Bronwyn,   age 15

> *No woman can call herself free*
> *who does not own and control her body.*
> *No woman can call herself free*
> *until she can choose consciously*
> *whether she will or will not be a mother.*
> MARGARET H. SANGER

Contraception

In my day, contraception was spoken of in hushed tones, if spoken of at all. Catholics were opposed to it, and others seemed not to have a great deal of information about it at their disposal.

Margaret Sanger, the pioneer doctor who strove to bring contraceptive information to the mass of humanity who needed it, was jailed repeatedly, reviled and ridiculed, and she was continually restrained from being able to disseminate contraceptive information and aid. Difficult as it is to believe now, Dr. Sanger was still being imprisoned well into the 1930s, and the Planned Parenthood Foundation she established was outlawed and closed down on numerous occasions.

So much for history. These days contraceptive information is abundant and available. It can be obtained through one's own doctor, through free clinics or through Planned Parenthood. It can be read about in women's magazines and in books like *It's*

Your Body: A Woman's Guide To Gynecology by Dr. Niels Lauersen and Steven Whitney. Many kinds of contraceptives can be purchased at the neighborhood drugstore.

However, even though contraceptive information has become more readily available and contraceptive methods have proliferated, the subject is still a difficult one for kids to tackle, I think. Most teen-agers are embarrassed about seeing a gynecologist, never mind discussing contraception with one, and I'm certain that in many parts of the country, doctors are still judgmental and reticent about discussing contraception with young patients.

When you reached twelve and thirteen, my own gynecologist, whom I consider to be a dear and enlightened man, asked me how I felt about his dispensing contraceptive information to you, should you ask for it. He said he always polled his patients about such things when their daughters reached puberty. I, of course, told him that as far as I was concerned, anyone intelligent and sensible enough to seek contraceptive information should be given it. He said many of his patients didn't feel that way.

Truth is, deciding which method of contraception is right for you takes a little planning and as much knowledge of what's available as you can glean. I've chosen to write about the most widely used methods (and a few of the ones being tested now) just to give you an idea of the range of possibilities. It is quite probable that different methods of contraception may be sensible for you at different times in your life. Many women take the Pill when they are young and very sexually active; switch to a diaphragm or a barrier method when married and when a pregnancy, even if badly timed, wouldn't be a big hardship; then they may opt for sterilization, when they feel their childbearing needs have been fulfilled. The important thing is that whatever a woman's sexual habits, life-style or age, there is some kind of contraceptive that is appropriate for her to use. Knowing all the options can help you make an informed choice.

The Pill

When the Pill first was released into general use, when I was in my early twenties, women greeted it as salvation: it was easy, it seemed relatively foolproof, and it presented no inhibiting problems in lovemaking. Unfortunately, ten years later, side effects and serious problems associated with Pill taking began to be documented—and many women, fearing long- or short-range problems, abandoned this means of contraception. Nevertheless, the Pill remains today's most popular and reliable means of preventing pregnancy.

There are now two versions of the Pill: the combination Pill, which contains synthetic female hormones, estrogen and progestin; and the "mini-Pill," containing only progestin. The combination Pill suppresses ovulation (the release of the egg, which is necessary for conception to take place) and creates a condition within the uterus that is unfavorable for conception. The mini-Pill makes the uterine climate unfavorable for pregnancy, too. The combination Pill is about 99 percent effective; the mini-Pill, the one most often prescribed for teen-agers and those over thirty-five, is about 97 percent effective.

The side effects noted by about 40 percent of Pill users are any of the following (by the way, it would be very unusual for one woman to experience more than one or two of these): mild headache, nausea, weight increase, irregular periods, decreased menstrual flow. In addition, there are a number of serious conditions that research has associated with estrogen, and that can pose a threat to certain Pill takers' lives. For example, blood clots, heart attacks, liver tumors, migraine headaches, gall bladder disease and breast and uterine cancer may all be linked in some way to estrogen.

Only a doctor can evaluate for you, basing his opinion on your own health and your own family history, whether or not the Pill would make sense for you. Despite the possible dangers associated with it, statistics suggest that there is still significantly lower danger to a woman from taking the Pill than from pregnancy and childbirth. In other words, with the help of a good doctor and all the statistics you can find, you must simply decide if the convenience and effectiveness of the Pill outweigh the possible risks.

I took the Pill for six years and experienced no annoying side effects. At the end of that time, I developed a thyroid problem which may or may not have been connected to Pill taking—I suppose I'll never know. Of course, in those days, ten years ago, the level of hormones in the Pill was vastly greater than now, so it's quite possible that even if my thyroid condition was related to my taking the Pill, lower-dosage pills might have saved me the problem. To be honest, I thought the Pill a great boon to life and lovemaking, and have never regretted taking it.

When you are weighing the possible risks in taking the Pill, you should be aware of one factor. Women who take the Pill and *smoke* face a significantly greater chance of developing heart attacks or strokes than nonsmoking Pill users.The 1977 Federal Drug Administration studies on this subject were striking enough to compel drug manufacturers to label Pill packets (both combination and mini) with the following warning: "Cigarette smoking increases the risk of serious adverse effects on the heart and blood vessels from oral contraceptive use. The risk increases with age and with heavy smoking (15 or more cigarettes per day) and is quite marked in women over 35 years of age. Women who use oral contraceptives should not smoke."

The IUD

More than three million American women have chosen the IUD as their contraceptive means. Basically, the *intrauterine device* is a copper or plastic coil that is inserted into the uterus itself, thereby setting up a hostile uterine environment, which inhibits conception. Some of the newer IUD's also release tiny amounts of copper or progesterone, which are said to add to the efficacy of the device's contraceptive properties.

Like the Pill, the IUD is about 95–99 percent effective; like the Pill, it has come under attack because of possible risks and side effects.

Although most women experience few problems from the IUD after the initial cramp of insertion, about 25 percent of IUD users give up on the device within the first year. Some women experience severe pain and continuous cramping, others spontaneously expel the device, others have too heavy menstrual bleeding or frequent spotting between periods. I tried the IUD twice. The first time severe pain accompanied its insertion, the second time my body simply spontaneously expelled it. Yet I have friends who have used this method of contraception for years, with only minor discomfort at period time.

In 1975, the FDA ordered the Dalkon shield removed from the market because of contraceptive failure and an unusually high incidence of miscarriages and infections. Although no other such problem has invoked government intervention, still IUD users have a five-times-greater risk than other women of developing pelvic inflammatory disease, or P.I.D. These infections can be minor problems, quickly cured, or in extreme cases they can be severe enough to lead to sterility. The women with the greatest risk of P.I.D. are those who have not had children, are twenty-five or younger, or who have had a variety of sexual partners. Thus there are valid questions to be raised abut IUD's when teen-agers are concerned.

Again, your doctor is best equipped to evaluate this device in light of your own physiology.

Barrier Contraception

Barrier methods include diaphragms, condoms, foams, jelly and spermicidal vaginal suppositories. In essence, all these methods form a barrier between the sperm and the egg, thereby making conception unlikely.

If you bear in mind how conception takes place, it's easier to understand how these barrier methods function. I know you've been through these data many times, but just for the record (and a reminder), here's how conception works.

An egg (ovum) is released from one of your ovaries, once during each monthly menstrual cycle. It is propelled on a journey through your Fallopian tubes and into your uterus. If a sperm manages to reach this egg and penetrate it, conception takes place, and the egg attaches itself to your uterine wall, where it begins its growth into a baby.

Obviously, if a means can be found to keep the sperm from reaching the egg, pregnancy cannot happen. The problem we all face is that with each ejaculation millions and millions of sperm are propelled into the vagina, and unless a barrier intervenes, they swim merrily into the uterus, where conception can take place.

Vaginal Spermicides: Foam, Cream, Jelly

Vaginal spermicides have been around for centuries. Because they act in the vagina to kill the sperm, they have been considered a staple, easy means of contraception since ancient times.

Modern vaginal spermicides act by blocking the cervix with a bulky material, and by killing the sperm. They are available in foams, creams, jellies, foaming tablets and suppositories.

The best part about this method of contraception is that it is easily available. Spermicidal foams like Emko and Delfen can be purchased in drugstores and chain stores. They are easy to use, inexpensive, need no prescription and are harmless. (Some people develop irritations from certain brands, but by and large the products do no harm to the body.)

An applicator filled with the spermicidal preparation is inserted into the vagina just before intercourse. Although this is simple, it is an inconvenience (particularly if you are not at home, in a comfortable setting). The high failure rate with vaginal spermicides is probably due to people's tendency to neglect using them, as much as to any inadequacy on the part of the product.

Condoms

Condoms (sometimes called prophylactics or rubbers) are thin sheaths that a man wears on his penis during intercourse. They are made of rubber or animal membrane, look a bit like a balloon, and conceptually are very simple: they trap the sperm as it leaves the penis, so that it cannot enter the vagina.

They are a very effective means of contraception *if* the condom does not break or slip off, and if it is worn during the entire act of intercourse, not just slipped on at the last moment before ejaculation. (The reason for this last admonition is that sperm cells can escape into the vagina even before ejaculation takes place.)

Diaphragms

The diaphragm, one of the most popular barrier methods, is a rubber cup-like device that covers the cervix or opening of the uterus. When it is filled with a contraceptive jelly or cream, the sperm has an almost insurmountable obstacle to surpass in order to reach the egg. With a diaphragm, you need have no fear of side effects, and for a teen-ager whose sexual experiences may be few and far between, it is a contraceptive solution that probably makes good sense.

The major drawbacks, with diaphragm use, are these: even though the diaphragm can be put in place ahead of time, if you haven't remembered to do so, the spontaneity of the act of lovemaking can be interrupted. With a diaphragm you must use fresh jelly for each sexual act, and leave the device in place for six to eight hours afterward. Although doctors say there is no discomfort from a diaphragm, my own experience, and that of a number of women I've discussed it with, is that leaving the diaphragm in place for the required number of hours can result in a feeling of tenderness and pressure that is quite unpleasant.

On the other hand, many women use diaphragms for a lifetime without major problems, and inasmuch as it is a method readily available and free of side effects, it may be one you should consider in order to see if it suits your needs.

The Rhythm Method

The rhythm method requires abstention from sex during a woman's most fertile period of the month. The system cannot be used by women with irregular periods or by women who *must* not become pregnant. It requires abstinence from sex for a minimum of ten days a month, and can obviously cause anxiety, stress and serious problems in a relationship due to the lack of sexual spontaneity it engenders. This method of contraception is the most unreliable of all.

The Morning-After Pill

The idea of the morning-after pill sounds fine—a drug to be taken *after* intercourse without protection has taken place. Unfortunately, the only one invented so far has quite a lot of drawbacks. So many, in fact, that it is prescribed only in emergencies, as with rape or incest victims.

The drug used is diethylstilbestrol (DES), a synthetic estrogen. If this drug is taken it will cause a spontaneous abortion, if pregnancy has occurred. The regimen takes five days to complete (two pills per day) and during that time the majority of women experience headaches, cramps, nausea and vomiting. This DES is the same very controversial drug that was used to prevent miscarriages, and which has caused such a high incidence of uterine cancer in the children of women who took it. Although it obviously carries no such threat when used as a pill to *prevent* pregnancy, nonetheless this drug doesn't always abort an incipient pregnancy, and when it doesn't work, a woman who has taken DES is generally told to have an abortion, as the results of DES are potentially dangerous to the developing fetus. It is also a synthetic estrogen drug, and as such it carries the same risk of blood clotting and heart problems as the Pill.

Sterilization

A great many couples who have decided they do not wish more children, or that they do not wish any children, are opting for sterilization. Obviously, this is not an option to consider at your ages, but it is something you should probably know about nonetheless. Either the man or the woman can be sterilized; however, the surgery is more major for the woman than for the man. Because sterilization is, for all intents and purposes, permanent, it is an option that must be very seriously considered before one undertakes the procedure—as a matter of fact, most states have rigorous stipulations that must be met before one may be sterilized. A person may think he or she is finished with childbearing, but a remarriage may cause that decision to be regretted. There has been some degree of success recently, due to new microsurgical techniques, in reversal procedures, but by and large one should be as certain as possible that the decision to sterilize is a sensible one, because it is more than likely permanent.

Vasectomy

The procedure of male sterilization is a simple half-hour surgery, performed in the doctor's office. The vas deferens, or tube which carries the sperm from the testicle to the ejaculatory duct of the penis, is surgically cut and tied off. Some discomfort and swelling generally follows the procedure, but most men resume their sexual activity within a few days of the surgery. If infection occurs, as it does in about 4 percent of the cases, it generally responds quickly to antibiotic therapy.

While researchers have found no evidence of health hazard in vasectomy, a small percentage of men (about 4 per 1,000) experience decreased sexual desire or even impotence. However, it is theorized that this decrease in potency is due to emotional problems rather than the surgery itself, as vasectomy does not affect male hormonal balance or orgasm.

Female Sterilization

Tubal ligation, or the cutting and sealing off of the Fallopian tubes, through which the egg travels to the uterus, can be done by several techniques.

In the laparoscopy (the most usual procedure) the surgeon makes two small incisions in the abdomen. He inserts the laparoscope, a sort of lighted periscope, into one incision to locate the Fallopian tubes. Through the other incision, he inserts instruments that cut and tie off the tubes. A newer technique called the mini-lap allows a similar procedure to be done through only one incision.

The older procedure, called a laparotomy, is larger-scale surgery, utilizing a larger abdominal incision and requiring general anesthesia. Once the only means of female sterilization, it is now used primarily in conjunction with another procedure (for instance, it may be done at the same time as a Cesarean section.) The laparotomy requires about two weeks' recovery time, while the laparoscope and mini-lap require only two or three days. In rare instances a woman may conceive ectopically (in the Fallopian tube itself) after a sterilization procedure, but this is most unusual. For all practical purposes, female sterilization is permanant and foolproof.

Improvements on the Way

A considerable amount of research is currently under way in an effort to achieve a perfect contraceptive method—no complications, no adverse side effect. While such a miraculous method has not yet been perfected, several interesting possibilities are being explored.

Cervical Cap or Sponge

The cervical cap, a device that can be left in place between periods, and that releases small doses of spermicidal substance all during the month, is being used extensively in Europe. A new cervical sponge containing a spermicidal chemical, which can be left in place for twenty days, is also being tested, and it appears it may be more comfortable and less problematical than the diaphragm. The search for a foolproof, comfortable, pleasing and safe form of contraception continues at all major drug companies, and there is every reason to believe that breakthroughs will come during your childbearing years. Remember, the whole field of contraception is only forty years old.

Depo-Provera

A derivative of progesterone called Depo-Provera can be injected into a woman once every three months, and provide safety from pregnancy. This is used extensively in Europe, but the FDA has not permitted its use here yet for purposes of contraception, because it can cause very irregular periods, and it has the same potential side effects as the mini-Pill.

Implant

Progestin can also be administered via implantation of capsules under the skin. These can be implanted in fifteen minutes in a doctor's office, and can prevent pregnancy up to three years before they must be removed.

Unfortunately, the capsules are visible beneath the skin of the forearm, and certain of the health hazards associated with other progestin-based contraceptives are also risked with implants.

Male Contraception

Injections of synthetic progestin, a female hormone, or androgen, a male hormone, can suppress sperm production in the male—but not totally, and not without inhibiting such production for a year or more after stopping the drug. Thus far, none of the extensive research done on this form of contraception has netted positive results.

Temperature Gauge

Science has known for some years that a woman's temperature changes at the time of ovulation (when the egg leaves the ovary and starts its journey to the uterus). Just before ovulation, the temperature drops; and immediately after, it rises (a change of about 0.5–1 degree F. or 0.15–0.3 degree C. takes place). The safest time for intercourse is considered to be seventy-two hours after this temperature elevation.

Many women on the rhythm method of birth control take their temperatures daily. A new device, unavailable as yet in the United States, can be worn like a wristwatch, and can record minute changes in body temperature, to help make judging more accurate.

Some Practical Thoughts

I would strongly urge you to read a book called *It's Your Body: A Woman's Guide to Gynecology* by Neils Lauersen, M.D., and Steven Whitney. It has a comprehensive and intelligent chapter on contraceptives that should give you a lot of vital information, and easy-to-understand diagrams, which should be very useful for you in helping decide what's best for you, even before you see a doctor.

There is, unfortunately, no perfect contraceptive yet on the market. To be absolutely honest, I don't know a single woman who doesn't lament the fact that the available methods are so *imperfect.*

However, despite the imperfections and inadequacies of contraceptive choices, there are enough different possibilities so that an intelligent choice can be made—and, considering the anxiety and heartache that can accompany unprotected sex, even imperfect methods are a boon to your well-being.

Having written all of the above, I realize that there is another slightly more esoteric contraceptive thought which is most important to come to terms with. In order *not* to get pregnant, *you must want not to get pregnant.* In other words, many girls have a subconscious desire to get pregnant. Perhaps they want to "catch" a reluctant boyfriend, or they want to do something truly rebellious. If this is the case, they forget to take their Pills, they take chances—and eventually they get pregnant.

Remember, if you want the right to lead a sexually free life, you must be willing to take on the adult responsibilities that go with the right. The most major of those responsibilities is that of not becoming pregnant when you are not in a position to have a child and give it the secure environment of a family.

I trust, my darling daughters, that you will utilize the knowledge and means that are available to you. If you combine these with good common sense, you should be able to make this very important area of your life, safe and tension-free.

———————————

Pregnancy is something that teen-agers should know more about. A lot of teen-agers are getting pregnant and having the child, without realizing all the responsibilities they will have to carry out as they get older. If a girl is willing to have sex, I feel that she should know as much as possible about how to protect herself against getting pregnant. I, for one, would not like to get pregnant until I have finished college, enjoyed my life and am ready to settle down and start a family.

Gigi,   age 15

Parents should openly talk about things like contraception . . . I guess it would make life a lot easier and a lot less scary.

Lola,   age 15

I think that with so many different methods of contraception available these days, nobody really has an excuse not to use one of them. Unless they want children, of course!

Bronwyn,   age 15

I think it's really irresponsible not to use contraceptives. If you intend to have sex . . . it's totally irresponsible not to learn everything you can about contraception. With all the un-wanted children in the world, and all the agony you could go through from an unwanted pregnancy, you should have your head examined if you take chances. The big problem is that a lot of kids don't want to talk to their parents about it, and they don't have any other grown-up they trust enough to confide in.

Bronwyn,   age 15

Kids aren't informed enough. For instance, I thought you couldn't get pregnant the first time! You know they don't start talking about sex education in schools until you're in the tenth or eleventh or twelfth grade, and that's crazy, because you've been hearing about sex since third grade! I guess it's still that "forbidden thing."

Lola,   age 15

If I were ever pregnant and unmarried it would be very hard to confront my mother with something like that. She would be very disappointed in me, and I know it would hurt her a lot.

Wanda,   age 15

> *If men could get pregnant, abortion would be a sacrament.*
> FLORENCE KENNEDY

Abortion

Abortion is so potentially trauma-filled and so personal a subject, I've deliberated and procrastinated a long while before tackling it. While I have unresolved doubts and mixed feelings about the emotional implications of abortion, I have a very firm conviction that we women must be absolute rulers of our own bodies.

I believe that a woman must have the right to *decide* if she will carry and bear a child. This right is, of course, best exercised *before* conception, in the form of taking appropriate contraceptive precautions to avoid pregnancy, and I wholeheartedly encourage you to learn all you can of the contraceptive options open to you.

But suppose a woman has taken every contraceptive precaution, utilized common sense, and still becomes pregnant? Then she must face an intensely personal decision in choosing to abort or continue an accidental pregnancy. The thinking which should probably go into that decision is what I'd like to discuss with you here.

Emotionally, abortion is a highly charged issue. I believe we women are preconditioned to the idea of motherhood—so much so that when we become pregnant, no matter what the obstacles we face, a few million years of biology swing into high gear, and we are fighting not just a moral battle but a biological one as well in trying to make an objective choice. I think it's quite plausible emotionally to "want" a baby, despite knowing the impracticality of having one, at a particular moment in your life.

In this age when women are marrying later and putting off childbearing almost indefinitely, it won't surprise me that there will be women who at thirty-eight wish they had given birth to the baby they chose to abort at eighteen—just as I'm sure others will be convinced that a youthful abortion saved their lives and emotional well-being.

Yet I believe that there are many factors a potential mother must take into account in making her decision that go beyond her own desires. For example:

Age. It is very hard to imagine a young teen-ager capable of successful motherhood. Each of us deserves the chance to grow to full womanhood before taking on the responsibility of another life besides our own. Motherhood demands both maturity and unselfishness. Bearing a child while a girl is emotionally and physically still a child herself could do serious harm to both mother and baby.

Financial capability. Affording the financial care of a child can be a very real problem. Getting started on earning a living for yourself can be difficult enough without the addition of children to support. Is it fair to give birth to a baby whose very existence may be threatened by severe financial instability? It's certainly a question which would have to be considered.

Single parenting. Raising a child alone is an enormously difficult task that places severe stresses on the child as well as on the mother. Whether it's right willingly to bring a baby into a single-parent home is a question that must be coped with as intelligently and as dispassionately as possible.

Religious conviction. Despite the erosion of people's strict adherence to religious conventions, there may be vestiges of guilt or of religious conviction that would seriously affect a woman's choice, and the emotional consequences of that choice.

Physical danger. Needless to say, beyond three or four months' gestation, abortion poses serious danger to the pregnant woman. Your own safety has to be paramount in your mind in such a situation.

Knowledge of what you're getting into. Few people faced with the choice of pregnancy or abortion know what the demands of motherhood are. Babysitting is the closest most of us come to parenthood before the real thing happens to us, and babysitting is a very temporary experience.

Do you really want to be a mother? There are many women who simply do not want to be mothers, even if they are financially secure, happily married, and mature enough to cope. I believe firmly that these women have every right to choose not to have children. It is an unnecessary injustice to both mother and child for a baby to be born to a woman who truly wishes not to be a mother.

The alternatives. Actually giving birth to a child which you have planned to give up for adoption could be both mentally and emotionally cataclysmic. I would think it horribly difficult to give up a baby you have carried and grown connected to for nine long months. There is a growing demand for such babies, of course, as there are fewer and fewer available for adoptive parents, so there is every reason to believe that a child would find a loving home in such circumstances. Nonetheless, the emotional toll deserves a lot of consideration.

I myself would probably have a very hard time coming to terms with having an abortion. I come from an Irish Catholic background, charged with emotional electricity where such things are concerned, and to be honest, I *wanted* my children from the instant I knew they had been conceived. Yet I abhor the Right-to-Lifers who seem to allow no rights at all for the pregnant woman. I feel certain that if I ever found myself in the situation of having an unwanted pregnancy, I would have the courage to end it. I do not underestimate the possible regret or sadness that the abortion decision might entail, any more than I can ignore the relief it might provide—it is surely a judgment that each woman must make most carefully for herself, weighing the pros and cons *respectfully* and paying careful attention to her own emotional needs and capacities.

What I do absolutely believe is that the right to continue or to terminate a pregnancy resides entirely with the pregnant woman: hers the responsibility, hers the right to choose. No woman should bear a child she doesn't want, or a child she cannot care for. I'd be hard pressed to imagine a God who would expect things to be otherwise.

When I was your age, abortions were performed in hideously unsafe conditions in back rooms or in foreign countries far from home and safety. Women were subjected to fear and danger, doctors were harassed and arrested, unskilled people performed abortions they were ill equipped to do properly. The entire situation was worse than deplorable. The people who seek to repeal the abortion reform laws seem to forget all this. The rights to safety of the mother appear to be last on their priority list; such rights would be first on mine.

Abortions have been performed as long as sex has existed. It is absurd to think that legislation can change that fact. The only change made by liberal abortion laws is in the humanitarian treatment they have afforded to pregnant women. Whatever your personal convictions about having an abortion yourself, I believe you and I as women cannot allow legislators or all the churches in the world to deny us the right to make our own choice on this very intimate subject.

The experience of motherhood is too profound to be taken lightly, too immense to undergo against one's will, and too intensely personal to permit others to usurp your right of decision-making.

I think abortion is good. I mean, not good in itself, but it's a good option if someone is in trouble, and they're young and they can't have the baby. I think it's okay to have an abortion if there's no alternative, but I think that if you are old enough and you have enough money, and you can support the baby, and you have a husband, then I don't think that you should have an abortion. I think then it's wrong.

Bronwyn,   age 15

I guess I'm not really for or against abortion. I don't consider it terminating a life—I just think it's an option you have to have. I think a woman should have the right to decide whether or not she's willing to carry a child for nine months, and care for it afterward. Sometimes the only logical thing to do is have an abortion. Maybe for financial reasons, maybe for emotional reasons. I can't see a fourteen- or fifteen-year-old girl carrying a child and expecting to take care of it properly. Or a sixteen-year-old girl, or a nineteen-year-old girl, for that matter, if she doesn't have a husband and a stable environment for the baby.

Lola,   age 15

Having to take care of a baby you don't want in the first place would be unfair to the mother and the baby.

Gigi,   age 15

I believe abortion is a necessary option to have, but I guess having an abortion would be kind of a painful thing to go through mentally as well as physically. I don't know—you might look back years later and think, Wow, what have I done here? I could have killed somebody who could have been our next President, or an Einstein or somebody the world really needs.

Lola,   age 15

I would never want to have an abortion. But I feel that under some circumstances (if I got pregnant accidentally and couldn't give the baby a home) I'd consider having one. Not that I would want to, but that is just how it would have to be. There's no use bringing a baby into this world if you cannot give him security and a family.

Gigi,   age 15

Observations about Aging

I seem to be blessed with little or no fear of aging. Perhaps because I was always younger than everybody else in school, in business, in life, I've enjoyed the growing-up of getting older. Then, too, my life has become considerably better since thirty, immeasurably better since thirty-five, and therefore I have high hopes that with advancing age goes advancing fortune.

I'm prompted to talk to you about aging for two reasons:

1. Women get programmed into .thinking that their desirablity is diminished with accumulating years—a thought that I reject most vehemently.

2. None of us learns, early enough, to protect and care for our own body, as a safeguard against the ravages of aging and of declining health, so it seems to me a worthwhile subject for a page or two.

To address the first idea: women have, from time out of mind, seen themselves through other people's eyes—most especially through men's. We've allowed our feet to be bound, our waists to be corseted, our breasts to be siliconed and a host of other curious adjustments to be made on our bodies. Beyond that, we've accepted the idea that our sexuality has a stopping point—that a line of demarcation exists, after which we are less desirable than we were before we crossed over that line.

I believe it is not only in *our* best interest to progress beyond such nonsense, but it is in men's best interest, too. It takes a lot of years to get to be a grown-up, and, believe me, there are a lot of compensations to be had in being loved by an adult. Experience—sexual, intellectual and emotional—is not to be sneezed at as a credential for loving, and experience takes a good long while to come by.

Regarding the second point: when you are young, you believe that your body is indestructible—that it can be pushed, pulled, worked, trodden on and generally abused with impunity. I'm not suggesting for a minute that you wrap yourself in cotton wool, and cease to enjoy the luxuries of indefatigable youth, health and vitality. What I am suggesting is that you learn what you can about the things that can contribute to keeping you in tip-top shape forever. Things like nutrition, exercise, clean air, sufficient rest, freedom from tension and anxiety—all the things we've been talking about in the last few pages. If you grasp all the knowledge that can contribute to a lifetime of healthy living and if you are able to maintain a healthy, happy sense of your own worth at every age, you have a lot of sensational years ahead of you.

Most important, how you evaluate yourself at any age, and therefore how you telegraph to others, boils down to the strength of your sense of self. If you love yourself and believe in your own worth, you'll be able to accept all the *contributions* aging has in store for you. If you know yourself well, you'll be able to evaluate your gains and losses as you go along, with a healthy sense of expanding vision. "You're not getting older, you're getting better" should be true for each and every one of us.

There is every reason to believe that your generation will have a vastly increased life expectancy over any past generation's prospects. Life expectancy in 1850 was thirty-seven years; today for a woman it is seventy-two. Who knows what will be the case in the year 2020? With all those years to look forward to, it's just good sense to try to learn all you can about how to make every one of them healthy, happy and filled to the brim with life.

It's sad, but people don't seem to like old people anymore. But I do. I really like old people. They know a lot and they have time to tell it to you.

Bronwyn,   age 15

I'm not sure kids worry about aging anymore. I don't even think about it.

Cee Cee,   age 14

I know a lot of old people that I help when I can. I go to the store for them and do favors, and they're really sweet to me. I try to help, because I think it's kind of hard to get old. Nobody seems to care about what happens to the elderly.

Cee Cee,   age 14

I don't really mind about aging because I am only fourteen, but maybe when I get to be thirty-five or forty, I'll start worrying.

Cee Cee,   age 14

First of all, aging is a part of life and it's something to look forward to. You can't stay the same age for the rest of your life, and who wants to, anyway! As you age you learn more about life, you discover more about other people and about yourself, too. So aging isn't bad at all.

Bronwyn,   age 15

Aging leads up to death, of course, and I think death should be rather interesting, so that doesn't scare me. Aging gives you a lot to look forward to, it seems to me.

                                            Lola,   age 15

I'm going to be a fabulous old lady.

                                          Bronwyn,   age 15

In our culture old people are put down; they're thought of as senile and useless. But in other cultures, old people are respected, because they've had many more years of experience and growth. I personally think that old people have an awful lot to tell us, because they've lived through things that younger people haven't gone through. I hope by the time I'm old, people's attitudes will have changed toward old folks!

                                            Lola,   age 15

I respect the wisdom that you acquire with age. I don't think that I know everything just because I'm a whole fifteen years old! I guess you never really stop learning, and hopefully I'll live to a ripe old age, and have lots of adventures and experiences that I can share with younger people. They better not treat me as if I'm senile!

                                          Bronwyn,   age 15

6

HOMESPUN PHILOSOPHY

One of the nicest things about getting to be thirty-five is that you are, more or less, a finished product. Replete with opinions, idiosyncrasies, experiences and an established, comfortable philosophy of life. Not that you have outgrown the ability to change, adapt and grow—but you no longer feel constrained to be tolerant of *everything* in order to learn about life. By that ripe old age you've made quite a few serious judgments and have developed values that make life orderly and sound, by your own standards. It is the pursuit of these values and standards that is, I think, the essence of a philosophy of life.

In talking to you via these pages, I've had the chance to confront many subjects head on and to delineate my own beliefs more explicitly than I might otherwise have done. After all, despite the fact that a life's philosophy is something *everyone* evolves, other than at times of moral siege one seldom has to define its perimeters.

This written conversation of ours has afforded me the opportunity to do just that: to define and delineate and reexamine where I'm coming from. I'm very grateful to you for being the catalyst of such self-examination.

Give what you have.
To someone, it may be better than you dare to think.
HENRY WADSWORTH LONGFELLOW

Generosity

"Cast your bread upon the waters" was always an axiom of my father's. There is a story in the family that during the Depression when he was young and poor—as it seems most of the world was at that time—he would leave home every day for New York with 20 cents in his pocket: a nickel for the subway each way and 10 cents for lunch (with which in those days, I'm told, one could buy a sandwich). It seems that as often as not he would give the money to a beggar on the street or to the apple sellers on the corner because he reasoned that they were "down and out" and needed a helping hand. Thus, it seems that most days his lunch consisted of an apple, and often he would walk the five miles home instead of taking the subway because that particular nickel had gone to someone who "needed it more" than he did.

Once I heard someone ridicule him for perennially being a soft touch and giving to a street beggar. "He probably goes around the corner to his Rolls-Royce," said the one who knew better. "He's just making a fool of you."

Papa smiled in that very gentle way he has, and said, "What I give, I give in God's name. If the man is reduced to begging on the street, even if he's as rich as Croesus, he's worse off than I am. It's not up to me to worry what he does with what I give him."

And all this brings me to the subject of generosity. The older I get, the more it seems to me that generosity of spirit is the wellspring of all the good that happens on this earth.

If we are generous with love, we are likely to get some back. Generous with time, we probably can do some good in it. Generous with money, we can help those less fortunate. Generous with information, we can teach. Generous with ourselves, we can learn. Generous with patience, we can help our children. And on and on and on.

I think that like Papa we can't worry what becomes of the progeny of our generosity. We can't be niggardly of either worldly goods or self, because such stinginess diminishes us as much as it withholds from those around us.

When we give with a good heart, everybody is enriched and expanded by the giving. If you are tempted to give a quarter to the man with the tin cup—do it. If you have an hour you can spare to help someone, or teach someone, or merely be with someone who needs a friend—do it. And if you can find it in your heart, do it graciously. A grand gift that's reluctantly given is tarnished and shoddy; a trifle that's joyfully bestowed is a mighty anthem.

Papa always said that no matter what you give away, it will return to you a hundredfold. Certainly, in his case, it is true. I have never know a man so genuinely loved and admired. It is an extraordinary legacy, my daughters. A hundredfold greater and more wonderful than the money he might have passed on to you had he chosen to lead a selfish way of life.

———————————

I think that it's terrific to be generous and to share things with others, because you should treat others as you want to be treated. If you are not generous, then others won't be generous with you, and when you want to borrow something or you want them to share something, they won't cooperate and you'll feel hurt. I'm pretty generous most of the time—except with my sister!

Cee Cee,   age 14

Most people don't really want to be bothered being generous, because they're afraid of getting hurt by not getting anything back. But generosity is a very important virtue and nobody likes greedy people. Besides, being generous and helping others gives you rewards and satisfactions, too. It's a good feeling to know you're making other people happy.

Lola,   age 15

Failed in business in 1831
Defeated in the legislature in 1832
Second failure in business in 1833
Suffered nervous breakdown in 1836
Defeated for Speaker in 1836
Defeated for Elector in 1840
Defeated for Congress in 1848
Defeated for Senate in 1855
Defeated for Vice President in 1856
Defeated for Senate in 1858
Elected President in 1860

Failure

Einstein once said, "Do not try to be a man of success, but rather to be a man of value." Wonderfully sage advice, don't you think?

We, in our time and place, are bred to achieve success. America is an aggressive, success-oriented place, and as society's complications escalate (to say nothing of inflation) there are more and more pressures on us to succeed. Which is why I'd like to take a minute to talk about failure.

The specter of failure, it seems to me, is with us all through life, although we seldom talk about it except in our mind's secret places. For every goal we strive to reach, there is a coexistent possibility of failure. For every test we take, every job assignment, every stressful confrontation, even every game we play, there is the incumbent possibility of losing. We don't dwell on failure much, perhaps because it reminds us of those long-ago childhood times when we flopped more than we succeeded. Lord knows, none of us would like to relive those experiences. But nevertheless our failures are plentiful in life, so they may be worth talking about for a minute.

171

I think we must never, never expect to fail—for a positive outlook is half the secret to winning—but when we do fail, we must be able to handle it. Whether it's failure to measure up, failure to perform, or failure to fulfill, we have to be strong and plucky and resilient to be able to cope with such happenings and carry on.

To tell you the truth, the best way I've found to cope with failure is to try again. Lots of first-time failures are replaced by second- and third- or twelfth-time successes; stick-to-itiveness is still one of the great wonder-workers at our disposal. Sometimes initial failures are really opportunities to change our tack and win by a different approach; think of all the scientific success stories that have grown out of trial and error. If you don't get a second shot at whatever it is you flubbed, best to chalk it up to experience, I expect. There's a profit-and-loss statement to life as well as to business.

The most important trick is, I believe, to try to avoid *feeling* like a failure. Feelings of helplessness and despair will only generate self-defeat. If you've failed at something *unimportant* to your life, it's not worth letting it get to you. If you've failed at something you really want to succeed at, you'll need all your positive energy to regroup and try again. In either case, a negative outlook can only hold you back from your final goal.

There's another aspect to failure you might want to consider. We can sometimes fail in the eyes of the world, but still be successful in our own game plan. Lincoln failed at everything he tried until the Presidency, yet he was an inordinately successful human being, a great contributor to humankind's reservoir of compassion and intelligence. The list of such "failures" is endless, and I think the lesson is important.

We must strive to measure our own success in life by our own standards, our own values. We must work at what we believe in even if none of the world believes with us.

It is quite possible to be a flop by the world's reckoning and to be a resounding success as a woman, wife, mother, worker, thinker, doer. As a matter of fact, it is quite possible to operate by standards most of the world isn't even lucky enough to possess! Einstein failed math, yet theorized relativity. Edison failed grammar school and invented the light bulb. Lincoln failed everything, and is immortal.

You are going to fail sometimes. You may flub a test when you expected to get a good grade; you may come in last in a contest you thought you'd win; you may lose a job, or an honor; you may be laughed at for doing something differently from your peers. It doesn't matter one bit. What does matter is how you respond to your failures, what you learn from them, what strengths they call forth, what depths of fortitude they unearth, what ingenuity they engender—these are the triumphs that can make those failures worthwhile. Believe me, a lot of good can come from that "I'm gonna show them!" attitude, which can grow out of having a flop.

The only failure I can think of which is truly a washout is the failure to try. "Nothing ventured, nothing gained" is deadly accurate. To become a woman of value, as Einstein suggests, is to venture many things, and not to let the fear of failure stand in your way. It seems to me that those who unduly fear failure are doomed to immobilized, stifled lives. Those who can both win and lose with grace have infinity as the limit of their possibilities.

———————————

I don't think you can blame anybody at all if you try your hardest at something and you just can't do it . . . well, it's not anybody's fault . . . and it's also not the end of the world. Everybody's going to fail at something, some of the time. You can't do everything perfectly. You can't do everything right, and you can't let it ruin your life just because you fail at something. So you have to keep a good attitude and remember to learn from your failures and try again.

Bronwyn, age 15

When you fail at something, I think that you should just face up to the fact that you've failed and go back and try it again. You have to keep trying if you want to make something work. You can't let yourself be discouraged, because if you do there's just no hope.

Lola,   age 15

The measure of a man's real character
is what he would do if he knew
he would never be found out.
THOMAS BABINGTON, LORD MACAULAY

Trust and Honor

Someone once said that the worst thing about being a liar is that you are doomed never to be able to trust anyone else. The same principle, of course, applies to all areas of honor. Honorable people tend to expect honesty in others, people of integrity give others credit for integrity, and so on and on.

I'm especially interested in trust, honor and integrity where you are concerned, my daughters, because these are words you don't hear very often anymore. Maybe they've just gotten momentarily lost in the shuffle of "being smart," "getting ahead," "being practical" and all the other things that are held up to the young as being the proper goals today.

In the old days (even before my time, if you can imagine anything so antique) people aspired to be ladies and gentlemen, and part and parcel of being ladies and gentlemen were quite a lot of enviable qualities.

Nobility of spirit. Even though a moral decision was difficult you were expected to make the "right" one, *and* you were expected to know what the right one was. If a damsel was in distress, a gentleman was expected to come to her rescue, or his honor was diminished. If self-sacrifice was required in order to do the honorable thing, then self-sacrifice was expected.

Duty. This was something everyone attended to. No big decisions here. If something was your *duty*—whatever that something happened to be—*you* dishonored *yourself* by not doing it. None thought themselves clever to have "gotten away" with a breach of honor. Instead, they felt themselves besmirched.

Integrity. In the olden days, this meant that a man's word was expected to be his bond, and that there were certain standards which society lived by that everyone knew about, observed and admired.

All of these principles—honor, duty, integrity, nobility of spirit—were so essential to the fabric of everyday life that to live without at least aspiring to them would have been unthinkable.

If these words sound a little antiquated today, surely the essence of their meaning remains valid. And that essence has very simply to do with developing a standard of conduct. I think it is doubly important that you have the courage to do so in an age where anything goes.

It's not so easy to have standards and stick to them when your peers expect less of themselves than you do. It isn't easy to decide what's right and wrong in an age that hardly acknowledges a difference between the two. Having decided which is which, it's hard to do the right thing all the time—especially if you can profit from doing otherwise, or if nobody's watching. Someone once said character is what you are in the dark.

When I was in high school, I was once confronted with such a "nobody's watching" decision. I wanted to be valedictorian at graduation and was running neck and neck with a very aggressive young man. It came to my attention that he intended to cheat on the final exam—the only thing that stood between me and the coveted valedictory. I was furious and confused. If he was going to cheat, wouldn't I be a dummy not to? Didn't I deserve the prize as much or more than he? Wasn't it God-awful unfair? I asked my parents what they thought I should do. *They said I had to make my own decision. They said that only I would know if I made a right choice or a wrong one*, since no one would ever know whether or not I cheated. But that was as it should be because, after all, I was the only one I'd have to live with.

Just so you don't have to die of curiosity about what happened, I decided not to cheat on the exam. As a result I got a lower mark than my adversary and ended up with an average two-tenths of a point less than his. Curiously enough, I felt pretty good about having had the courage to be honest, even though I didn't win in the eyes of the world. I've never regretted the decision.

In a way that experience has served as a model for me throughout my life, I suppose. In my heart of hearts I've always known the difference between right and wrong, and I've always felt a good deal better about myself when I chose the right. Even, by the way, when I lost out on some prize by doing so.

I'm not a Goody Two-shoes. Let's just say I've seen enough to know that law and order are better than chaos, civilization better than anarchy . . . honor immeasurably better than dishonor. After all, when the votes are counted, I have to be the kind of person I'd like to live with, even if nobody else is looking—and trying to be honorable goes a long way toward achieving that end.

The trouble with cheating—even a little—is that it can be habit-forming. Let's say you cheat on a test and get a good mark. It's awfully easy to say to yourself that it's dumb to study, if cheating works so well. Next step is to cheat a few more times, and the end result becomes that you "get by" the course, but you haven't learned the material, so you've ended up *losing*, when it all nets out.

Trust—being trustworthy yourself and being able to trust others—is so central a part of healthy living that it's hard to understand how it has gotten such an old-fashioned reputation. Let's look at it from a totally pragmatic point of view. What would happen if you had to be suspicious of everything I told you, because you knew I couldn't be trusted? If every time I told you a story, or gave you some information or advice, you would have to take it with a grain of salt? Think how complicated life would be if you had to check out everything I said or be suspicious of any advice of mine.

Imagine if you multiplied that suspicion times all the members of the family, and then times all your friends and acquaintances. Imagine if you couldn't take anything *anyone* said on face value, because honor had gone out of style and trust was passé. Wouldn't life be absolutely horrible? Wouldn't you be overwhelmed by tensions and confusions, *and* wouldn't you feel angry at being cheated all the time?

I know that's a rather extreme example, but maybe not too far off the mark. After all, if the old values eroded, if anything went, if honor and truth and trust were replaced by expediency and dishonor, civilization would be in big trouble, and we as individuals would have suffered a dreadful loss.

I do not mean to suggest that your generation is not honorable and trustworthy, by the way. I mean simply to suggest that you kids are being bombarded by corruptions and an awareness of the world's seamier sides far more than any generation before you. TV brings everything—good and bad—right into your living room, and your generation is expected to sort through it all with many fewer moral guideposts to help you.

I think about the best you can do toward arming yourself against moral confusion is to create a set of standards for yourself that you believe in and live by. Believe me, my dear children, life will present you with many dilemmas—some of them with far-reaching consequences. If you've developed a strong sense of morality, those decisions will be easier for you to see with clarity, and to make with confidence.

Trust is something you must earn.

Gigi,   age 15

I think that everybody should be trustworthy and honorable. It's very important to trust each other, because if you don't trust, then you have no basis for any kind of important relationship. Mother/daughter, boyfriend/girlfriend—whatever the relationships, if you don't trust, you have nothing.

Cee Cee,   age 14

Parents have to learn to trust their kids' common sense. The smartest thing a parent can do is to trust his child, because if someone trusts you, and you know they believe in you, you'll try hard to live up to that trust. The only kids that parents can't trust are the kids who know their parents don't trust them.

Lola,   age 15

Responsibilities in the Home

I have a feeling that whenever the words "responsibilities in the home" surface, everybody groaningly thinks of walking the dog or taking out the garbage. Because by the time they reach your ages, most people have had plenty of experience doing both, I thought it might make sense to talk about home responsibilities on a more philosophic level.

Living in a family has a lot going for it—support systems, love, laughter, camaraderie. It also has some pain-in-the-neck aspects—sisters who wear your clothes, tie up the telephone, use the ironing board exactly when you want it. You know how it works; there's no way four or more people can live in an enclosed space without getting on each other's nerves sometimes.

Because I'm so convinced that the pluses of family life outweigh the minuses, I've made a list of some household responsibilities that help make communal living better, more workable, less aggravating. I'd love to hear what you would add to the list.

Scheduling. A little organizational talent applied to things like TV watching and bathroom traffic can help a lot. If you, Cee, have the bathroom at 6:00 A.M., when you first get up, and then Bronwyn has it at 7:00 A.M., when she begins to percolate, nobody feels shortchanged. With a little planning along this line most every potential tug-of-war in the family can be averted and the noise level around the house can go down several notches to everyone's delight.

Letting people know where you are. This is a big anxiety-producer and a responsibility you are both really wonderful about. Knowing that you will always make certain I know where to find you at any given moment helps my head enormously, especially in this city, which provides so many potential safety hazards. Joe and I have the same responsibility to you, of course. It's just a important that you know where to find us.

Little thoughtfulnesses. I'm sure you've never thought of thoughtfulness as a household responsibility. Neither had I until a moment ago! But when you get right down to it, we all do have a responsibility to each other that goes above and beyond the call of duty.

Your offering to walk the dog, Bron, when it's not your night to do so; your offering to clean the house, Cee, or do grocery shopping; my helping you clean the animal cages; Dad's driving you where you'd like to go—you know the kind of things I'm talking about. They make life brighter and sweeter, and in a way that's a very nice thing to be responsible for.

Chores. Without going into infinite detail, I guess the truth is that divison of labor in a house is as important as division of labor in a business or government. It is simply fair. The best way I know of doing this is listing all the tasks that need doing and dividing them up so that each person does the ones least odious to him or her. Some people like ironing better than sewing, or cooking better than cleaning, or shopping better than animal care. It makes sense to pass out chores in as equitable a way as possible, for the sake of everybody's disposition and also for the sake of doing things well. After all, we tend to do chores better if we don't hate them.

Where Mom fits in. In the traditional household, Mom did everything around the house and the daughters helped her, while Dad went to work and the boys mowed the lawn! Our household is less traditional—Mom and Dad both go to work and we have neither boys nor a lawn to do.

In our kind of household (and I think, if current research is correct, there will be more and more of them) the biggest problem we all face is not having enough time. Time to spend with each other, time to do all we'd like to do, time to slow down and smell the buttercups together. If I were to attempt to do all the traditional chores alone, I'd have no time at all left over for the important moments we want to spend together. So by your pitching in to help, you give me more family time.

By the way, I personally believe that it's important for me to do things like cooking, or sewing that important button on that important dress—the little nurturing things that make you feel loved at a particular moment. But the rest of the chores around the house—the dishes, the bed making, the picking-up of debris—will go much faster if they're divided up fairly among all of us, so that there's time left over for the important and enjoyable stuff. I love to sew, Cee Cee loves to clean, Bron loves to cook, Dad doesn't mind walking the dog, even if he doesn't love doing it. When everyone pitches in, no one person is overburdened.

The main thought I'd like to get across is the idea of pitching in with *goodwill.* It isn't fair to grumble and moan every time a chore appears, or to step aside conveniently in hope that someone else will do it. It isn't fair, either, to expect others to live with your mess, until the moment when inspiration strikes and you decide to clean up.

As you know, I don't believe in bugging you about keeping your rooms neat. As far as I'm concerned, your bedrooms are your domain, and whatever condition it pleases you to keep them in is fine by me—provided, of course, that you don't ever expect me to burrow into the debris! On the other hand, in the communal rooms of the house—living room, kitchen, hall, baths—it's only fair that we each do our share to keep order for the common good.

If you think for a minute about the philosophy behind such division of labor, it makes all the sense in the world. We all share a prescribed space. We all need comfort and prettiness and a sense of order in that space. The only way to achieve it *fairly* is for everybody to pitch in.

To tell you the truth, I think it all boils down to treating your own family with the same graciousness and courtesy and thoughtfulness you use with outsiders. It's awfully easy for family members to take each other for granted, but life is so much nicer—more loving, more pleasant, more filled with emotional riches—if we don't.

If everyone lives in a community and a family is like a little community, I think, no matter how many bodies there are, you should divide up all the chores that need doing, so that nobody gets stuck with too many. I do think parents should realize that school is like going to work; it's a big job and a big responsibility, and sometimes you just feel too tired to do chores, too.

Cee Cee,   age 14

As a member of a family, I think your responsibility to the family takes in a lot of things. You should try not to invade each other's privacy. And you should be able to do what you want, with what's yours. If you want to cut the sleeve off a T-shirt, I think it should be allowed, because it's obviously important to you to wear it that way. If you want to mess up your room and keep it that way, I think that should be okay, too—as long as you don't mess up the rooms you share with others, because that would interfere with other people's rights. If you mess up the bathroom and leave it that way, when everybody else needs to have it neat, that's not fair.

Lola,   age 15

Everything in a family should be divided up pretty much equally. I mean, there are always things that each person can do well—a kid can't go out and do the shopping when he's eight years old, but he can pick up around the house, or maybe wash dishes. I admit I don't do as well as I should with responsibilities around the house—I try to duck them but I know it's not fair of me to do it.

Bronwyn,   age 15

I think life is a test. One big test. If you send your kid out and say, "Come back at eleven o'clock," and the kid shows up at one, you know that this kid is not an adult.

Bronwyn,   age 15

Graciousness and
Good Manners

Emily Post, the official etiquette expert in my day, once said that good manners meant never giving offense to anyone; it's a simple definition, but not bad. If you begin to think about other people's comfort in most social situations, your own ease will probably take care of itself. Besides, thinking of manners as synonymous with consideration makes them seem less contrived and more human.

It is essential, of course, not only to know the basic rules of social etiquette, but also to expand this knowledge into a philosophy of life. Graciousness hasn't anything to do with wealth or station. One can be as cared for in a cottage as in a palace if the spirit is there. It has to do with going out of your way to convey warmth, and with having a real desire to please those around you. It has to do with anticipating others' needs, and with thinking of their well-being. I do believe that these traits

185

come fairly easily to women, by the way. We are nurturers by nature, and our instincts help us care for people comfortably.

When Women's Lib began to be talked of openly, the first thing we heard was "Now that they're equal, we won't have to pull out chairs or open doors for them anymore." What a shabby and silly response. Pulling out chairs, opening doors, and letting women go first—these are niceties of life, small gracious gestures on the part of a man that can be gracefully responded to by a woman. How discouraging it would be to think that equality has to destroy good manners on our part or theirs. The courtesies we show to each other, male and female, add gentility, pleasure and prettiness to life. As such, they are worth caring about.

The particular nuances of current custom may not be the same as years ago, but the principle remains the same. You needn't curtsy in 1980, but on the other hand, a warm and gracious handshake can add considerable attractiveness to your life. You needn't carry calling cards (other than those of business) but a warmly personal and prompt thank-you note can return enormous pleasure to someone who has been thoughtful enough to send a gift.

There is practicality, too, in all of this. I believe good manners are a stabilizing influence. They can at times carry us over difficult social hurdles with our self-esteem intact. They can also add an equilibrating force to a world that is tough and fast-paced, often curt and insensitive.

Yes, I would take the time to read Emily Post and Amy Vanderbilt and the newer experts like Charlotte Ford and Letitia Baldrige. They have quite a bit to say that's useful. I would also try to tune in to the people around me. Try to sense their needs a bit and to observe the little niceties that give pleasure. You'll find that once you are alert to courtesy, graciousness and good manners, you will make your own life better and easier.

It has taken mankind millennia to become civilized. Putting

all those eons of learning into practice in your own life can be more pleasurable than you can imagine.

———————————

Everybody should care about good manners and graciousness because that's just the way it is. People watch your manners and they judge you by how you eat, and talk and answer a phone, and shake hands, or meet somebody—so you owe it to yourself to have good manners, so you can make a good impression.

Cee Cee,   age 14

I think gracious gestures like saying "Thank you" or sending a thank-you note—in other words, being thoughtful and doing favors—are all the kind of things that make life nicer for everyone, so they're very important.

Cee Cee,   age 14

*So long as we love, we serve; so
long as we are loved by others
I would almost say that we are
indispensable; and no man is
useless while he has a friend.*
ROBERT LOUIS STEVENSON

The Art of
Being a Friend

You hardly need my pointers on this subject. Your close friendships are of such long and loving duration that it is obvious that both of you have developed an understanding of what it means to have and be a friend. Nevertheless, it occurred to me that through a lifetime of friendships, one learns a bit about the *process,* the art form if you will, of friendships. Having been greatly blessed in this category of experience, I'd like to contribute a few thoughts of my own.

You must be a friend to have one. Friendship involves give-and-take. The balance often shifts at times—one being more on the giving end, at other times more on the receiving end—but it all evens out over the long haul.

There is an etiquette to friendship: a line that separates genuine interest from intrusion, information-sharing from unsolicited advice, attention from nosiness. You can enter into a friend's life only as far as she wishes you to enter, so you must be alert to these perfectly legitimate boundaries if the friendship is to prosper. For example, if you take it upon yourself to tell a friend she's fat, odds are she'll be hurt and offended. If on the other hand *she* confides in *you* that she has a weight problem and asks your advice, then you might feel freer to speak constructively about the situation.

Friendships change with time. Some deepen, some dissolve, some go into a holding pattern. There are also seasons to friendship, certain times when great closeness is appropriate, other times when distance is more comfortable for both. When friends are single and footloose, they can spend much time together. When either or both marry, or when one moves away, the friendship goes into another phase, no less warm, but certainly less constantly manifest.

Honesty. My most special and cherished friends know a great deal about me—and I about them. Such deep-down honesty is essential in true friendship. You can't wear your heart on your sleeve with every passerby; personal confidences are for friends, not acquaintances. But within the confines and security of real friendship, there is a great comfort in being able to be truly honest about how you feel and who you are. Rabindranath Tagore, a gifted Indian philosopher and poet, once wrote to a friend to thank him for knowing his imperfections and loving him still. That's about the size of it—only if we are honest about who we are can we have the joy of knowing we are loved despite our faults.

Choosing friends. Some choices seem cosmic. Occasionally in life we meet someone we seem always to have known and loved. Perhaps such friends are left over from other lifetimes—who can say? There have been a few people in my life for whom I had such an instantly intense affinity, but in most cases it takes a while to know enough about someone to consider her a friend. Some of your choices may be disappointments; of course not all friendships work out exactly the way you want them to. But experience will probably teach you to choose wisely and well.

My only advice to you about the choosing of friends would be this: listen to your instincts—your heart and brain working in harmony. Don't trust just anybody, but don't be overly wary either. Love yourself enough to select the very choicest people as your soul's companions. The ones who are rich in spirit, intellect and heart are more desirable than those who are rich only in fame or money. Don't be fooled by effusion. Judge people by how they behave toward you and others, rather than on how vociferously they proclaim their friendship.

Loyalty. If someone is your friend, be loyal. I think we have an obligation to protect our friends, not only by speaking well and honestly of them ourselves, but also by demanding that others do so when they are with us. People who gossip to you about others are highly suspect material for friendship. Secret-keeping falls into this category, too. If a friend tells you something in confidence, that knowledge should, I believe, be kept sacrosanct.

All this may sound a bit complicated. Truth is, it isn't. If you seek out the best and most trustworthy people, and are open to such people when they come to you, the rest should be easy.

Friends are enriching and fun. You can learn from them and with them . . . you can enjoy them and grow with them. If you nurture your friendships, they can and will bring great joy to your life.

I think your openness, intelligence and good instincts will help you choose friends wisely. I have no doubt that your warmth and lovingness will help you enjoy the fruits of such friendships long and fully.

Friendship vs. sisterhood. Obviously I don't know anything firsthand about men's friendships, but my observation suggests that few men are lucky enough to enjoy the same close friendships we do. It may be that their programming makes closeness harder to achieve; it may be that they are trained into self-reliance more than we; it may be just a function of our particular society. It must be a great loss.

For whatever complex reasons, women seem to take easily to friendships. They listen to each other's tales, triumphs and traumas. They offer each other advice, and they share accumulated wisdom. I've often wondered if this sharing came about because of our status as Number 2—a sort of underground mutual-aid society—or simply because we are nurturers by nature, and get a primal kick out of mothering and helping.

When I lived in Charlotte, during the two years in which I was pregnant with you both, I had two women friends who were salvation for me. Our lives drifted apart when I moved north; and I hadn't heard from either in ten years until a week ago, when one telephoned to say she was in town and wanted to have dinner. I've been flooded with memories as a result of that meeting: memories of friendship and of that strange, almost familial bond that can form between women—that bonding which at a certain point in one's development can mean survival in a confusing world.

The kind of bonding that I'm talking about is distinctly different from the friendships women form with men. I think that women turn to each other for solace and for shared experience. I think we speak a coded language that allows for comfort and ease. I think the bond within that cipher world is strong and universal. I think it is a world which no man can enter.

Yet I must tell you, my dear daughthers, that I am wary of the feminist concept that "sisterhood is powerful," and I've been trying to figure out why; for at the same time that I've been having such loving feelings about my women friends, I've been reading a feminist book about "sisterhood" that has set my teeth on edge.

I find the idea of a powerful sisterhood a little scary. I think it conjures visions for me of a battalion of marching women, strong in their union and potentially dangerous; after all, what's the need of asserting your power unless you intend to use it *against* somebody? The chauvinism disturbs me, too, as if somehow being part of this powerful sisterhood makes you part of an elite corps. Such separateness troubles me, for in my heart of hearts I believe that the salvation of family and of civilization itself depends on men and women coming closer to each other, increasing understanding, reaching out and touching spirits. Separateness, threats of power, chauvinism—none of these encourages communication, and communication has to be the key to a better future.

Someone once said to me plaintively, "I wish I could talk to my husband as honestly and with as much assurance of understanding as I can to my women friends," and I knew just what she was feeling. There is an intrinsic understanding between those who have shared experience, which needs few words; it is restful to be able to communicate via telegraph, leaving out all those excess syllables of explanation. Yet I persist in believing that the best of all worlds would be one in which such perfect understanding could be achieved between men and women and I'd like to plead the case for any enlightenments that could lead us in that direction.

These days, I think, boys and girls are developing real friendships. Cee Cee, you and Gigi confide in your boyfriends, it seems to me, with absolute candor and honesty. Bron, you treat your boyfriends to the same open, direct communication you use with your girl friends. In my day, girls and boys played so many roles with each other that they seldom knew each other's real feelings about anything. Now, it seems, each sex is genuinely interested in hearing what the other has to say. What a mighty step forward!

It is true that we receive from the best of female friendships support, understanding, sharing, trust and love of a special kind. I'm very hopeful that perhaps your contemporaries will find the means to talk to your husbands "as honestly and with as much assurance of understanding" as other generations

have done with their own sex. I believe the future rewards
would be phenomenal.

----

*I guess being a friend isn't as easy as it sounds. Everybody's got
friends and everybody tries to be a friend, but it's a pretty
complicated thing to do. You've got to learn to understand the
other person's feelings, to accept their faults, and to care about
their needs. To try to understand how they feel and try to see
their point of view. But, I guess mostly, being a friend just
means being thoughtful and caring.*

Lola,   age 15

*I think being a friend means helping the person who is your
friend when they have a problem. Comforting them, maybe.
Being a friend is mostly a question of being there when you're
needed. If your friend needs someone to laugh with, to cry
with, or talk to, or to gossip with, or to giggle with, you should
be available. Come to think of it . . . giggling is the best part of
friendship.*

Bronwyn,   age 15

*I think that to be a friend, you have to trust the other person,
care about the other person and be able to just come out and
tell the other person how you feel or what you are thinking
about, no matter what it is. Friendship means knowing you are
liked and cared about by somebody trustworthy.*

Cee Cee,   age 14

*My friends are very important to me. They are one of the most
important things in my world. I know that my friends care
about me and I certainly care about them. Having friends is
very important at my time of life because you can talk with
your friends about anything; you can go places with them to
have fun and you can do things with friends you could never
do with parents. Friendship is about the best thing that can
happen to you.*

Cee Cee,   age 14

When God measures a man, He puts the tape measure around the heart instead of the head.

Help When
You Need It

My Aunt Helen once told me, "If the good Lord intends to save you from destruction, He'll send someone to give you a helping hand." Despite the fact that I believe we must take responsibility for our own lives, when I think back on the close calls I've had in this life (and I expect all people have them), it seems to me she was quite right. The thought prompts me to write to you about help—for help, small or large when you need it, can sometimes make all the difference in both survival and quality of life.

Have you ever noticed that people who love each other help each other, be they friends or family? Sometimes they do so at the price of their own comfort or money, and sometimes (hardest of all) at the cost of their own peace, quiet and privacy. It's like my minding Alexis for you, Bronwyn, on Saturday mornings, when you'd rather sleep than babysit. Or my helping you

194

build a model of the Globe Theatre for school, Cee. Or your cleaning the house, or walking the dog for me, when I'm on my last legs. All those myriad little unselfish acts we all treat each other to add up to kindness, generosity, love, family and friendship—and on a grand scale, it seems to me, to community and civilization.

I've been hearing a lot about the "self" generation lately . . . about the "me first" syndrome of modern society. Frankly, I can't imagine either of you generous-spirited young women falling into such an unidimensional pattern, but perhaps the whole trend is worth talking about, since it seems so pervasive.

I would never suggest that you forget your own needs and lose yourself in the plight of others—there are very few of us born to be Mother Theresa—but I don't think it can hurt for you to give a little thought to where total "self"-centeredness eventually leads. It seems to me that while taking good care of your own needs is healthy, out-and-out selfishness is not, for it can quite effectively set you apart from others. After all, if you give nothing, surely no one will want to give to you; if you talk only of your own escapades, you soon bore everybody else in the room; if you close yourself into a cocoon of self-interest, how can you ever be open to compassion or friendship, generosity or love? It seems rather obvious that if no one ever chose to be at least a little bit unselfish, there would be few noble deeds, few great love stories, few instances of man's higher nature breaking through. I'm being a bit simplistic, of course, just to make a point, but I'm sure you see where I'm driving.

I'm not asking you to sacrifice yourself unthinkingly for others' sake—little need to burn at the stake these days, or to go to the guillotine for your friend—but rather to look around you and sharpen your awareness of who in your immediate vicinity could benefit from a helping hand, a kind act, a smile, an unselfish gesture. The more generous-spirited acts you perform, the more they become second nature, and the more reward you yourselves will reap from your own strengthened spirit.

Thinking back over a lifetime, I find that certain individual acts of kindness people treated me to stand out in bold relief despite the years. I remember, when you were tiny and we were poor, that Papa, knowing I hated ever to accept money from him, yet sensing that there wasn't always enough to go around, would hide a ten-dollar bill under a cookie jar or lamp for me to find later—always, of course, denying knowledge of the magical origin of the "found" money. You can't imagine how very loved that gesture made me feel, sometimes at moments when my spirits were at the lowest ebb. My mother, knowing how unaffordable the constant stream of necessary new clothes for you girls was, would turn up with skirts and coats and dresses she just "happened" to pick up. My sister, Conny, too, took on nearly adult responsibilities while still a teen-ager to help us all to manage and prosper.

When you get right down to it, it's not the actual specifics of the help that matters, it's the closeness of spirit such little and big helps engender that is the real HELP rendered. Recognizing such unselfish acts when they are directed your way takes a little strengthening of sensitivity and observation, too, I think. It's awfully easy to take for granted what people give to us, or do for us . . . after all, we're each the center of our own universes, and it's easy to forget to be grateful for simple kindnesses. If you give some thought to the motivation behind what is done for you day to day, you might be awfully pleased to realize how many people love you enough to help you when you need it.

If we are going to reserve the right to express our anger over the bad that people dish out (and as you know I'm a firm advocate of doing so!), then shouldn't we be just as expressive about the bountiful good we're treated to daily? The friend who helped you with your homework . . . the one who invites you to the show you've been dying to see . . . the person who tips you off that your teacher is on the warpath . . . the teacher who gives you an extra twenty-four hours to finish that horrendous report . . . the grandmother who bothers to remember when she's at the store that you just love earrings . . . the grandfather who is always willing to stop what he's doing to pay *attention* to you . . . the sister who lets you wear her new shirt even though she's convinced you'll probably do it irreparable damage—these aren't your rights and privileges, just kindnesses that are freely given.

I've been helped in life, in love, in business, in learning. I've been given more than, strictly speaking, I deserved, on a thousand occasions. Perhaps if that hadn't been the case, neither you nor I would be here to tell the tale. What I'm advocating to you, my loves, in this rather rambling soliloquy is a slightly more activist policy than simply counting your blessings. I'm suggesting that having counted them, you multiply them, by passing them on. The day will come when a helping hand from someone will mean to you the difference between success and failure, happiness or unhappiness, maybe even life and death. The best way I know to say thank you is to pass the good along.

O Lord,
Thou givest us everything
At the price
Of an effort.
                    LEONARDO DA VINCI

Keep on Keepin' On

Bob Dylan, the poet mover and shaker of my generation, wrote a song about how to keep on keepin' on. Every once in a while its lyrics flash into my mind, because it seems to me that in order to keep on, we must equip ourselves with special replenishments for the journey.

Much of the time we are totally immersed in the plugging-along. Life is mostly full of everyday responsibilities, everyday chores, people to be cared for, things to be handled, things to be done. While this is fine, and there is fulfillment in successfully meeting these mini-goals daily, most of what we spend our time at isn't much fun. That is why I think it's important to keep something close at hand that nourishes your heart. Let me try to explain.

There's an old proverb that says, "If you have two loaves of bread, sell one and buy hyacinths to feed thy soul." It is this feeding of the soul that seems to me increasingly important as I grow older. Whether your own personal pleasure is to knit an afghan, read a cherished book, paint a picture, make a pot of homemade tomato soup, plant a seed, or some other more esoteric possibility, I believe there must be found some moments in a busy life for personal replenishment. Such pleasures renew the wellspring of energy that makes the "keepin' on" possible.

Many's the day I've survived a grim and trying office experience knowing there was something I longed to enjoy waiting for me at home. Writing these notes for you, for example, has given me great, great pleasure . . . more, perhaps, than you could imagine. When I'm writing, I feel particularly close to you—a very lovely feeling.

As you grow older, you will often find yourself with miles to go before you sleep. It's okay; sometimes those miles have much to show you, many treasures to unfold. But along the road it doesn't hurt to stop and smell the flowers. Such stops don't slow you down, they simply let you travel on, refreshed and replenished.

Some people develop hobbies to fulfill this need, some possess a passionate interest in a subject they study with relish. Some fill the bill with friendships, and for all, most certainly, the biggest single source of such personal fulfillment is love. All these possibilities are means of keeping a life in balance. They help establish an equilibrium consisting of a bit of work, a bit of pleasure; a dose of practicality, a dash of poetry. The idea is, I think, to maintain as best you can the balance between what you *must do* and what you *like to do*.

Often this is easier said than done, by the way. The practical needs of life are quite enough to keep you busy. Most especially so at certain times—when you're getting started on a job, or having a new baby, or striving for some particular success. Yet these are probably the moments when you most need replenishment; most need a source of tensionless, contented strength to draw upon.

You are, after all is said and done, your own natural resource. Inside you are all the tools, the potentials, the reservoirs you will need to construct a happy and productive life. Like a magician's hat, your own body and brain are a never-ending source of useful substances to be magically produced at need. By providing yourself with pleasurable moments—peaceful, tension-free times of doing things that truly please *you*—I believe you refresh and replenish that magical reservoir of yours as surely as snow from a mountain refreshes a spring with cool clear water. After all, it's nice to know, when you have those miles to go before you sleep, that you are well fortified for the journey.

> *It does not do to leave a dragon*
> *out of your calculations*
> *if you live near him.*
>   J. R. R. TOLKIEN

The Unexpected

To be perfectly honest, almost everything in my life has been unexpected. Someone once told me I was *incident*-prone. He wasn't far off target.

It seems to me that one of the greatest gifts we can possess in this life is *responsive flexibility*. By that I mean the ability to change and grow as change and growth are needed. Very structured people, those who engrave their life path in cement, are doomed not only to a lifetime lacking in surprises, but also to the probability of being a dinosaur in an evolving landscape.

The ability to grow and evolve will be more important to your generation, I suspect, than to any other one in earth's long history. Think of the progress—technological, medical, scientific, psychological—that has happened in this single century. When my parents were born, there were no radios, no airplanes, few automobiles; and electric power had begun to be supplied only forty years before. Space travel happened in *my* generation, so did television and laser beams. God alone knows what progress will mark your life-span. What we do know is that progress is accelerating. There's been more of it in this century so far than in all the centuries that went before. At the rate we're going, miracles will soon be commonplace; which brings me to my thoughts on the unexpected.

If I were you, I'd expect surprises and be open to them. Surprises of intellect and technology, surprises of spirit and vision. Knowing you both, I'm pretty sure you won't get too bogged down by the old ways. It's my hope for you that no matter how wonderfully well-ordered your life gets to be, you will always stay loose enough to think new thoughts, embrace breakthroughs and respond to invention. Loose enough to learn quickly, to keep an open mind, and to drink deeply of all life's wonders, and that you will have the courage to explore the seemingly implausible, and to investigate the ideas that stretch your mind to its outer limits.

People with closed minds are doomed to ordinary lives. Not terrible, you might say, and I agree. But on the other hand, an open and inquiring mind is a passport to realms you may not yet have dreamed of. Who knows, after all, which way your own destiny lies? The more windows you open up in your soul, the more chance there is of something surprising coming in.

Let's imagine the future for a moment . . . increased life-span, space travel, TV you can talk back to, telepathy, bionic transplants—and, on the dark side, overcrowding, pollution, ecological trauma and the threat of a nuclear age. We haven't really a clue to what life will be like on this planet of ours in twenty years.

I think the only way we can prepare ourselves for such a jumble of potential experience is by firmly establishing our own confidence in ourselves and in our ability to grow and adapt. If you strengthen your belief in yourself by whatever means are open to you, you will need fewer cement props, fewer permanent security blankets to help you carry on. By carrying your security deep within you, your whole being will be free to soar.

The best way I know of to prepare yourself for the unexpected is to take life as it comes, with a sense of adventure, a sense of humor and a weather eye out for opportunity. We never know from which quarter opportunity will come, or what guise it will take. Expanding your knowledge, talents, reflexes, sensitivities and especially your powers of observation is the best and surest preparation. After all, you can only respond to any opportunity according to your ability to perceive that the opportunity is there.

Well, when the unexpected comes up, like somebody dying, or something surprising happening to you, you just have to deal with it then and go on from there . . . you can't let anything throw you.

Lola,   age 15

I don't really sit down and think about the future very often. I mean, even planning a week ahead isn't really my thing. You don't know what's going to happen tomorrow, so how can you plan for something that's going to happen years from now? I guess I'm pretty optimistic about my future, though. I know I'm going to have a good life no matter what happens. I usually manage to make the best of every situation so I figure I'll just keep on doing that. I have no idea what I'm going to be when I grow up, and when I finish school. I have no idea what kind of job I'm going to get, or if I'm going to get a job, or if I'm going to be married and have twenty kids, or if I'm going to be doomed to suburbia forever. But I know that whatever I do, I'm going to enjoy it, and I'm going to be happy because I can usually manage to turn things into something good or useful.

Lola,   age 15

With this situation in Iran and all, I do worry about wars quite a bit . . . I wonder if maybe life is going to be totally different ten years from now. Maybe we'll have to learn how to speak Russian or Chinese. That would be really awful . . . I have enough trouble with English! I'm a little worried about our ability to win a war, too. We don't seem to have the fighting force, or the loyalty, or the dedication that the U.S. had in its past wars. Vietnam seems to have changed everything. This time it could be even worse. With nuclear war, with the possibility of war being fought here in America, people will practically want to commit suicide if it looks like a fight is starting. I just feel that somehow the future is going to be pretty strange.

Lola, age 15

I think the future is really going to be pretty interesting. It brings more wisdom, brings more of everything! But there's no looking into it. I don't know what is going to happen, which makes it all the more exciting and adventurous. But no matter what happens, you know everything that comes will give you more wisdom and more things to tell your grandchildren or your great-grandchildren.

Bronwyn, age 15

Okay, Mom, this is your future! Did it turn out like you expected it to? When you were a kid, did you always wonder what was going to happen—if you were going to get married and have two or three kids and live in suburbia? Well, this is your future. You've already seen part of it—how's it doing?

Bronwyn, age 15

I don't know, I wouldn't want to hurry up the future. I don't want to go through it any sooner than I have to. I'm enjoying right now, and I'm living for now. But whatever the future holds for me, I'm going to find a way to deal with it, and I'm going to enjoy it!

Bronwyn, age 15

I am looking forward to the future, because I'm going to get older and I am going to get a job and I am going to settle down, maybe. I doubt it, but maybe! Things will all be electronic then, and I'll just have to push a button and a maid will come out of the closet and clean. I can't wait for that. I'm looking forward to the future because everything will be new, and like science fiction movies with all kinds of mechanical gadgets to make life easier. I'm really looking forward to all the improvements the future will bring.

Cee Cee,   age 14

Great things are done when men and mountains meet.
WILLIAM BLAKE

The Task That
Couldn't Be Done

When I got home last evening, Bronwyn, you were lying on the sofa curled into a ball, miserable, hopeless and half asleep. The cause was exams. You had so much to study that you had psyched yourself into exhaustion, just thinking about what needed doing. By the time we had tackled the studying for an hour or so, two things had happened. You'd realized how much you already knew, and you'd decided that the rest was handleable. It was a perfect example of why action is better than inertia. Action accomplishes at least part of the "hopeless" task and it puts the rest of it into perspective. Action reinforces your own good opinion of yourself, and strengthens your will to succeed. It eliminates the psychically debilitating option of running away, and moves you closer to where you need to go. Inertia erodes your sense of self, distorts your vision of the difficulty of the task, impairs your will to overcome obstacles, offers the illusion of options you don't really have (I'll run away from school and never go back!). And, perhaps worst of all, it makes you feel like a failure.

My father had a lovely custom when I was a child. If I was faced with a hopeless task, he would swoop in and say, "My, my, that does look impossible, doesn't it? Well, it shouldn't take so long if we do it together." A wonderful use of positive psychology. First, he agreed with me that the task looked awesome; that made me feel vindicated for my bleak outlook. Next, he offered help—a big relief. Last, he made the work seem do-able instead of hopeless. I've lived to learn that behind this simple statement was an enormous wellspring of wisdom.

My mother, with her characteristic efficiency, could take the most monumental project and somehow whittle it down to handleable size in record time. There was a larger-than-life-size force field about her that made me feel that no project, no matter how immense, had a prayer of withstanding her dynamism. Because I believed so thoroughly that *she* could make the walls of Jericho crumble if she chose to, I, too, was somehow magically imbued with a belief in my own capacity to win through. It seems clear to me now that much of my belief in my own ability to succeed in life is directly traceable to my mother's confident competence. In other words, my parents' commonsensible courage in facing the hard stuff was a lovely and permanent inspiration.

All through your life you will be faced with a smattering of tasks that seem too monumental to contemplate. Tasks in business, in child-rearing, in loving, in living. If by the time the important ones come along you've stocked up on fundamental belief in your own ability to overcome difficulties, you'll be like the man in the old poem "who tackled the task that couldn't be done. And he did it." If, on the other hand, you've learned to duck the tough stuff, to decide early on that you can't, and therefore *won't* try, you'll have no firm foundation of belief in your own strength and stamina.

I learned from my parents' philosophy by practicing. Every time we overcame an obstacle "together," I learned to believe that one day I could go it alone, and maybe even help someone else to do the impossible. I'm not suggesting, by the way, that you eliminate common sense and cautiousness when you evaluate the feasibility of tasks that come your way. I know you'll use both in analyzing the difficult situations life presents, so you can decide when discretion is indeed the better part of valor. If somebody asked you to move the World Trade Center a little bit to the left, I doubt that you'd buckle down to it! But if you take a good hard look at tasks as they pop up, and decide if the goal is sensible and the reward desirable, you can go to it with confidence in your own brain and brawn.

The moral of the story is, I think, that most of the world's progress has been the result of people who took on the impossible. Like Columbus, sailing to a place that might have existed only in his imagination; the Pilgrims, who traveled to a land full of unknowns; the pioneers who went west in covered wagons; the prospectors who dug for gold in the Yukon. Or the Curies, the Martin Luther Kings, the peace marchers. They all took on the impossible tasks, *and they did them.* By and large they were quite ordinary, everyday people. Everyone who ever found a cure for a disease, invented a better mousetrap, climbed a mountain, taught a retarded child to dress himself or a blind one to read Braille has put into practice what I'm talking about. These little miracles are all around you. Tributes to people's hard work and intestinal fortitude. Remember the wonderful story of "The Little Engine That Could" that you loved when you were small—that story of a little train, trying with all his might to get over a big mountain, is a splendid metaphor for life. "I think I can, I think I can, I think I can" is what he kept telling himself as he chugged up the hill—and he was right, *he could.* And so can you.

When you are looking the most worrisome tasks in the eye, it sometimes helps to remember that "This, too, shall pass." I guess we've all had the experience of lying in bed at night, worrying about some fearsome thing that's to happen the next day (somehow odious tasks grow larger as night grows darker!) and then being astounded the very next night to realize the crisis is over and life is back to normal. Crises are part of life. They come, and happily *they go*. It's not so easy to remember that, when you are in the middle of a pickle, but it has sometimes helped me to say to myself, "By Thursday, this will all be behind me."

Some of the hard tasks tackled in my life have been fruitful, and I've profited from them. Others have been just plain hard work with no apparent reward at all. Sometimes I've overcome all obstacles, and sometimes I've been a big flop. In the final analysis, I think, it doesn't much matter. You grow through it all, you live and learn; and you as a human being increase in stature, in strength, in confidence, in maturity and in clarity of vision.

By the way, I would like very much to help you with your impossible tasks, my dear daughters, when they pop up and while I'm still around to do so. Don't ever hesitate to ask me for aid when you need it. After all, whatever the task is, "It shouldn't take so long if we do it together."

Being Direct

We live in a world in which being direct has few advocates. We are taught politics practically from the cradle. "Don't tell Mrs. Tibbet her hat is dreadful." "Tell your teacher how much you love being in her class." You know how it goes. We learn to be manipulative because it seems to be an acceptable mode of conduct, and because it gets you things.

I'd like to write the brief for the other side. Not because I think life would be improved by telling little old ladies that their hats are ugly, but because I think that constantly practicing dishonesty erodes our sense of reality, weaves a web too tangled to be comfortable, and eventually leaves us with no sure knowledge of where truth ends and lying begins. Let's say someone asks you if you'd like to go to her house for the weekend. You don't want to go, but you think she'll be mad if you say so. So you procrastinate with an answer and finally make up some silly excuse at the last minute. Result: she still is

210

pretty sure you didn't want to go in the first place; she's huffy because now it's too late to invite someone else; you've ended up fretting for three days over how to handle it! A simple "No, thanks, I appreciate your inviting me, but I really like to spend my weekends in the city" might have made everybody's life simpler.

What if people ask you a question they don't really want to hear the answer to? you might ask. I'd say that the fact that *they* asked the question exonerates you from guilt in giving an honest answer. At the worst, they will be temporarily annoyed with your reply and perhaps regret asking, but at least they will know they can rely on your candor. Who needs a friend who tells us only what we want to hear? You'd be surprised how often someone has heartily thanked me for telling him something no one else would.

If it's so easy to be direct, why don't people do it more often? The shortest distance between two points is still the straight line, but the politically sage often choose the most circuitous, roundabout answers to questions. Well, the truth is, those who don't answer directly are probably afraid to do so, afraid of the commitment a single yes or no answer implies. Instead, the politician responds with "Maybe yes, maybe no, maybe something else," thereby assuring himself of a way out, if yes or no doesn't turn out to be a profitable stance. While this may seem like a clever ploy, it is bound to backfire sooner or later.

The clever politician simply brands himself as one who cannot be trusted—not so clever an achievement in the final judging.

Beyond all this, obfuscators waste time. Because they do not take the shortest distance between points, they doom you to the long way around, thereby taking up precious time you might not want to waste. By hiding everything in a cloud of vapor, they make judgment confusing and unnecessarily complicated and therefore waste both your time and energy in unraveling what they've tangled up.

Let's take a for-instance. Let's imagine you have a date Saturday night and you have a ton of weekend homework, too. You'd like me to help you do part of the research that's needed, so you'll only have to do the studying. Instead of asking outright, you spend Saturday moping around the house, whining and complaining. By Saturday night you feel pressured and explosive, and I want to hide in a closet every time you come near. By the time I figure out what's got your temper on edge, a whole day has been wasted that might have been used constructively to get the job done. The point is, of course, that asking straight out generally saves both time and aggravation.

There is a great deal to be said for clarity. Clarity of thought, clarity of speech, clarity of vision. By their own design, obfuscators are doomed to dissembling and diffusion. Never to cut incisively through the meat to the bone of the question means you are left nibbling at the edges and the outer wrap, a situation that seems to me effectively to keep you away from the crux of any matter.

I believe that the relentlessly politic ultimately confuse themselves. Truth and fiction become such a comfortable mélange to them that their grip on reality can weaken and their connection to the truth can become as indirect as their arguments. Surely, clear, direct thinking helps lead to clear, direct conclusions. The man who lives by clouding the truth in his dealings with others must eventually be hard pressed to recognize the truth for himself in his own life. If you are direct and honest in your opinions and appraisals, chances are you will be trusted. Not necessarily liked, by the way, but most likely trusted.

There are, of course, times when the direct approach can get you clobbered . . . just as there are times when you may *want* to tell the little old lady her hat is gorgeous just because it's kinder. I certainly believe you have to use your judgment in determining when and if to tell those little untruths. Yet in principle and in practice, direct thought, speech and action is ninety-nine times out of a hundred the way to go.

Life is filled with decisions, choices and questions, most of which demand of you either an answer or an action. I would like to hope that in the years to come both of you will, within the perimeters of your own personalities and styles, find it best to be clear, forthright and as direct as possible.

I think people should be direct, because first of all it gets everything off your chest. If you just say what you mean, it's better than beating around the bush, because when you beat around the bush, you can easily be misunderstood. If you just come right out and say what you mean, it's a lot easier for all concerned.

Bronwyn,   age 15

Being direct also helps you out if you're shy, and you don't always know how to ask for what you want. If you learn to ask for things directly, I think it can help keep you from feeling withdrawn and alienated from your environment.

Bronwyn,   age 15

Being direct isn't always the easiest thing to do. Just coming right out and saying what's on your mind is pretty hard. I guess sometimes it helps to beat around the bush, and sort of hint at what you want. But if you want to get it over with, if you have something to say that's not too pleasant, being direct is the only way to do it. Sometimes people get hurt, of course. I think the best bet is to be direct as long as you use a little tact. You know, like Mary Poppins always said, "A spoonful of sugar makes the medicine go down."

Lola,   age 15

You should be direct, in everything that you do and everything that you say. You should just come right out and say everything that you feel, no matter how the other person thinks. It's the only honest way to be.

Cee Cee,   age 14

7

LEARNING

Whatever desire for knowledge I possess seems to me a direct legacy from my mother and father, who had an infinite capacity for making the quest for knowledge seem the most joyous of undertakings. It was a great and forever gift, one I would dearly love to share with you.

*The object of education is to prepare the young
to educate themselves throughout their lives.*
ROBERT MAYNARD HUTCHINS

Learning vs. Education

Somebody should have patented my mother's system of education, for she had the remarkable ability to make learning desirable. History became one long adventure story, geography an escape to the exotic, poetry a means of exercising the emotions, reading a way to make anything possible. Instead of children's stories, she read me mythology—what better tales than those of giants and gods to fill a child with awe and wonder? Instead of Dr. Seuss (I was a child long before his delightful time) I was reading Robert Louis Stevenson, and Arthur was the Prince Charming in my fairy tales. I learned the order of succession to the thrones of France by hearing the stories of the king's mistresses buried under the Royal Oak. I learned that Catherine de'Medici brought her own personal on-staff poisoner with her to her marriage, because her husband had put his mistress's initials on the royal silver instead of her own— and a host of other odd, gossipy tidbits. History, as gossip, lives far more easily for a child than history as an endless succession of faceless dates.

I mention these long-ago learnings only because I think the methodology was brilliant. Education was a game; knowledge was a tangible reward; learning was a joy. Just as it should be. Yet I have a feeling that kids today are often turned off by the peanut butter-and-cement consistency of much modern schoolwork; so little sense of drama and intrigue about it, and so much sloshing through swamp. I wonder how it deteriorated so. I wonder how my mother knew so much better than many educators how to make learning a glorious adventure.

I sometimes think if the kids of your generation could somehow empty their heads of the perception of schoolwork as you've known it and magically substitute a sense of adventure and a lust for knowledge, the future of mankind would be irrevocably altered. Years ago, Cee Cee, as I was watching you play Store, always the favorite game of your very commercially oriented brain, I realized you could figure 8 percent of anything at lightning speed in order to add tax to your imagined purchaser's bills; at the very same time you were having terrible trials getting percentages and fractions straight in school. The rather obvious conclusion? You *liked* figuring out taxes, so you were a whiz at it; you hated learning math at school, so it slowed you to a standstill.

An intriguingly innovative educator named John Holt, who is devoting his life to American educational reform, provided a most provocative indictment of our school system in his book *Instead of Education*, by saying:

Almost everyone who goes through school comes out believing:
   1. If I want to learn anything important I have to go to a place called school and get someone called a teacher to teach me.
   2. The process will be boring and painful.
   3. I probably won't learn it.

School is, of course, a place you go to, to learn, but learning happens to you every minute of every day of your lifetime. Somehow in our society "schooling" and "learning" have gotten lumped into the same cubby, and they don't necessarily belong there. Mark Twain once said that you should never let your schooling interfere with your education. And Henry Adams said, "While I was being educated, I went to school."

If you think of education as a lifelong quest for knowledge and useful information, it's a far more enticing proposition than most kids imagine. It's a snap to learn if you love the knowledge you seek, of course. For instance, Bronwyn, memorizing a complex part in a play is a breeze for you because acting is your great love. Learning how to operate a cash register and keep books, Cee Cee, was more fun than work for you. Both these "learnings" were easy because they were desirable, and knowledge that you covet for yourself is enjoyable to accumulate and, quite honestly, the most likely to stay with you through a lifetime.

I do not mean to suggest by this that you should limit your studies only to the subjects you like best. I firmly believe that exposure to arts, language, science, math, history, etc., is an important broadening process. Unless you taste a bit of each of the fruits of the tree of knowledge, you can't possibly know which ones belong in your personal fruit salad.

What I do mean to suggest is that once you find subjects, ideas, studies which excite or intrigue you, you should allow yourself the pleasure of delving into them fully. I'd encourage you to think, write, talk and read about the things in life which excite you, thrill you, race your blood, or tickle your fancy—no matter what these things be—for by so doing you not only take control of your lives, but you give yourself the best shot at accumulating lasting and useful knowledge. You are far more likely to achieve important levels of learning when pursuing one subject dear to your heart than by pursuing ten which don't race your motor.

You Are Your Own Teacher

I suppose what I'm really saying to you about learning is this: love yourself enough to educate yourself. Find what intrigues you and fill yourself to the brim with that knowledge. Open your eyes, ears and powers of concentration to all of what is around you. You can learn psychology from observing the actions of the lady opposite you on the bus, see what you can figure out about her from her body language. You can learn from TV and movies; it's such a palatable way to absorb information. You can learn from the older people you know—every living human probably has at least one "something" you'd be interested to hear about. You can learn from books—they've got it all. You can learn from your friends, from walking in the park, from reading subway posters. You can even learn from yourself, by paying attention to your own intrinsic talents and potentials.

If you learn to look on life and all that surrounds you as a sort of sacred repository—a place where all the accumulated knowledge of mankind is kept, much like the contents of the lamasery in Shangri-La—a remarkable thing will happen to you.

You will suddenly realize that the amount of knowledge you can accumulate is bounded only by the extent of your curiosity and the indefatigability of your own stamina. In a way that realization is a two-edged sword, for it precludes forever the excuse that "I don't know how to do that," and substitutes instead, "I didn't bother to learn how!" But nonetheless it is a fabulously creative way to live your life.

The important thing for a parent to do if a kid is not trying to do well in school is to find out why. Maybe there's an explanation.

                                        Cee Cee,   age 14

I feel good if I'm keeping up in school, because I like to learn as much as I can. I think that's what it's there for—to educate us. But sometimes you get a little disillusioned because it seems schools are only there to make us bored to death and to keep us off the streets for eighteen years.

> *Lola, age 15*

One of the problems with school is that kids get turned off by a bad teacher here or there, and then they get turned off to school altogether—without realizing that there's a lot of learning available in school that you can make use of in life later on.

> *Lola, age 15*

I think that school should be run this way—you can either take morning classes or afternoon classes, because a day can start at 8:45 and you can have five classes up until 12:45, and that's not so bad. I'd go home, do my homework, watch my soap operas and really enjoy life!

> *Bronwyn, age 15*

My biggest quarrel with school is that I feel like there are about five hours' worth of stuff that's useful and the rest of it is nonsense. To have to hang around for eight hours, being bored by gym and study periods and art and shop, isn't exactly thrilling. It seems to me the time could be put to better use.

> *Bronwyn, age 15*

If I could reinvent the educational system, I'd make a lot of changes. I'd make it so that you could wear what you want; teachers wouldn't be so boring; there'd be more fun in learning; I wouldn't have the curriculum exactly the same every day. I'd use modern tools like television and movies to teach with, too.

> *Cee Cee, age 14*

If teachers would sit down and actually talk to their students as if they're people, too, then school would be a lot better. For me, everything depends on the teacher. You know how I hate English, but I had a great teacher and English was my favorite subject.

> *Bronwyn, age 15*

You know what constitutes a great teacher as far as a kid is concerned? Somebody who talks to their students, and who really listens—one who doesn't have a rigid idea of what's going to happen every day. I like open discussions in class-rooms—they're much better than just being lectured. When teachers really listen and respond, you feel as if you are an important part of the process. Otherwise it feels like "Them vs. Us."

Lola,   age 15

The school I liked best was one in which the teachers seemed to be very warm and friendly toward the kids. It wasn't a very structured environment. I learn better if I'm not scared to death of all the rules and regulations.

Bronwyn,   age 15

The most pressured thing about school is keeping up your grades. Also figuring out about what to do when you grow up, and figuring out how to get into a good college.

Lola,   age 15

All that stuff that teachers threaten you with doesn't make any difference to kids' behavior. It just turns everybody off.

Bronwyn,   age 15

My school is a nice one, because it's laid back and it has a relaxed atmosphere for a private school. You can really talk to the teachers person-to-person. Calling them by their first name makes you feel more like a person—like someone whose opinion counts.

Lola,   age 15

I think it's important to have discipline in the classroom. But if one person does something wrong and the teacher punishes the entire class (as they always do), that's unfair.

Bronwyn,   age 15

I think the teacher or the principal or somebody should sit down and talk to any kid who gets into trouble a lot, and try to find out why. If they find out what's going on, maybe he can be helped. I don't think anyone is ever helped by being punished. It just makes whatever is wrong worse. Everybody gets angry and nothing gets solved.

Bronwyn, age 15

Isn't communication really the key in life, though? I mean if more people communicated and found out why *things are happening the way they're happening, then there'd probably be less trouble. But teachers and headmasters and principals don't seem to try to communicate much. Whatever they say is pretty much a one-way street.*

Bronwyn, age 15

Poetry

I can hear you groaning already. Poetry is, I know, passé as far as you are concerned, but I'd like you to hear me out anyway for three reasons.

1. I have cherished poetry throughout my life.

2. I think you may have suffered a great loss in never having been taught to love one of the most rewarding uses of our language.

3. You might just miss out on one of the closest things to magic this life has to offer.

When I was little, my parents loved poetry. They read it to each other and they read it to me. My father proposed to my mother by sending her Shelley's

> The fountains mingle with the rivers
> And the rivers with the ocean,
> The winds of heaven mix for ever
> With a sweet emotion;

Nothing in the world is single,
All things by a law divine
In one another's being mingle—
Why not I with thine?

I can't tell you how romantic I thought that, as a child. I suppose I still do. At any rate, because I heard it recited, poetry was a living art form. We compared notes about it, shared new finds with each other, wept (only a little ashamedly) over the most maudlin varieties. I remember one of my great favorites had a poor husband and wife trying to decide which of their sleeping brood of seven could be spared to a wealthy man who wished to adopt one. To this day I can't get past the part where they decide not to give up their "wayward" son.

"For He who gave,
Bids us befriend him to
the grave . . .
Only a mother's heart could be
Patient enough for such as he.

It gets me every time.

For years I memorized a verse or two nightly before bed, and at one point could boast having memorized the entire *Rubáiyát,* if not ever quite in the right order!

My grandfather, when he was very old and almost blind and could no longer read, would sit for hours and recite poetry to himself or to me. He had the most prodigious memory I've ever encountered next to my mother's. It seemed to be an enormous comfort to Grandpa to have all that knowledge tucked away securely inside, where no one and nothing could interfere—not even old age.

Then and there I decided to tuck away as much as I could, too. You'd be amused to know how often it pops out. Seldom in important places, but always as a comfort. Everything reminds me of some verse, of some long-neglected poem. When my most loathed employer used to badger me with his pomposity and self-importance, I would picture him as Shelley's Ozymandias, whose "vast and trunkless legs of stone" stand forgotten in the desert despite the words "Look on my works, ye Mighty, and despair!" he'd had inscribed on his monument.

When I run, I unbore myself with a few choruses of Tennyson's "The Charge of the Light Brigade" or Thorpe's "Curfew Must Not Ring To-night"; and Yeats's "Cuchulain's Fight with the Sea" has gotten me through more than one deadly dull meeting intact and happy.

Here's the secret, I think. Poetry is the repository of all of mankind's finest emotions, most glorious language, most agile intellect. It is incisive and it touches brain and heart, with all the debris cleared away. It chronicles courage, heartbreak, love, death, honor with the extraordinary perceptiveness of a poet's intuition. It defines time and cultural confusions. It touches hell and heaven, and it teaches moral fortitude while showing us the dazzling clarity of vision only artists and poets ever see.

Consider what you have in the smallest chosen library:
A company of the wisest and wittiest men that
could be picked out of all civilized countries,
in a thousand years . . . .

RALPH WALDO EMERSON

Reading

My mother was a book person. Not only did she read every-thing she could get her hands on at an astounding rate, but she made a very special point of passing on to me what books she thought I could appreciate at each successive age. *Nobody's Boy* one year, *King Arthur* the next. *Gone With the Wind* when I was lost in the throes of thirteen-year-old romance, *War and Peace* when I had pneumonia and needed a lengthy escape route. The book list grew as I did. Looking back, I realize what a prodigious feat this book selection was. Not only did my mother mentally catalog vast numbers of literary goodies with me in mind, but she intuited exactly the moment when I would be thirsting for specific finds. She also introduced me to my beloved library, and feistily insisted that the horrified librar-ians give me grown-up books from the time I was seven. I was not relegated to the lowly children's stacks when I had bigger game in mind. It was a lovely gift.

About a month ago, while rereading Sigrid Undset's *Kristin Lavransdatter* for the sixth time, I had a vivid flashback of my mother handing the heavy green-bound *Kristin* to me when I was fourteen, with the kind of reverence reserved for sacred things. Suddenly, I realized that the gift of books and words she had given me has altered the entire course of my life. It has not only put a goodly portion of mankind's accumulated wisdom where I could reach it, but it has also given me a lifetime of comfort and pleasure.

So I'd like to take a minute to talk about love of reading, love of words. To love your own language, to taste and feel its nuances, to possess it sufficiently so that language can be called on to do your bidding in a pinch—to be on such intimate terms with words that you can speak them or write them, or think them or retort to them, with agility, speed, style and precision: this is a legacy worthy of kings.

Words are necessary for thought, and the finer the clarity and definition of your words, the more subtle your thinking can be. We are judged by our use of language. With sufficient command of it we can cross the boundaries of class, time, education, wealth and status. We can protect and defend ourselves. We can touch the stars.

If you love to read, I firmly believe all doors are opened to you. Whatever you wish to taste of is there to be feasted upon. What you wish to learn is there to sustain you.

My mother once told me that there is no aristocracy in this world but that of achievement. I believe this to be so. I believe, too, that the road to achievement is paved with books and words. Everything is easier and better if you have these treasured tools at your disposal. Whatever achievement you may yearn for in life—be it fame, fortune or simply the pride that comes with a job well done—words can help you get there and help you express your pleasure once you've earned it.

Find them for yourself. If there is no great teacher in your immediate sphere, find the works of a great one who has committed his knowledge to paper. Study words—their roots, their nuances, their possibilities. And once you've learned them, think with them, speak them, write them, love them.

Without words there is no language for the heart and mind— no communication. With them, the accumulated knowledge of all ages past is yours.

8

CHOICES

There is a poem that goes like this:

> To every man there openeth
> a high road and a low
>
> And every man decideth
> the way his soul shall go.

What it's really saying is, I believe, that the choice of who we are, and what we become in life, lies in our own hands and is continuously reinvented at those moments when two roads diverge and we must take one or the other.

Most of the choices and pressures you will face in life will represent hard work for the soul; my heart is with you in your efforts to choose well. I hope that perhaps some of the thoughts in the following chapters may be useful in helping you find the path that will make all the difference in deciding which way your soul shall go.

*Sex is a natural function
like breathing or eating.*

WILLIAM MASTERS

Sex

Considering that sex is one of the most important and fulfilling ingredients in life, it's very sad that parents have tended to prepare their children badly for it. I was always sure I'd do better than most, but the same strange phenomenon overtook me in the process that, I suspect, stymied other parents. It goes something like this: just at the time of life when sex becomes important to your children, they clam up about it. The same kids who questioned you at five and seven, and sported their sensual knowledge to less enlightened children at ten, are strangled with embarrassment at thirteen. You try to tell them about masturbation during the sexually sporadic teen years. They look aghast. You try to tell them how not to get pregnant. They think *you think* they're being promiscuous. You try to talk about boys. They'd rather die first. You try to explain the longing, the lustiness, the utter sexuality of being a woman; they excuse themselves and leave the room. You are the last person on earth they'd like to talk to about any of the above.

I started writing this when you were thirteen and fourteen. I had only a sketchy idea of what you thought about boys, other than that you thought of them a good deal. I was not certain you'd know where to find a good gynecologist when the time came that you needed contraceptives, despite the fact that we'd discussed it. I wanted to tell you that if you ever found yourselves pregnant, I would help you in any way I could—and a hundred other things about sex—yet every time I broached the subject, you headed for the door. I felt I had gone wrong somewhere, but I just wasn't sure where!

Fortunately for us all, after a year or so passed, and you began to really get the hang of being a teen-ager, you started talking again and we've now had a chance to exchange quite a bit of information. I don't know how it makes you feel, but it certainly makes me feel better!

You see, in my day sex was a somewhat nonexistent experience for the young. I remember vividly my own suppressed but resilient sexuality—and the lack of information I had about it. In those days anything that had to do with sex was considered unacceptable for discussion or even for thought. We were a generation admonished never to touch ourselves "there" and we were made to understand that sex was not an appropriate topic for "nice girls" to talk, think or learn about. I was so obedient that I never masturbated until I'd had sex . . . and then felt guilty about doing it but continued relentlessly nevertheless.

I spent most of my teen-age life being groped at (nice girls didn't grope back, in those days), soul-kissing, as it was then called, and living a life of unidentified but fierce sexual frustration. I wanted to know more, but felt somehow guilty that I was curious. I remember unearthing a book about how animals mated and reading it stealthily behind the stacks in the library, only to feel somehow sullied by having done so.

By the time I finally managed to rid myself of a virginity that

I had long since wanted to discard, I felt so guilty that I immediately convinced myself that I must be hopelessly in love with the man who had deflowered me. A most precipitous and, as it turned out, erroneous judgment—and one which, I'm afraid, was quite a commonplace error in those times.

In those days—now they seem very long ago—there was little information about sex readily available. You couldn't go to the store or library and find *The Joy of Sex* or any other informative literature. As a matter of fact, our local librarian was fired for buying a copy of *Peyton Place,* so you can imagine how much sexual reading matter was available! There was much moral, religious, parental and societal pressure against girls experimenting with or even thinking about sex, and much double-standard nonsense afoot among the boys and men of the world. "I want my wife to be a virgin when we marry," and other similar silly-business was considered sensible, standard morality. Men could play around and should for experience's sake—women, never. This, of course, was as ridiculous as it was impossible, but nobody seemed to notice.

Which, of course, brings me to another peculiarity of my generation. Boys had all the privileges. What they wanted or didn't want was all that counted. Women were raised to understand their needs and wants and to cater to them unflinchingly. Nobody was busy catering to us!

We were bred to gaze adoringly at any male, no matter what his I.Q., sex appeal or common sense, and tell him he was wonderful—relentlessly. If we told him that often enough, if we listened in rapt attention while encouraging him to talk only about himself, if we flattered him within an inch of nausea, he would "like" us and ask us out on more such dates. What a dumb system! It meant that we spent a lot of time with people with whom we had nothing in common, lying to them about our interest in their conversation, and then wondering why we felt so disappointed in boys as a species.

Why all this subterfuge? And why does it still exist in part today? Perhaps because of a basic difference in the way in which teen-age girls and teen-age boys approach sex. Teen-age girls still tend to crave emotional closeness and commitment to go along with sex, while teen-age boys are very often just looking for the "experience" of sex (at least, until they grow up to be men). I don't mean to suggest by this that girls aren't just as lusty and curious as boys; simply that they are more involved with the idea of "romantic" love at this age. This inequity, of course, evens out later on in life, when both men and women are seeking someone to love as well as to make love to. But in teenagerhood, I suspect, the whole thing is just a little lopsided.

I wish I could give you some magical advice to get you through this tricky time, but lacking magic, perhaps I could offer some thoughts about sexual decision-making, in the hope they may prove useful:

How do you figure out which boys to get close to? It's easy to say "Just follow the same guidelines as with girls," but it's more complicated than that, because at your age girls are very anxious to attract boys—any boys. Boys are interesting, an unknown quantity. They are different, attractive, strange, desirable, and they are in charge of the dating process, so they must be enticed.

The first advice I can give you is to *trust your own good instincts.* Listen to that little voice inside you that *knows* good from bad, wise from unwise, right from wrong, not-quite-right from okay. When not-quite-right comes along—be it boy or girl or situation—pass it by. We all often give the benefit of the doubt to people or situations that don't deserve it. Trust your own good instincts. If your instinct says, "There's something wrong with that person," even if you can't put your finger on *what's* wrong, steer clear. I bet you'll find that inner voice is amazingly accurate and protective.

If you can learn to be a good judge of friends—male or female friends—all choices in life get a lot simpler and less confusing. Some people can be trusted. Others can't. Being around the trustworthy ones will provide stability and sense to your life. The other ones bring uncertainty, worry and often disaster. Remember that you really can recognize the difference in people if you want to; if you believe in yourself enough to want *only* the *best* for *you*, you are likely to choose boyfriends with the same attention to character as you use with girl friends.

I think, mundane as it sounds, you should keep your eyes and ears open . . . *keep your reality in high gear.* When you meet a boy or go out with one, *listen* to what he has to say and evaluate him honestly in the light of his own actions. It's fine to excuse the annoying foibles of someone you intend to have a very casual relationship with; not so fine to do so with someone you feel seriously attracted to. If you have a pretty strong sense of your own worth, you'll be less likely to accept less-than-okay behavior in someone you are close to.

How do you know when to experiment with sex? I think that *deciding when to experiment with sex, and to what extent, is a very personal choice.* One you should do in your own good time and with someone worth sharing with. After all, even if you are simply anxious to learn about sex rather than being in a very serious love affair, you are still sharing your own very precious, very personal self with a boy or man when you go to bed with him, and you would be best off sharing with someone capable of appreciating your specialness.

How do you cope with societal and peer pressure? While I believe that sex is as natural as breathing, that doesn't mean I think it's as easy to figure out. Not only does sex seem confusing and full of question marks at your age, but there's a good deal of sexual pressure being generated from *within you* at this time, as well as that which is generated by your peers. Simplistic as it may sound, perhaps the best way to approach this internal kind of sexual pressure is to accept its naturalness and to try to understand where it's coming from. I have a feeling that part of the problem you are facing is that sexual decision-making for your generation seems to have been taken out of its natural context—that of being the natural extension of a relationship—and relegated to the status of a pragmatic command performance.

It seems to me, from what I read and hear, that the sexual revolution which my generation longed for and initiated has ended up doing just the opposite of what was intended: it seems to be placing *more* sexual pressure than ever on the young. What our generation wanted was the opportunity to be more intimate *within* our relationships; your generation seems to be suffering from having divorced sex from relationships altogether. In each of these instances, the end result is alienation, rather than the desired natural closeness. I have a feeling the real key to working your way through the maze of teen-age sexual confusions may center on getting to know a boy really well, as a friend. Let me explain what I mean: *without* the pressure of immediate sexual decision-making, a young man's friendship could help you learn a lot about yourself and about the perceptions, needs and desires of the other half of humanity. Such a friendship can allow sexual exploration to be the eventual and *natural* extension of your learning about each other. When you think about it, the desire to gain more intimate knowledge of another person because you feel attracted to him and genuinely *care* about him is a far cry from being pressured into sexual intimacy simply because the "group" expects it of you. Sex as a logical extension of an intimate relationship seems to me a potentially *unpressured learning experience.* Sex as a tension-ful experiment you are forced into by peers is a far less happy prospect.

If you are feeling pressured to engage in sexual activity that makes you feel *uncomfortable,* it may be that you simply haven't yet connected with the right young man or the right relationship with a young man. If such is the case, I think you have every right to demand the opportunity to proceed at your own rate of speed, and with your own right of privacy. Sharing

your body with another human being is a very important act of
intimacy. It should be done only when it has the potential to
please you and give you some measure of fulfillment. The very
words *peer pressure* suggests tension that someone else is *im-
posing on you* . . . not a very pleasurable-sounding situation,
and certainly not one that is conducive to sexual enjoyment.

No matter how perplexing it all may seem at the moment,
truth is, sex isn't just something to learn about, like chemistry
and physics; or to experience, like Disneyland. Sex is something to feel, and to feel good with—a very important area of
your growth and pleasure. You deserve to be able to take your
own good time learning about it. If you allow sexual intimacy
to develop on the basis of friendship and affection, it will be, as
it should, a natural evolution—not just a series of hit-and-run
incidents.

To be honest, going to bed with "just anybody" isn't good
enough at any age, yet the pressure that seems to be plaguing
young people these days is that of having to do so, just to be
able to say you did. That's such an unfair and unfortunate
setup, my darlings. You would do yourself a giant favor by
letting nature take its course in a slightly less tension-ful and
more old-fashioned way. By that I mean starting out your sexual investigations by knowing some young man well enough to
care about him, before you get tangled up in decisions about
sexual intimacy. If you wait until you really feel *the desire to
be intimate* with someone, rather than being pushed pre-
maturely into something you're not ready for, the whole process will probably happen quite naturally.

My major concerns for you sexually are these: that you be in
touch with your own sexual self and do whatever is best for
your own personal needs; that you, to the best of your ability,
choose your partner or partners with good sense; that you become knowledgeable about contraception; that you learn as
much as you can about your own sexuality—your own physical

and emotional being—so that you can enjoy deeply and abundantly the many pleasures of being a woman.

Guys say, "If you really cared for me, you'd have sex with me." Then girls say, "If you really cared for me you'd respect my feelings about this." So I guess the whole thing is pretty much the way it was twenty years ago.

Cee Cee, age 14

There's still a double standard about sex, but it's not as rigid as it once was.

Gigi, age 15

The first time kids learn about sex is from their friends. Then your parents come along and tell you about it, but it's a little too late, and your parents are mostly embarrassed and then they throw a book in your lap! Books are okay, but the whole system isn't terrific!

Lola, age 15

I don't think the idea of getting misinformation about sex is as much a problem as parents think, because there is so much information around—movies, TV, books, magazines. Sex is everywhere.

Bronwyn, age 15

There's a lot of worry about it. If you're a virgin, you're scared because you don't know what it's going to be like. You hear so many different stories. First of all, you hear the medical side of sex from teachers; then you get the mechanical side from books; then you see these awful things from porno movies or books that just make sex seem like something horrible and common. It's very confusing.

Lola, age 15

These are the things girls look for in boys. Cute is the first thing. That's the first thing you think about, I don't care what anybody says. A lot of girls say the first thing that they think about is honesty, or some other ideal, but I think before you get to the honesty, you look for "Cute!"

Bronwyn,　age 15

You should evaluate a boy the same way you would evaluate a female friend, don't you think? Look for the same kind of good characteristics.

Cee Cee,　age 14

You want to know, Do they seem polite and interested in you? Do they reach out their hand and say something rude, or do they reach out their hand and say "Hi, I'm Joe Smith, I want to get to know you"?

Lola,　age 15

I think most boys aren't looking for friends, they're looking for somebody to have sex with. Up until a certain age, that's true. I think there's a lot of pressure on them to find out what sex is all about, so therefore they almost have to do it. I mean, they feel that they have to. I wish there were more just nice guys you could have a friendly relationship with, before getting pressured about sex.

Bronwyn,　age 15

I think kids don't want to talk to parents about sex because it's a very private thing.

Cee Cee,　age 14

A boy can have sex with as many people as he wants and not get a reputation, but a girl can't—so it's still the double standard.

Cee Cee,　age 14

It's more open about sex nowadays and people talk about it more now, but there's an awful lot of pressure on kids to have sex, just like there used to be pressure on them not to.

Gigi,   age 15

Girls all look for nice boys who can be a friend, but there aren't too many around. There are some, though. You feel really good when you find one, too. Most of the nice ones are a little older.

Bronwyn,   age 15

Kids are at fault, too, when it comes to talking about sex. They don't ask the right questions because it's embarrassing.

Lola,   age 14

"Mommy, where did I come from?" "Oh, the stork brought you." Isn't that ridiculous! You've got to tell your kids the truth. From the beginning.

Bronwyn,   age 15

I think that boys expect too much these days, because a lot of girls do have sex with them—for the wrong reasons. You know there are some who just do it with anyone, because they don't want to be rejected. But boys have their problems, too. It seems like any boy who's over the age of fifteen and is still a virgin is a social outcast. I guess it must be really hard on them, because they have to claim they've had sexual experience, or they're ridiculed. I think most guys are 90 percent talk and 10 percent action. Most of them don't really do half the things they talk about. They just want to put up a big macho image, because they think that's what's expected of them.

Bronwyn,   age 15

I kind of like innocent guys, but no guy wants to be one of those! The double standard still goes on, you know. Guys are expected to have sex and at an early age—and to experiment a lot. But it just doesn't happen that way most of the time in real life. A lot of times guys are scared, just like girls are, but they're afraid to admit it. It's a pretty dumb system in a lot of ways. Everybody wants to learn and nobody wants to have to pretend, but everybody gets pushed into roles and games.

Bronwyn,   age 15

I think that sex should be a very special, intimate thing between two people. I don't think it should be plastered all over bulletin boards, and I don't think that everybody in the world should know about what you're doing. It's really nobody's business except the two people involved. I think it should be special.

Gigi,   age 15

Sex is a wonderful thing, but everybody has to pick the time that's right for her. Some people are ready for sex at fifteen or sixteen, and some aren't ready for it until their twenties, or until they're married. Some have old-fashioned values, some are scared. But at least people seem to be a little more honest about sexual matters now than they were in the old days.

Bronwyn,   age 15

Some people have old-fashioned ideas about sex and that's all right with me, too. I guess the decision is up to each person. I don't think anybody's exactly "outcast" because she's decided to remain a virgin forever, or because she's decided to find out about sex at twelve! I guess today—at least with the friends I have—they accept pretty much whatever each person's personal decision is. I know I have really good friends who are virgins and intend to remain virgins for a while, and I have really good friends who are far from virgins. I guess today everybody has more choices than in the past.

Lola,   age 15

If you've been going out with a boy for a long time, he really pressures you to go to bed with him. You know how it goes: "If you care about me, you'd have sex with me." But then you just say to him, "If you cared about me, you'd respect my wishes about not having sex." There's a lot of peer pressure, especially if you're a follower.

Bronwyn,   age 15

I think it's very wrong that kids my age are having sex as if it's nothing. I think sex is something that shouldn't be played with.

Wanda,   age 15

I think it's very true about that "little voice" inside you. My little voice has helped me quite a lot. I don't think that it's horrible to have sex, but I really believe what they say: "Once you have sex you'll never go back to holding hands!"

Wanda,   age 15

I hate to sound chauvinistic but I do think it takes guys a lot longer to grow up than girls. And I think a fifteen-year-old girl is about eight years older than a fifteen-year-old guy. Emotionally, mentally and in every other way, and it's not really fair to either of them. I think guys spend so many of their younger teen years thinking only about sex. They don't think about anything else. So it's hard to have a mature relationship with them.

Bronwyn,   age 15

> *Youth is wholly experimental.*
> ROBERT LOUIS STEVENSON

Drugs

I must tell you going in that I have no experience of drugs whatsoever. I have many friends and acquaintances who have used or are using them; I am a child of the fifties and the sixties, so I lived through the genesis of the drug culture. I've heard Tim Leary's drug soliloquies and I've read Coleridge. Not very impressive credentials, I'm afraid, when embarking on such an important subject. But as I believe it to be, in truth, a broader question than that of drugs alone, perhaps some of my experience at living could be valuable to you.

Inasmuch as this is the only note I've attempted to write on a subject about which I haven't any firsthand experience, I decided to do some research before putting my thoughts on paper. I was both fascinated and startled by what I found out. According to my various sources, the drug experience of your generation is more than widespread; nearly everyone tries drugs—some continue, some grow beyond them.

242

It seems teen-agers resort to drugs for various reasons: to be accepted by the crowd, to feel grown-up, to get away with what's forbidden, to be able to say things they wouldn't ordinarily say, to feel more intensely. Interestingly the sheer *pleasure* of drugs seems to be far less important than the pleasure of being accepted by the group.

Why and when do they stop? Sometime between teens and twenties the stronger and saner realize the danger of continuing into pills or heavier drugs, and the weaker and more vulnerable become dependent, addicted, sick, crazy or dead. In other words, most teen-agers are self-protective enough to stop before it's too late to stop.

What about the efficacy of drug classes in school and of parental warnings? These seem pretty futile. The scare tactics used by parents and anti-drug filmstrips are disproportionate to the reality most teen-agers see around them. Parents warn them that pot will mess up their minds, but they see their friends smoking it with no seeming ill effects, so they disbelieve the warning.

I don't know whether or not either of you has experimented with drugs. If you haven't, there seems a pretty good chance of your being tempted into it at some point in your life. So I'd like to spend some time telling you of some of the potential dangers of drug use. Perhaps they will make you better understand why parents worry.

Unscrupulous people. Drug dealers are very low on the human ladder. The people who traffic in dope are unscrupulous, criminal, untrustworthy and, by the way, uncatchable if anything goes wrong. By using what they supply, you are taking into your body substances which may or may not be safe, may or may not be what you think they are, may or may not be the dosage you expected.

The old adage of there being no honor among thieves applies nicely to drug dealers. You can't for a minute imagine that the same kinds of people who hook kids on heroin and run the world's seediest prostitution rackets and all organized crime are trustworthy on any level of life . . . including the level which could touch your life. I won't bore you with the stories of the kids we all knew in the sixties who freaked out on the wrong dose of acid or the wrong grade of hash. Suffice it to say, when it comes to drugs, you're playing with a rough and tacky crowd.

Physiology. There is physiological evidence which suggests that your chromosome patterns can be altered by continued use of drugs, even marijuana. I suspect not enough research has yet been done for definitive data to be available. Maybe you should read up on the subject at the library so you will have as much information as exists at your disposal. *The Ups and Downs of Drugs* by Kathleen Elgin and John Osterritter, M.D., is pretty informative and fair-minded. No one would, I think, willingly mess up his or her own body or those of any unborn children if there was a choice in the matter.

We do know that drugs alter your body chemistry. Some speed it up, some slow it down, some set up chain reactions, some like psychedelics can lie dormant for years and then manifest themselves randomly at a future moment. I don't even believe in ingesting Red Dye Number 2 in your hot dogs if you can avoid it, so I'd certainly suggest to you that you find out exactly what any drug you are considering will do to your body or brain. It's only sensible to know what you're dealing with before you deal.

Your brain. Your mind exercises control over your actions, voluntary and involuntary, every instant of your life. There's a great deal to be said for being in control of yourself, of your actions, your thoughts and all your resources—it's simply the safest and surest way to be. When you are under the influence of drugs or alcohol, you are no longer exercising complete control. The reason people say or do things when drunk or stoned that they wouldn't ordinarily is that their inhibitions and normal signaling systems have been momentarily short-circuited.

In other words, your brain has been altered, your responses have been impaired, your nervous system has been tampered with.

Yet society holds you just as responsible for your actions while stoned as for those when you are in complete control, as well it should. In other words, if you run over someone, have an accident, injure yourself or others, you must pay the penalty. Drunks have been causing a lot of damage for centuries; I suspect drug users will simply inherit this dubious mantle.

Illegality. Since you've recently seen *Midnight Express*, the story of a young man imprisoned and tortured in a Turkish jail for trying to take drugs out of that country, I don't suppose there's much point in belaboring this fact, but drugs—selling, buying, using—are still illegal, here and internationally. You can get yourself into one hell of a mess by being careless or indiscriminate.

I've been thinking a good deal about this subject, for some time, because I know it is one that is of prime importance to your generation. I know that people your age are subject to huge amounts of drug pressure from friends and from older kids who are setting the standards for your contemporaries. Most of this pressure will hit you spontaneously—you'll be at a party or in a group, or at school, and you'll be offered drugs and have to say yes or no on the spur of the moment. Because you are human and part of this culture, the odds are you will experiment. Because you are smart and self-interested, I'm pretty sure you'll then make fairly good judgments about what's right for you and what isn't.

I am personally utterly opposed to the use of drugs. I am also very much aware of the fact that you both must wrestle with this question for yourselves: you must choose if you wish to experiment, must decide how much and how long to do so, must bear the consequences of your own actions, must inevitably decide this and all questions for yourselves. I trust you, by the way, to do so with intelligence and self-interest.

Rather than advice on this very volatile subject, I'd like to offer you a few thoughts for consideration:

Any "high" that can be induced chemically can be induced by exercising control over your own mind. Meditation, yoga, many disciplines permit you to experience a similar freedom from the pressures of life, far more safely than do drugs. Should you wish to explore such mind-expanding possibilities, there is a great deal of literature and a few good teachers who can help. All you need is an open mind, a keen curiosity and a willingness to practice the disciplines needed to open these extraordinary vistas to you.

Whenever you gamble with your own being, your own potential, your own body and brain, you owe yourself the protection of common sense and of foresight. It's unwise to gamble with what you can't afford to lose. This applies not only to drugs or drink or sex but also to the process of living.

There is a good deal to be said for having the courage to stand alone. Having the courage to do what's right, against the herd, is an essential element in mature living. Somebody once said the most valiant gesture in the world is having the courage to spit in the eye. It's a lovely thought. All through life, if we maintain the courage to do what's right for us and for those we love, no matter what pressure is brought to bear on us to conform, we are way ahead of the game. Drugs, rest assured, will not be the last potentially dangerous temptation you will face. Whenever such things appear on your horizon, I would encourage you not to fear, but to be wary; not to conform, but intelligently to choose; not to accept blindly, but to judge as best you can.

My very dear daughters, you are no longer children. You are your own people. Whatever admonitions, warnings, guideposts I can offer you about drugs are just that—guideposts. Decision-making must be yours. That is the great joy and the great responsibility of adulthood.

The best allies you will possess for now, and for the rest of your lives, when it comes to sane and happy living are your own good instinct and your own common sense, for these are with you when parents and society are not. You will face many temptations and many crossroads; perhaps that's why nature has designed us so that we carry our self-protection with us wherever we go.

Drugs are a danger. Try to be as smart as you can where they are concerned. Your mind and body are all there is of you, and you are very, very special and very, very loved.

———————

I don't have a lot of firsthand experience about drugs. I did smoke a joint with a friend of mine, for the experience of getting high. I didn't like it too much. I didn't like the thought of being out of control. I think kids who do heavy drugs or even just a lot of marijuana are asking for help. I guess they feel like they can't get it from anything else, so they're trying to look for a way to escape from their troubles in the real world.

Lola, age 15

I had a lot of guilt the day after I first smoked pot. All I could think of was, Uh-oh, I've ruined myself for life. So I never did that again—I suppose because I didn't think it was all that great. I kind of like natural highs. Life the way it is every day is pretty wonderful, so I don't think I need drugs to make myself happy.

Lola, age 15

If parents would only realize that instead of punishing their children for taking drugs, they should try to find out the reasons for it, then maybe a lot of problems would be solved. I guess it's a pretty painful experience to find out that your children have been doing drugs. I guess all I can say is that if parents find out that their kid is on any type of drug at all, for any reason, they should try to communicate about why before

*they start screaming and yelling. You've got to let your kids
know that you care, even if they've screwed up. Let them know
that you're really concerned—not just mad. That you don't
want them to hurt themselves.*

Bronwyn,   age 15

*I personally think drugs are a way to fight against your par-
ents, too. A lot of kids do it to rebel or because they're too scared
to say no to a crowd or friends. I think most kids are "followers" and that is how they get screwed up with drugs.*

Bronwyn,   age 15

*Drugs are very bad because you can get hooked on them, and
they are not good for your system at all. Most people take drugs
because they are sad or because they have problems, so they just
take drugs and think that everything is going to be okay. But
instead they end up with more problems because the drugs
themselves can be really harmful. I think kids are getting
pretty smart about this stuff, because they've seen a lot of
people mess themselves up with drugs that were supposedly
"harmless." We've all seen kids with burnt-out brains by now.*

Lola,   age 15

O, God! that men should put an enemy in their mouths to steal away their brains!

WILLIAM SHAKESPEARE

Alcohol

When I was your ages and a little older, drinking was the "in" thing. Most people drank at parties, many had a cocktail or two before dinner each night; drinking was something everybody looked forward to getting to be old enough to do.

I, like the rest of my friends, felt very grown-up when I had my first drink, and for a while I thought it wildly sophisticated to order a drink on a date, or to drink at a party. There was only one problem. I didn't like it; didn't like the taste, didn't like what it did to my stomach, didn't like the woozy out-of-control feeling it produced. In short, as far as I was concerned, drinking was not for me. Yet I felt very out-of-it, and people seemed to think I was a spoilsport if I didn't participate in drinking. I can remember feeling like a fifth wheel at a lot of social gatherings when I was in my teens and twenties, for in my college days everyone seemed to think it essential to be tipsy for the weekend, in order to have a good time. It took me a long while to grow comfortable with my own nondrinking, but along the line I had an opportunity to *watch* a lot of drinking as a sober observer. It was quite a revelation.

I've seen people I cared about mess themselves up with alcohol. I've seen marriages and families destroyed by it. I've seen people make damned fools of themselves. And finally, I've seen people completely destroy their lives with excessive drinking. I have a feeling most people my age have seen similar tragedies—which is what prompts me to talk to you about the whole subject of alcohol.

I've been reading lately that there is a growing alcohol problem among kids of your generation. I imagine drinking simply provides another means of escape from a less-than-perfect life, and if that is so, most all of what I mentioned in the chapter about drugs might apply here, too. The biggest problem I see with escaping via chemical routes is that when you come back down to earth, whatever problem you had still exists. Alcohol doesn't change anything—it simply obliterates the problem, for the moment, and numbs the responses. You've only delayed the inevitable and maybe messed yourself up in the bargain. If there is something in your life so intolerable as to make you want to escape it, there are surely better means at your disposal than alcohol. Seeking counseling in whatever form it may be available to you—parent, friend, teacher, priest, minister, rabbi, therapist—at least is a constructive step toward finding a solution, which could make escape unnecessary.

The biggest difference between the problem of drugs and drinking is this, it seems to me: drugs are a sporadic part of life, even today. Drinking, on the other hand, is a very constant escape hatch. People drink at lunch, people drink after work, people drink at parties—drinking is an accepted ritual of the American social scene. As such, the person with a drinking problem can masquerade for a very long time as normal, and can rationalize that his or her problems are okay.

I've often had heavy drinkers explain to me laboriously that there's a *big* difference between constant heavy drinking and alcoholism. Drinking, they say, enhances their personalities, makes them feel convivial, helps them loosen up, while alcoholism is something else altogether. I'm not at all sure that's true. I think heavy drinking is always suspicious. You must wonder why the drinker needs chemical aid to be convivial—surely it would be better to avoid dependence upon an outside substance to alter your personality. I've never known anyone whose personality was *really* enhanced by being drunk—I've known lots who "thought" it was. Alcohol, after all, alters the accuracy of your perceptions of yourself, too, so you can't judge correctly *how* you appeal to people.

I can't see a thing in the world wrong with moderate drinking. Wine with dinner, a drink or two in a social situation, or when you are relaxing at home, doesn't seem to be harmful at all. Some alcoholic beverages, like wine, may even have very beneficial qualities. Even though Joe and I drink only an occasional glass of wine or beer, I find it perfectly understandable that other people enjoy drinking considerably more than we do.

However, I do find lots of things wrong with heavy drinking. It is dangerous, it is offensive, it is a potential killer. To drink heavily and consistently can alter your personality, your intellectual performance, your sex life and your brain cells—all for the worse. With every excess drink, the alcoholic puts himself further out of control of his life, further from reality and closer to oblivion. He systematically robs himself of home, family, job, self-esteem and, if he continues long enough, of life itself. While the alcoholic is not doing all of this consciously, of course, the results are just as devastating as if he'd put a gun to his head.

Alcoholics Anonymous has probably had more success in treating alcoholism than either the medical or psychiatric profession. Because AA is entirely composed of recovered alcoholics, they manage to combine a sort of spiritual healing (there is a great warmth and camaraderie among the members, as well as belief in God) with group therapy (everyone is encouraged to tell his story to a supportive and empathetic audience) and clubbiness (the AA meetings often become the hub of the alcoholic's universe, a place to gather with friends, to discuss similar problems, to find enjoyment and companionship). The result is AA's truly remarkable record of help for both alcoholics and their families.

I thought you might be interested in seeing the twenty-five warning signs that indicate a serious drinking problem, according to AA—and I think most people would agree that they should know! A person needn't have all of these signs to consider himself or herself a possible alcoholic. I'm told that just a few of them could be a definite sign of trouble.

1. Do you drink heavily after a fight or quarrel?
2. Are you under a lot of pressure?
3. Do you drink more liquor than you once did?
4. Do you have memory lapses after an evening of drinking?
5. When drinking with friends, do you try to have a few extra drinks that they won't know about?
6. Do you feel uncomfortable without drinks on certain occasions?
7. Do you rush to have your first drink?
8. Do you feel guilty about drinking?
9. Do you become irritated when other people discuss your drinking?
10. Do you increasingly have blackouts (memory lapses)?
11. Do you continue to drink after your friends have stopped?
12. Do you have to have a reason to drink?
13. Do you say things drunk that you wouldn't say sober? Do you regret having said those things?
14. Have you tried to control your drinking?
15. Have you made promises about controlling your drinking and failed to keep them?
16. Do you avoid your friends while drinking?
17. Are financial problems increasing?
18. Do people tend to treat you unfairly?

19. Do you eat little and erratically while drinking?
20. Do you have the shakes in the morning?
21. Do you find you can't drink as much as you were once able to?
22. Do you stay drunk for several days at a time?
23. Are you depressed?
24. Do you hallucinate?
25. Are you frightened after drinking heavily?

Even if a person is *not* an alcoholic, excessive drinking can be dangerous. According to government studies *it doesn't take as much alcohol as you think to impair your faculties.* More than two drinks in an hour will affect your judgment, your perception, your vision and your ability to think straight. The police tell us you shouldn't drive if you've had more than three ounces of alcohol in one hour.

In other words, the problem with alcohol is that once you've had two or more drinks, your judgment is impaired enough so that it will be difficult for you to judge when to *stop* drinking, and your inhibitions will be lessened so that you won't *want* to stop.

It all boils down to the simple common sense of moderation. Drinking moderately can be pleasurable and even beneficial. Drinking heavily can be dangerous and addictive, and can mask many psychological problems that need attention. It can also kill you.

The AA guideposts about alcoholism are probably a pretty good way to evaluate where heavy drinking ends and alcoholism begins, but perhaps common sense is just as good. If a person must drink to feel good, it's suspicious. If a person cannot stop drinking and still function, it's very suspicious. If drinking is a major support system in a person's life, he or she is an alcoholic and needs help badly.

One of the great tragedies of alcoholism is that in our society it is easy to accept the too-heavy drinker as normal. Many women marry a man knowing he drinks too much and thinking they can encourage him to stop after marriage. This is a really unfortunate mistaken judgment, for alcoholism is an illness. Whether mental, emotional, physical or all three has not been fully determined. But everyone, including AA, considers it an *illness*. As such it must be treated by a professional. No matter how well-meaning, friends and family can't fix the problem. They can, however, encourage the alcoholic to seek professional help and they can start by *not* putting up with excessive drinking and pretending it's okay.

I hope with all my heart that you will never have the misfortune to get mixed up with excess alcohol, either in your own life or that of someone you care about. If you do, I hope you'll have the courage to seek guidance and help from those who are equipped to give it.

Alcohol doesn't do anything for you that I can see, except make you sick or dizzy. It doesn't even taste good.

Bronwyn,   age 15

Usually kids don't really drink hard liquor, they just drink beer. Mostly all kids drink beer, but I think drugs are a much bigger problem. I think kids get into drugs and drinking mostly because they are curious, or because they want to escape bad parents or bad house problems.

Cee Cee,   age 14

Kids use drugs or drinking or whatever, as an escape—but when they find out that it doesn't change anything, they either get deeper into drugs or they'll try to stop because they see friends who get really screwed up by it.

Cee Cee,   age 14

Peer Pressure

Since this is a topic *you* have suggested, I must believe you are facing a substantial amount of peer pressure at this moment, probably more than I can even imagine.

Even though I don't know the exact dilemmas you are facing or the parameters of the peer pressure being exerted, I do pretty much know the drill. Every generation, including mine, faced pressure to do things that were scary, questionable, dangerous or simply forbidden. In my day one of the most popular lunacies was hazing at fraternity and sorority initiations. In order to get to be one of the crowd, people were subjected to all manner of indignities, from swallowing live fish to being beaten or buried or worse. Aside from causing a fair amount of terror, this stupidity cost enough kids their lives so that eventually campuses outlawed hazing, and it has now passed to eternal, and well-deserved, oblivion. The point of the story is,

255

however, that a lot of people were injured and humiliated by succumbing to the pressure to "belong."

While belonging has a lot going for it—nobody wants to be left out in the cold—nobody wants to be compromised or put in jeopardy by it either. Whether you are wary of danger or simply unsure of whether something is right for you, all you can really do is evaluate the situation sensibly and try to come up with an answer that's right for you at that moment. Remember, the fact that something appears to be right for the whole world doesn't mean it's necessarily your cup of tea, or that the timing is right for your best interests.

All of which brings me to some possible thoughts to bear in mind when trying to wend your way through the peer pressure system.

1. Do *you* truly want to try whatever it is, or are you doing it to please someone else?
2. Is your instinct telling you yes or no?
3. Will you be putting yourself in danger rather than simply being adventurous?
4. Are you feeling pressured to do something you feel is against your own best interests?
5. If you had a magic wand and could make the opportunity go away, would you?
6. Why is the group pressuring you? For your good or their own amusement?
7. Does the fact that you are feeling pressured suggest that deep down you'd rather not do it?
8. If it's so good, why do you have to be pushed into doing it?
9. Is the standard of behavior of the ones who are pressuring you as comfortable for you as yours is?

Honest answers to these questions might help clarify where *your* own head is at—and that is really all that counts here. Remember, you needn't demand of yourself that you be perfect, or that you always make the right choice; just that you do the best you can. If you ask the right questions, your own instincts will probably give you the right answer. Truth is, in matters of conscience, safety or just personal conviction, the will of the majority has no place whatsoever.

———————————

Peer pressure isn't nearly as bad as parents seem to think it is. Anyway, I've never experienced peer pressure. Maybe it's because I've got a brain and don't just follow the crowd, automatically.

                                        Bronwyn,   age 15

I think you have to be a "follower" to get taken in by peer pressure. But peer pressure's not as important as parents seem to think it is. They blame everything that kids do on peer pressure, and most kids just want to do their own thing . . . whether anybody else is watching or not.

                                        Lola,   age 15

I don't do what people tell me to do if I don't want to do it; I just say, "If I don't want to, I just won't!" And if friends don't like it, it's just too bad.

                                        Cee Cee,   age 14

9

WORKING

Most of the women of your generation will probably work outside the home. I don't think you can have any idea how remarkable that seems to me, since when I was your age almost every woman grew up to marry and have children . . . period. Working was done before that inevitability happened, or if one's husband had financial difficulties, or if one was divorced or widowed. In the first instance, the jobs available were primarily secretarial and clerical; and in the latter two instances, there was something slightly suspicious and shoddy about the fact that a job was *needed!*

So things have changed. After twenty years of working, I've lived to see young women coming out of graduate school with MBA's held high, so confident of their place in the business community that they don't even anticipate a problem. And yet I remember lunching, not so many years ago, with a smart and determined girl who had just instituted the legal proceedings against the Harvard Business School which helped make her the first woman "allowed" into that hallowed male sanctuary.

I have lots of notions on the subject of being a working woman, as you might guess. I think that while you will have a somewhat less prejudicial environment in which to prosper professionally, you will also have a world of intense competition, heightened aggression, lowered moralities and a more confusing male/female interchange than we did. I think you'll also expect of yourself that you do it all well—be a great titan of industry, mother, wife, etc., etc., like the wonder women we read about in magazines—and that is a disquieting demand to make upon yourself.

At any rate, I've put some thoughts on paper for you to cogitate. They are as much philosophic as they are practical, for I believe that you will spend a goodly portion of the rest of your lives working at something, and I would, with all my heart, like to encourage you to make it something you both like and value.

Have thy tools ready.
God will find thee work.
CHARLES KINGSLEY

Choosing Your
Life's Work

My working life has been, like most people's, the result of circumstance. I grew up, got a job (in advertising, because I could write and draw) and proceeded to take advantage of opportunities as they came my way. After I was divorced, when you both were very tiny and we needed money badly, I worked at anything people would offer, just to survive. I wrote, I drew, I even painted portraits. I learned advertising, sales promotion, publicity and marketing because they were means of support. The more I knew, the more I could earn. And to be fair, I also had talent. It turned out that I was very good at these pursuits, so I worked very hard and prospered, but at no point did I *choose* my career; rather it seemed to choose me.

Few people know what they want to be when they grow up, no matter what they tell you later, when time and success have clouded their memories. Most people simply must earn a living. They do so by whatever means are available to them, dependent on their inclinations, talents and exposure. This is an acceptable system as far as it goes, but I believe that people sometimes get locked into the wrong slot and then stay stuck because of economic necessity, inertia or fear of the unknown. I'd like to raise a few random observations about it all.

Exploration. I would like to encourage you, while you are still in school, to allow your imagination free rein. Explore the areas you *think* might provide you with a career, no matter how extraordinary they may seem; the more you expose yourself to open minds, interesting people and varied opportunities, the more possibilities will occur. Give yourself a chance to try your hand at the pursuits that intrigue you. You may *think* you want to be an actress, a model, a veterinarian, a silversmith, a designer, a musician, a nuclear physicist, a genealogist or an expert on duck decoys! But until you've given it a whirl, you can't know for sure if you have a strong bent toward any such pursuit. Talk to people who are already following that road; ask questions, touch their environment, see if it feels good to you.

You may not yet know what you want to be when you grow up, but if you stay in close touch with yourself, you probably will know quite definitely what you *don't* want to be. You already know a lot about your own strengths, weaknesses and peculiar gifts. The decision-making process should be easier if you follow your own instincts about what's *good* for you, rather than society's dictates about what's acceptable for someone in your station in life. You will spend a lot of years working. You'll do yourself a giant favor by finding a means of earning a living which gives you pleasure as well as financial reward.

Summer jobs. One means of checking out the great world of working is via summer employment. Sometimes, if you're lucky, you can get a job in a field that has potential future interest for you. If that happens, you may get an opportunity to see the field in action, talk to people already working in it, and to get a feel for whether or not a particular profession is right for you.

Most often, summer jobs are fairly menial: waiting on tables in resorts, mailrooming in a huge corporation, delivering something for somebody in a retail store. Not very inspiring, I'm afraid, and sometimes downright discouraging.

I remember, Bron, the first time you had a job in our office. You were trying to fill in for our receptionist and were so frazzled by nightfall on the first day I think you fell asleep at eight o'clock. Obviously, as you learned later, it wasn't a fair test of what working was all about. After all, you didn't know where to find anything and you had a dozen people demanding things simultaneously; so you were very discouraged.

The point of the story is that while summer jobs are not necessarily a perfect barometer of what is to come, there are some terrific benefits to be derived from them. They can teach you what disciplined work is all about; they can give you a taste of the heavenly independence that comes with earning money; they can show you a bit about what the world of commerce looks like on the inside; they can help you meet people and they can give you a feeling of being in an adult world. All very worthwhile things to tuck under your belt.

Courage to change. Now let's suppose you've decided to become a doctor, and then, after a few years of practice, you discover that you are ill suited for being constantly around sickness and suffering. In other words, you've invested time and money in becoming something you don't want to be. What do you do then? First and foremost, you must believe in yourself despite the setback; then you can examine your options. Could you bear the thought of remaining for forty years in a profession you dislike? I would hope not. Do you have something else in mind? How much training will you need in a new field of endeavor and what's the best means of getting it? And so on and on. In other words, positive action in the face of such a dilemma is the most productive way out of dead center.

In such an instance I'd opt for following instinct, regardless of time, money, public opinion or incumbent difficulties. Some of the world's greatest contributors changed their professions in midstream, or simply didn't figure out what their profession was meant to be until midlife. There is a wonderful philosophic statement, sometimes called "The Serenity Prayer," that's really quite appropriate for a crisis of the sort I've just described:

> God grant me the serenity to accept
>   the things I cannot change;
> The courage to change the things I can;
> And the wisdom to know the difference.

It generally takes courage to correct a mistake in any area of life. Your profession is an important enough category for the exercise of courage to be worth it.

Dreams vs. fantasies. For many years, when you were very young and I was struggling desperately to support us all, I had a dream. I was realistic enough to know that for a good many years to come (most likely until you were grown) it would be necessary for me to work very hard at what I knew best in order to feed, clothe and house us, and to assure your future. Please understand that I didn't begrudge this effort at all. Frankly, I was grateful that I had a profession that could afford us all some security; many other women in a similar position did not. However, in my heart of hearts I knew that the work I did was not fulfilling. It was a means to an end, a security system, no more than that. So I had a dream. I promised myself that when I was forty and you were grown, secure and launched in the world, I would chuck business and embark upon a new career—one that would allow me fewer obligations, more pleasure and freer creativity. As you know, I have written and painted since childhood, but through all these years I have done both for commercial purposes, and therefore to other people's specifications. So before my muse becomes too old to express herself, it has been my hope to give her freer rein.

The reason I can tell you of my dream is this: there are times in our lives when we find ourselves in circumstances—professional or otherwise—which are not what we would choose. In such difficult times it helps to have a dream. There were many dark days when my dream kept me going. Many moments when I might have felt self-sacrificial or trapped if I hadn't known, in my heart of hearts, that this was simply a phase of my life I was passing through, not the whole of it.

What You Should Seek in a Career

Work you like to do. The happiest professionals I know are those who genuinely like what they do for a living; who daily wake up knowing they will spend the next ten hours at a task they find either joyous or fulfilling on some level of their being.

Achieve according to your need. The goals of achievement should be set according to *your need*, not society's criteria. Do you remember a conversation we had about money, years ago when you were both tiny? Cee Cee, you said you would need a lot of it in life to buy a limousine. Bronwyn, you said you wouldn't need much at all, just oats for your horse! The simple accuracy of the statement tickled me, and in a way I think it still holds true. You each have vastly different needs. Clearly you must choose your life paths with those needs in mind.

Strike a balance. Few of us manage to have balanced lives: lives in which business and ambition play a part—but only a part; in which love, marriage, children and personal happiness are given equal time. It is tough, by the way, for a woman to find this balance. It will be several generations before we have acceptance enough, and systems enough, to allow us time for such an enviable harmony. I fear that because yours is the first generation of women freed for action, that very action itself may overwhelm other subtler and more potentially fulfilling areas of your life if you aren't careful. I would hope that in the face of such obstacles you will at least seek a balance in your life—a balance between professional pursuits and your loving and living as a woman.

A final thought. I'd like you to know that it matters not one whit to me which profession you choose. It matters greatly to me that you find happiness and fulfillment. Should you find both as a wealthy brain surgeon, a struggling actress, an obscure poet, a carpenter or something I've never even dreamed of, I would wish you well, and feel great pride in your having had the courage to make your own way.

I like the idea of working, because it means independence and that's important when you get grown up. I don't know if I'll like work, never having tried it, so I'll just have to try it and see, and hope for the best. But working isn't easy, because when I had to do a job for you, at your office, it was a lot of responsibility.

Cee Cee, age 14

I think most kids know what they want to do when they grow up, or at least have a good idea about it when they get to be high-school age. In ninth or tenth grade you start thinking about your future because that's when the teachers start telling you to think about what you're going to do with your life, so you start thinking about what you can do or want to do. It's not really a pressure, it's something you look forward to because it means independence.

Cee Cee, age 14

I want to work, but I don't ever want to own my own business, because I couldn't handle it, I'd die from the pressure. I'd rather have someone telling me what to do. But I definitely want a career.

Cee Cee, age 14

Whatever my career is, I'd like to be at the top of it.

Cee Cee, age 14

I'm having trouble managing the mansion.
What I need is a wife.

ELLA T. GRASSO,
Former Governor of Connnecticut

On Being
a Woman in Business

When I got started in business, women by and large were secretaries. They were trained to type and take orders and eventually get married and leave the work force behind—in other words, they weren't taken very seriously. Oh, there were a few who'd made it beyond those boundaries: some of them amusingly like the stereotypes—big hats at the office, tough and assertive—others merely smart and hardworking. But they were a tiny elite corps—too tiny to be of any great importance, and odd enough to be the butt of much humor on the part of their male colleagues.

Not so anymore. In my twenty years in business, I've seen everything change: the work force, the ambitions, the tactics and the women. I've seen a certain amount of respect begin to filter through the male business community. It's only a beginning, of course, and although we've come a long way, baby,

267

we've got a lot further to go before we ever get to "even," but nonetheless it's been a giant step for humankind.

Inasmuch as you will one day be women in the working world, I'd like to tell you how I believe being a woman could hold you back. Yes, it's true. Despite all the changes that have taken place, business still qualifies as a man's world.

There are quite a few obstacles you'll have to overcome as a woman that wouldn't affect you if you were a man. Some come from outside pressures, some from inside you. A few of them may surprise you.

Women have not been bred to be chairman of the board. Traditionally, women have been bred to be auxiliaries, to be content with being helpers, not movers and shakers. Because of this programming, women make different demands on themselves in business than men do. They expect less of their destinies, and often settle for less than their male counterparts would, given the same potentials. I firmly believe that women must start *believing* in their own unlimited potential, in order to be able to reach it. You can't very well get up the corporate ladder if you don't really believe you belong at the top.

Women are also bred to be painstakingly conscientious—a characteristic that often keeps us in the ranks of the workers rather than the managers. By that I mean that our tendency is to dig in and do every job *ourselves*. We must learn to manage, to delegate responsibility, to see the forest rather than just the trees that need pruning. It is something of a joke among men that if you hire a woman she'll work herself to death for you and never demand an assistant. That kind of foolishness is something we, not they, must bring to an end.

We have been trained for generations to be wives, not corporate presidents, so I expect we are heir to more guilts about family obligations than are men; few men would feel guilt or remorse at having to leave the children home to go out to work.

There is not yet a network of female executives for women to turn to as mentors, although I believe that is rapidly changing.

Whoever started the myth that women don't help each other along is going to be in for a big surprise in the next few years.

Women have not been taught the jargon of business or the tricks of the trade. We've been kept away from money management (which is particularly odd, because we've always tended to be good money managers at home) and from the power that such money management carries with it. This is a small issue, but an important one. It is important that we learn about money: mutual funds, money management, banks, insurance, stocks, bonds, real estate, home ownership. We may not need all that information, but if we women understand money better, we will not only make better use of it, but we will also find creative ways to make more of it!

We sometimes learn to mistrust ourselves once a month, because men do. I once heard a brilliant writer who worked for me say she was concerned because three days out of every month she wasn't at her best. I asked her if she knew any men who were perfect 100 percent of the time. The best method I ever discovered to deal with the myth of period-induced irrationality was quite frontal and funny. When a man in my office told me he could always tell when I had my period, I challenged him to tell me the next time he noticed my menstrual-nuttsiness. It's been several years now and he's never once guessed right!

We are often torn between love and business, while men take both in stride and don't feel they are mutually exclusive. We are taught we must be subservient to be loved. Men learn just the opposite.

We have not yet developed role models for our business behavior, and business training programs seldom take women's special strengths into account but are rather designed to suit men's needs.

Many women aren't really sure it's okay to have ambition. I imagine most ask themselves at some point in their business life if any man *really* wants to be married to the chairman of the board . . . or if their newfound success will alter their desirability. I think we wonder, too, if it will be lonely up there at the top, and what we'll have to give up to get there. I even think we sometimes wonder if there is something wrong with us that we want to be king instead of queen.

Or conversely, we may wonder if there's something wrong with us if we lack the ambition to be an overachiever—what if we just want to work at something fulfilling and do a good job at that? Will we then perhaps feel guilty that we are leaving home and hearth, not for an all-consuming ambition, but for a whim?

Most of what I've discussed has to do with the built-in problems women encounter by virtue of the fact that they *are* women. But what about external pressure? What are some of the prejudicial judgments they are up against in the male-dominated business world? I've compiled a list to help you recognize some of them. Needless to say, these are just possibilities; I hardly think you'll be bombarded by all of them! By the way, they're all quite handleable . . . perhaps more so if you know what to expect:

1. Men won't let you into the "Club"—by that I mean that you, like all minorities, will be an outsider, at least initially.

2. Men will want to take you to bed and you'll have to learn how to by-step this gently, when it makes sense to do so. Many will try to control you, using sex as a weapon.

3. Male superiors will probably judge you by a different standard from the one they use for themselves or for male employees. They may try to pay you less, although fortunately time and law are changing such inequity these days.

4. You may be annoyed to find that some men will evaluate you by how you look rather than by how you think, but remember, men, too, are judged by their appearance.

5. It is possible that men will be tempted not to take you seriously. That can be changed by your own attitude and talent.

6. Some men will feel threatened—particularly if you are working over them. It's up to you to help alleviate such unproductive inferences by being a fair and professional boss.

Now for the good news. We've got a lot going for us that *they haven't*. We are women with a matriarchal society behind us; in this country women have much to say about how life is conducted. We've been programmed to be enduring and to work hard, both powerfully useful tools. We tend to be adaptable as a species, and we have a multidimensional attitude toward life. We trust our own intuitions more than men do; we operate quite comfortably on an intuitive level of consciousness. Women haven't yet been pigeonholed into a specific business pattern, so we don't necessarily have to do things *their* way. We have a woman's perceptions in a world in which almost everything is sold to women. All our psychological eggs aren't in one basket. Our self-esteem is probably not entirely contingent upon success in business; don't underestimate the importance of this fact in protecting our egos, and therefore our performance and stability.

I had a big leg up in business. Now that I look back, my parents made me feel early on that I could grow up to be anything. With my mother an early feminist, and my father compassionate enough to believe in equality and justice, even though I was part of a generation bred to grow up, get married and have children (and that was certainly my intention until circumstances intervened) I still had great confidence in myself. It really didn't occur to me that being a woman would be a handicap on any level. Without a doubt, that positive programming has stood me in good stead every day of my business life. If you believe in yourself—believe that you deserve to be successful—it will be a lot easier for you to succeed.

To sum up, as you head into your working future I would encourage you to consider the following things:

What have you got to offer? Be honest. After all, you are unique. What has everybody else got going and how do you measure up comparatively? You'll probably find certain areas in which you are average and certain areas in which you are super. Playing up the super ones can help enormously in reaching your goals fast, and—more importantly—can help you pursue a career that will make you happy!

Think about what you *could* achieve, if you chose to equip yourself better. Maybe you are artistic, but untrained; or an animal lover, who might do well as a veterinarian, with the proper education. A little training could give you another whole set of potentials. College and graduate school couldn't hurt, and might give you the advantage over other qualified job candidates. Or consider spending a year in a specialized training school. Or a year working part-time in your field. The keyword here is preparation. It may make all the difference.

Check your own commitment incentive. Try to decide what is most important to you—home and family or career—and then strike a balance. Learn to *integrate your job with your life,* so that you stay in equilibrium.

Talk to someone objective about your career goals; seek advice from women with similar goals who have experience to offer.

Above all, learn to know and love yourself, so you will see clearly what's best for you and will enjoy the doing of it to its fullest measure.

10

JUST MY OPINION

I'm sure you'll get a big kick out of my admitting it right out front: the following sections are just one woman's opinion—mine.

The subjects couldn't be more random, but they are each in their own way important indications of who I've grown up to be, so I hope you'll forgive this bit of self-indulgence.

Patriotism

I've been giving a lot of thought to what I could say to you about patriotism and love of country. I grew up steeped in such things and they come naturally to me. I've always loved the United States—its ideals, its idiosyncrasies, its guts and its people. I have great faith in the mix of races and creeds and intellects that came here. Peasants and aristocrats, farmers and statesmen—in immigrant waves or dribs and drabs, they all came here to do better, to make their children safe, to forge a brave new world. Irish, Scots, Germans, Italians, Poles, Africans, you name it—all brought their strengths and weaknesses to mingle into a hardy new race . . . like fresh shoots grafted onto old stock, to help the future bloom and flourish. In many ways the United States is a paean to belief in the future against monstrous odds.

But I have to admit that despite this emotional commitment I feel for my country, for me, and for a lot of other Americans,

274

Vietnam was an end to innocence. For the first time we came
face to face with a war so cruel and stupid that there was no
explanation or redemption for it: a war not fought to win, or to
save the world for democracy, or to protect our shores, as we
have always believed our wars to be. Vietnam was a very big
shock to our vision of who we are as a nation.

With the loss of innocence, with the ugliness we were wit-
ness to, came a terrible demoralization for all of us, I think. We
Americans had finally seen corruption up close; we had not, for
once, been on the side of the angels. With that realization came
a terrible, terrible anger. For we felt we had been tricked by the
government we'd loved and trusted. Let me tell you what I
think that precipitated in our national consciousness.

If our government could thus betray us, use our boys as cannon fodder, napalm villages and continue an absurd travesty
for political expedience, many felt they would pay that government back by rescinding their trust, reneging on their part of
the patriotic equation. Like a child who finally decides to pay
back an abusive parent by rescinding love, I believe, many
withdrew their psychic support of America. As Senator Daniel
P. Moynihan said of the Kennedy assassinations, "We might
learn to laugh again, but we'd never be young again."

So much for what I think has happened up to now. What
worries me is the future. I, too, have reluctantly given up my
unmitigated patriotism. I, too, am questioning everything. But
what worries me most is that I see us possibly throwing away
the baby with the bathwater. In our embarrassment at having
been duped, I fear we have taken on political cynicism that
may be unfair and unconstructive.

It's okay to say that our country messed up, that there is
corruption in all levels of government, that there are a lot of
bad guys in high places. But what then? If we lose sight of the
ideals of America—the sense of purpose, of gutsiness, of helping the underdog, of fighting for the right, believing in our own
moral leadership, and believing in our ability to leap tall build-

ings in a single bound—who will fight the good fight? After all, if you don't believe, Tinkerbell dies. If we don't love America and what she stands for (even if she doesn't always measure up) I think we're done for.

Maybe it will help if we try to separate the issues and deal with them one at a time. There are three separate entities to be considered, I believe:

1. *Our American ideals:* the Declaration, the Constitution, all the good and the brave and the brilliant that have gone into making us the movers and shakers, and very often the saviors of the world.

2. *The reality of government* as it currently exists—the good mixed with the corrupt, the selfless with the self-serving, in a government we voted into office and can vote *out* of office if we put our minds to it.

3. *The American people:* the real idealists. The rich and the poor, the educated and the ignorant, the brains and bone and sinew of what America really is.

The ideals, I believe, are still intact. Whatever divine spark motivated the Founding Fathers when they created our set of standards and goals, they did a remarkably inspired job. Two hundred years have only proven the validity of their precepts— they are as worthy of being followed in your generation as they were in my grandfather's grandfather's.

Without question the second point, *the government,* needs a lot of work. It needs more seekers after the truth, and fewer seekers after fortune and power. It needs more statesmen, and fewer politicans. It needs more morality, and a hell of a lot less expediency and intrigue. We all know that. Yet we must be careful of how cynically we view our government, too. For if we believe it to be utterly corrupt, we may begin to believe that only corrupt people should be elected, as they are the only ones suited to cope with the system. If we believe that all is lost, we won't fight so hard at salvage. If we think the cause is hopeless, what's to prevent our walking away from it, instead of standing to fight and to fix it?

And *we can fix it,* my children. People have performed greater miracles in times past, with less than we have to work with. We need smarts, and determination and commitment and sacrifice and a firm belief in the future, to do it. We need to write our Congressmen and our President and let them know where we're at; we need to learn everything we can about our elected officials; we need to vote as if our lives depended on it. And finally, we need to be strong enough to defend our position in the face of passivity, cynicism, corruption and ridicule.

The third element—*we the people*—has to be the answer. I believe with all my heart that the vast majority of Americans are smart, tough, interested, hardworking citizens who believe in truth, justice and all the old ideals. We've been kicked in the teeth a lot lately, but we're still feisty enough to throw Nixon out on his ear, to turn out in record numbers for a critical Presidential election, to seek to root out the shoddy and the sinister whenever we find it.

We still have the best, most prosperous, most comfortable and most vital country in the world to call ours. We can't let America or ourselves down, by being knocked out by the hard punches. We have to fight back, because we've got everything at stake—and because in the final analysis we are still the land of the free and the home of the brave, and to maintain that stance in a crummy world is a job for the strong and the vigilant and the courageous.

My father used to say that the Lord judges the sins of the warmhearted and the cold-blooded with a different measure. I believe we still, as a nation, fall into the category of the warmhearted—the cosmic do-gooders, the ones who take in the tempest-tossed and try to give them an even break. So I'm hopeful that perhaps, in the final judging, some of our sins may be mitigated by some of our generosity and compassion.

In God we trust, after all is said and done, but since He is notorious for helping those who help themselves, we are going to have to get our act in order. It falls to the lot of your generation to do just that if we are to make it into the next century intact. I have great faith in you and your contemporaries. We are passing on to you a time of crisis and that's awful—but then for other generations there was Bunker Hill or Anzio or Heartbreak Ridge or Surabachi. It's never been easy to be the torchbearer.

We are also passing on to you, I believe, the best equipment there has ever been to deal with what you face. Never has there been a generation of Americans less likely to take any wooden nickels. You're the best educated, best prepared, least innocent of us all. You are bigger, smarter, less programmed and more aggressive, and it seems to me that through all the world's history, nature has tended to provide great leaders and great statesmen in time of crisis. I think your generation will produce such leaders.

I don't envy you the responsibilities you face, any more than I envied us our air-raid drills, or Korea or Vietnam. I wish you well with all my heart and I have faith in your good judgment and your righteous indignation, both of which can be helpful in sorting things out reasonably and soundly. What I wish for you is a whole new kind of patriotism.

A patriotism that doesn't say "My country, right or wrong," but rather "*My* country. I'll do everything in my power to help it to be right more often than wrong." If you decide to throw your heart and energy into making your country the best, you have it within your power to help do so through common sense, practical idealism, strength, intellect and hard work.

In my own lifetime I've seen American *people* change the face of this nation. I've seen kids march through the streets to end a war; I've seen thousands march to bring civil rights to minorities. I've seen blacks make their way to the front of the bus, and along with women to the front lines of business. I've seen the power of the people. Power to change, power to overcome.

The hallmark of a democracy is, after all is said and done, the *nonhelplessness* of its citizens, the power of the people.

Never forget that. In such a form of government, you can dissent, you can be heard, you can vote. *You can make a difference.*

How to Address Your Letters

The Honorable Ronald Reagan
President of the United States
The White House
1600 Pennsylvania Avenue NW
Washington, D.C. 20500
(*Dear Mr. President:*)

The Honorable George Bush
Office of the Vice President of the United States
Executive Office Building
Washington, D.C. 20501
(*Dear Mr. Vice President:*)

The Honorable Strom Thurmond
President Pro Tempore of the Senate
127 Russell Senate Office Building
Washington, D.C. 20510
(*Dear Senator Thurmond:*)

The Honorable Thomas P. O'Neill, Jr.
Speaker of the House of Representatives
2231 Rayburn House Office Building
Washington, D.C. 20515
(*Dear Mr. Speaker:*)

The Honorable [*Senator's name*]
The Capitol
Washington, D.C. 20510
(*Dear Senator ——————:*)

The Honorable [*Congressman's name*]
The Capitol
Washington, D.C. 20515
(*Dear Congressman* ——— ———:)

———————————

I've traveled all over the world. I've seen places where blacks live on one side of the town and the whites live on the other side of the town. When you see crazy things like that you sort of begin to understand that the U.S. is a pretty cool place to live. It really offers an awful lot. But it's not perfect.

Lola,   age 15

The problem is, I don't feel that one person *has power to change the world or the country for the better. No one person can do anything. No matter how hard they try.*

Lola,   age 15

Most people these days don't do courageous things like the kids did in the sixties. Most people don't want to make waves. A lot of the demonstrations and the peace sit-ins and that wonderful stuff that happened in the sixties is admired by the kids now, but very few people are willing to put themselves on the line to fight for anything.

Bronwyn,   age 15

A lot of people think that the eighties is going to be another explosive generation like the sixties, because people will again say, "Hey, I want to change that. That's not good enough. I want to make it different." But what I'm wondering is—because of Vietnam and because of Watergate and because of the corruption that we see—I think most kids are giving up on it, and saying, "It's a bummer, and therefore I'm not even going to try, because one candle can't change the darkness."

Bronwyn,   age 15

A lot of people have given up on the U.S. I mean, so many awful things have happened. You can't trust people anymore—the crime rate is millions of miles high, and nobody feels that they can trust the government, and nobody feels like individuals really count. I mean, if you want to get something done, if you want to talk to someone, there's red tape to get through just to talk to a president of a minor company, never mind the government.

> Lola,   age 15

But who's gonna change the world if we don't? That's a good question. I wish I had a good answer.

> Bronwyn,   age 15

The only people who ever change things are revolutionaries and activists, people who get up on soapboxes and risk themselves. Sometimes they're radicals, sometimes perfectly ordinary people that you wouldn't believe had the courage of their convictions. Some people really put their money where their mouth is. I mean, you can lick envelopes for a cause, if you really believe in it and that's all you know how to do.

> Lola,   age 15

I've always had these wonderful dreams about doing something to change the world, but I don't know how to do it.

> Bronwyn,   age 15

Everybody says, "If you want to change things, you can write to your Congressman." But I'm pretty sure all you'll get back is a letter from his secretary—with a signed picture of the White House.

> Lola,   age 15

They don't talk about politics much in school. I asked my teacher if I could talk about Iran and she said no. They don't

*discuss politics in school seriously enough so that kids can
make up their minds about world problems. It's just crazy.
Because politics is a really important subject.*

Cee Cee,   age 14

*With politics and with the state of the country, mostly kids
worry about the possibility of war. We don't feel as if we can
do something about changing the government, to keep us from
having a war. We don't think just being able to vote is going to
change things much at all, because with everything you see on
TV—Congressmen and Senators taking payoffs and stuff—it
doesn't seem there's much integrity in politics. You don't really
know anything about how to protect yourself and your country, even if you want to.*

Bronwyn,   age 15

*As long as you're willing to put your money where your mouth
is, I think that's okay. As long as you're willing to talk up what
you believe in, you can still help without being a revolutionary.
That in its own way is being an activist, you know. Trouble is,
most of the time I'm not even sure what I believe in.*

Lola,   age 15

*If everybody figured that nobody could change anything, the
corrupt would inherit the world. Right? Because people who
are corrupt are always busy changing things, they're always in
there doing their thing, and making things turn out their way.
If nobody works in the other direction, how do you keep everything from going under? You don't. We think it's really a responsibility we have to figure out what to do to help.*

Bronwyn and Lola,   age 15

The Draft

During the recent *Sturm und Drang* over the reopening of draft registration, there was a picture on the front page of a number of American newspapers that disturbed me deeply. It showed a young man, leading a group of picketers, carrying a sign that read "Nothing is worth dying for." I'd like to tell you why I believe he was wrong.

Your generation is pretty far removed from the threat of loss of freedom. You have been insulated by two generations of safety, since World War II. Yes, in answer to your unspoken question, I remember Korea and Vietnam very well indeed, but I don't believe that people in the United States really felt threatened by loss of freedom during those conflicts, as other generations had during the previous war. Perhaps that was because my parents' generation (and my own, by osmosis) was closer to the immigrant experience—to the reality of people fleeing oppression and pogrom. Because of that close connection to the horrors of tyranny, I believe earlier generations had a more visceral fear of losing freedom, and therefore, perhaps, a more visceral sense of the need to go out and defend it.

I am very much in sympathy with the disillusionment your generation seems to feel toward everything having to do with the military; Viet Nam and the threat of nuclear war are both strong deterrents to enthusiasm for the whole military establishment. Yet I feel there is a valid case for both the draft and the kind of passionate, sensible patriotism that says, "There are, indeed, things worth dying for." I'd like to explore with you just what these very valuable things might be.

First of all, when one fights or dies for his country, he is not doing so to defend an arbitrary landmass, but rather an ideal of freedom, a way of life he believes in, and the lives and property of the people he loves. I think that's a very important thought to come to terms with. When anyone fights in a war against an enemy that threatens any or all of these things, he or she (and I believe if there is ever another war, both men and women will be called upon to help, ERA or not) is sacrificing to protect some pretty important and practical stuff.

No one in his right mind is in favor of war—but there is a strong case to be made for the maintenance of enough military preparedness to deter any world power from starting one. It is naïve, I think, to believe that we can disarm and remain safe in a world in which victory still goes to the strong. Human nature seems to be both volatile and warlike, and where money and power are concerned the stakes are high. As long as other countries continue to make and stockpile weapons, I can't see how we can do less than they and still expect to survive, if push comes to shove.

I believe in the draft, because I believe the strength of our army has always lain in its being peopled by *ordinary citizens*, not mercenary soldiers. The very mix of people, from rich to poor, educated and uneducated, of all ethnic and social backgrounds, has provided to our army the same melting-pot strength and robust sensibleness that have built our country. I am wary of mercenary armies, for they are traditionally populated by military elitists at the top and sadists at the bottom. Neither classification seems to me compatible with our needs as a country for a sound, sane defense force. Civilian armies tend to want to win as quickly as possible in order to get back to the business of living; mercenary armies have no such incentive, and that, in itself, makes me nervous.

Much as I hate to imagine it, I think you may very well, in your lifetime, have another world war. If so, it will surely be the most threatening war this planet has ever experienced, for the capability now exists for us to destroy ourselves. Beyond that, our own nation is in a somewhat weakened and confused condition both in ideology and leadership. Your generation may well need to defend the lifestyle and the freedoms you now take for granted; you may well need to protect the people you love by rising to the occasion. If that happens, I suggest to you, my dear daughters, there will indeed be things worth fighting and dying for. Not for the sake of sacrifice or idealism, but for the very practical reason that somebody will have to do it if life is to go on.

Let's bring it home to a very practical analogy. If someone attacked our home today and threatened us, threatened you— would you expect Dad and me to fight to protect you, even if it meant putting ourselves in mortal danger? You bet your boots, you would—and well you should! It is our duty and our responsibility to protect you at all costs to ourselves—and what's more, because we love you, we would *want* to protect you.

That's what it's all about, don't you see? All this rhetoric about the "right and wrong" of the draft, and about "what's worth dying for," in the final analysis isn't worth a hill of beans. When the chips are down, it is our *duty* and *desire* to protect those we love, and to protect the ideals and the freedoms, which in turn protect us all. So we do it. Not because anyone welcomes the task, but because we are responsible adults, and as such there are certain values and possessions very much worth fighting for. All wars are not Vietnam, all wars are not hopeless or expedient. If there is a next one, I believe it will threaten us all. If that is the case, I cannot see how any self-respecting man or woman will be able to turn away from the responsibility of helping protect us all.

As to the question of drafting women, I think it is something of a tempest in a teapot. During World War II women weren't drafted, but countless thousands of them took jobs in war-related industries to try to help out. I don't believe that even if drafted, women will be sent into combat unless they volunteer. There are plenty of noncombat ways for a woman to work in a war effort, and frankly, with a few exceptions, I think we are ill suited as a sex for combat. I think there are only a few Zenobias and Boadiceas among us, and the women who are militarily inclined will most likely seek to participate actively in combat without any help from a draft. The rest of us, I expect, would just do whatever we could to help.

What I am suggesting to you, my dear daughters, on this rather sobering subject is this: if we do not take the defense of our freedoms seriously, there is every reason to fear that we will lose them. I believe absolutely in the theory that those who do not learn the lessons of history are doomed to repeat them, and one historical lesson stands out loud and clear: when great nations become lax in their patriotism, flabby in their morality, and slipshod in their defenses, they cease to be great nations. We must not let that happen here.

Just after the signing of the Declaration of Independence, Dr. Franklin said to John Adams:

What a dream; two hundred years, and I wonder, I wonder how I shall find them then: those Americans to whom the name American will not be new. Will they love liberty being given it outright in the crib for nothing? And will they know that if you are not free, you are, sir, lost without hope? And will those who reap this harvest of ideas be willing to strive to preserve them as we so willingly strove to plant them?

I believe with all my heart that we must protect what has been given us, and pass on to our children a nation no less strong and no less safe and no less free than the one that was passed to us. That goal, it seems to me, is both a sacred trust and a sensible idea—and as such very much worth fighting for.

If New York City or California or some place in the U.S. gets attacked—if my country were under siege—I'd feel a responsibility to try to do something about that. Maybe not to kill people, but I'd try to figure out what I could do.

Bronwyn,   age 15

I think wars don't solve anything.

Gigi,   age 15

The trouble is, what do you do when somebody attacks you? Do you fight back? The problem is there are some crazies who are in power in places in the world, so war could *happen. Also, if you put a whole bunch of people in a room, there's going to be an argument somewhere along the line in that room! If you multiply that aggressiveness times all the countries of the world and you consider the crazy people who are in power who could push the button—you could have another war.*

Lola,   age 15

I think wars should be fought by the people who are responsible for them—the leaders. If we're going to have a war, let's get the President to go fight.

Bronwyn,   age 15

There's all this talk of glory in fighting for your country, and protecting the American way—and some of that even makes sense. But you've got to remember that when you're out there on the battlefield, it's just you against the world, and I don't like the sound of that.

                                             Lola,   age 15

Patriotism all depends, I think, on whether or not you are threatened. Now we've never had a war on our soil, but that doesn't mean we couldn't. And I think you'd feel very different about fighting if the troops were marching through New York City. And that's what happened in every country in Europe. I mean, there were actually people out there trying to destroy your family and your way of life—so what do you do, you fight back, right? Philosophically, nobody wants to. I'm sure nobody ever wanted to fight, in a way. But it becomes a question of fighting in order to protect yourself, and to protect the people you love, and then there isn't any choice anymore.

                                             Lola,   age 15

All right, I guess if somebody was going to drop a bomb on New York, I'd shoot him, because it would affect me and my family directly. But if they're just fighting over in Iran or in Germany or whatever, I'm not going to want to go over there and get involved.

                                             Bronwyn,   age 15

Our heroes died in childbirth.
Our geniuses were never taught to read or write.
WOMAN'S RIGHTS POSTER

What Is ERA and Do We Need It?

The Equal Rights Amendment:
   Section I: Equality of rights under the law shall not be denied or abridged by the United States or by any State on account of sex.
   Section II: The Congress shall have the power to enforce, by appropriate legislation, the provisions of this article.
   Section III: The amendment shall take effect two years after the date of ratification.

That's all there is to the controversial Equal Rights Amendment—a simple, forthright declaration of human rights as they apply to women.

The reason I'd like to take some time to discuss ERA with you is that so much confusion seems to be gathering around it—so much volatile rhetoric and misunderstanding that I'd like to get down to basics and tell you as best I can what I know of it.

Why Do We Need ERA?

When the Constitution was framed, women were considered an inferior sex. Even a man as enlightened as Thomas Jefferson said, "Were our state a pure democracy . . . , there would still be excluded from our deliberations: . . . women, who, to prevent depravation of morals and ambiguity of issues, could not mix promiscuously in the public meetings of men." In other words, women were not deemed capable of having rights. Our rights were expected to be decided entirely at the discretion of men. In essence, this meant that like children or cattle, women belonged to their husbands, to do with as they would.

For more than one hundred years, the courts systematically rejected women's attempts to remedy this unfair situation. Women attempted to make use of the Fourteenth Amendment, which gave every person "equal protection of the laws," as a means of gaining fair treatment in the courts, but it was not until the Nineteenth Amendment was ratified, in 1920, that women gained the right to vote, and therefore began to be listened to as a potential political force.

Since then, women have striven to have rewritten those laws which are discriminatory on a sexual basis. The trouble is that we must challenge these laws *one at a time* in the courts, and this can take an enormous length of time. Did you know that until a very short time ago some states did not permit a woman to own property? If she inherited some, it automatically became her husband's. Did you know that a woman is currently, under the law of the country, *not* an equal citizen with a man? At the rate we are going, it could take two hundred more years to eradicate gender-based discrimination from our country's laws, and even then without ERA we have no guarantee that such discrimination will not reappear.

What the Fuss Is All About

As I see it, the reason the whole issue has become so fuzzy is that a lot of hyperemotional rhetoric has confused people. People are reading many peculiar issues into what is a simple fifty-word statement of human rights. The draft issue is currently the most volatile case in point. Opponents of ERA say that if it is passed, women can be drafted—not a very pleasant thought, I agree. On the other hand, is it really fair to expect men to be the only ones who do their share in a national emergency? I think we might bear in mind that conscription into the Army does not necessarily mean combat duty. Surely, no woman who is not fit for combat duty would be expected to serve on the combat lines. No woman with a small child would ever be drafted—remember, there are common-sense exceptions to the draft, even for men. Physical disability, child-dependent responsibilities and hardship—all constitute reasons why a man may *not* be drafted. It doesn't seem likely that women would be treated less sensibly.

Opponents of ERA list other problems, some of which are really rather amusing. They worry about unisex bathrooms popping up—a rather ludicrous fear, don't you think? It seems highly unlikely that our entire social system as it applies to lavatories would be disturbed in the least by women having equal rights under the law! Opponents claim women will no longer have the right to financial support for their young, or to alimony. Truth is, the current system of support for wife and child is woefully inadequate. Less than 20 percent of the alimony and child support awarded to women by courts ever really gets paid to them. It is probable that if ERA passed, and women's legal rights were strengthened, there would be *more* likelihood of reforms which would actually bolster a woman's legal position rather than erode it.

ERA opponents fear the destruction of the family, as if by getting equal legal rights, women would somehow be forced out of the home and into the labor market. I believe this fear to be unreasonable. Economic necessity, as well as the flowering of women's sense of self, is already altering the complexion of the family, with 58 percent of women working outside the home, as well as inside it. ERA or not, this trend is likely to continue.

Family life tends to evolve from generation to generation; most children don't get up in the morning these days and milk the cows or plant the fields, as they once did—yet the family system has managed to carry on despite these changes in lifestyle. Inasmuch as history has shown us that the family system tends to regroup, find new options, and adapt itself to progress, I see no reason to suppose that equal rights will alter the future family in any deleterious way.

What the ERA Would Do

Very simply, the Equal Rights Amendment would end discrimination against women based on sex, in all areas of life. The ERA would end discrimination against women in academe, athletics, job selection and financial remuneration for work done. If a woman has the capability of being a construction worker, a jet pilot, a general, a professional football player, a judge—or a wife and a mother—she could pursue that goal with the complete protection of the law.

- It would assure equal pay for equal work: a condition which is far from having been achieved.
- It would discourage the channeling of women into the lowest-paid jobs on the employment scale.
- It would allow women the same credit potential as men.
- It would assure equal property division in a divorce.
- It would encourage a rearranging of the Social Security system so that a working woman's family would get the same benefits as a man's.
- It would strengthen the legal climate in which women are working for many legal reforms, like reducing the incidence of wife and child abuse.
- It would allow women a stronger legal voice in working toward the formation of quality child-care programs.
- In short, it would assure women the same protections under the laws of our land as are currently assured only to men.

Where Does ERA Stand?

Thirty-five of the thirty-eight states necessary for ratification have already voted for ERA. Because the seven-year period of ratification, which ended in 1979, now has been granted a three-year extension, it is possible that some of the fifteen hold-out states (Alabama, Arizona, Arkansas, Florida, Georgia, Illinois, Louisiana, Mississippi, Missouri, Nevada, Oklahoma, North and South Carolina, Utah, Virginia) will ratify before the 1982 deadline.

Human Rights

One of the major problems ERA faces is, I believe, that the majority of women already feel they *are equal,* and therefore can see no reason to get excited about the issue. It is sometimes hard to feel passionate about "other people's" problems. As middle-class, educated women, we find it difficult to feel any serious abridgment of our own rights, yet inequities do exist and *shouldn't.* Perhaps that's the long and short of it. Equal rights for women is a fair and sensible concept. As such I believe it is worthy of consideration and support.

What it all comes down to, I believe, is common sense and *human rights.* It is hard to believe that any intelligent person would feel that every human being *shouldn't* have equal rights under the law.

I came upon an anonymous quotation addressed to women recently that moved me deeply. It read: "Our heroes died in childbirth. Our geniuses were never taught to read or write." It was said in reply to the often-heard slur that women haven't accomplished as much as men have, over the centuries. I was greatly touched by it, for it made me remember that until this century, women were not considered worthy of being educated, or of being permitted to vote, or of being able to use the courts, or of designing their own destiny. For the sake of those who have gone before us . . . for the sake of self-respect . . . for the sake of our daughters in all generations to come . . . I would urge you to give the equal rights issue some conscientious thought.

"Equality of rights under the law shall not be denied or abridged by the United States or by any State on account of sex."

In deciding if you are for or against ERA, your generation, like mine, is being called upon right now to decide how you feel about that simple concept.

Footnote

If you wish to learn more about ERA you might contact any of the following organizations for information.

ERAmerica
1525 M Street, N.W.
#602
Washington, D.C. 20005   (202) 833-4354

League of Women Voters
1730 M. Street, N.W.
Washington, D.C. 20036   (202) 296-1170

National Organization for Women
425 13th Street, N.W.
Washington, D.C. 20004   (202) 347-2279

National Women's Political Caucus
1411 K Street, N.W.
Washington, D.C. 20005   (202) 347-4456

Women's Equity Action League
805 15th Street, N.W.
Washington, D.C. 20005   (202) 638-4560

Business & Professional
Women's Association
2012 Massachusetts Avenue, N.W.
Washington, D.C. 20036   (202) 298-1100

This whole misunderstanding about equal rights is absurd, because nobody wants man and woman to be the same. "Equal" just means that you have the same rights as men, it doesn't mean you're the same as they are, but everyone seems to be confused by what's going on between the sexes.

Bronwyn,   age 15

For ages, tradition has said that man is superior and woman is submissive. I think a lot of women are trying to blame every single man in the world for this unfair idea that they were brought up with. It's really not fair to men to feel that way. Most men are trying, I think, to adjust to equal rights. I think most men agree with Women's Lib and the ERA.

Lola,   age 15

I happen to think that a woman can be a big business person—a business tycoon—and still be a lady. And I don't know what's wrong with a man for opening a door for you. It's just good manners. I'm getting really angry that Women's Lib is ruining the politeness men and women used to show each other.

Lola,   age 15

I think the majority of women want and believe in equal rights, but they don't want to associate with the Women's Libbers who seem to hate men so much. It doesn't mean that you're not equal because you happen to think that it's nice for a man to open a car for you.

Bronwyn,   age 15

I understand that everybody needed equal rights because women didn't have any rights, before. It's hard for us to know that now, because in our generation everybody has equal rights, but in the early days women weren't even permitted to vote, so it's understandable that they had to fight back. Women in some states until about ten years ago couldn't own property. But now that they're treated as equals, I don't see why those militant women have to be so nasty to men. I really like men.

Bronwyn, age 15

I think burning bras is the dumbest idea I have ever heard of.

Cee Cee, age 14

I don't want ERA, because it'll mean I'll have to go to war. I don't see why giving up exemptions from the draft is going to make women better off.

Cee Cee, age 14

I think the Women's Libbers are asking too much, and they're speaking for everybody. I don't think the way they do, so I don't understand why they're speaking for me. I think more women feel as I do than as these militant Women's Libbers do.

Lola, age 15

The reason that I think the whole ERA thing has gotten out of whack is because of these militant women who are really angry and hostile and who really want to hurt men. It's as simple as that. They really are angry with men, and they want to get back at them. They're screwing it all up for everybody else.

Bronwyn, age 15

Well, let those Women Lib people go to war. If they want to go to war, let them join up! I think a lot of women will just get pregnant so they don't have to go.

Cee Cee, age 14

I think men and women are both being stupid about this ERA, because they have gotten tangled up with "Okay, if you're equal, then we don't have to be gracious or mannerly toward you." Well, that's crazy. But a lot of women are going along with it. A lot of women are saying, "Don't light my cigarette, don't open the door, don't pull out the chair, don't do anything gentlemanly," so it's getting spoiled for everybody, ERA or not.

Cee Cee,   age 14

11

ENVOY

> *I've been through it all, baby.*
> *I'm Mother Courage.*
>   ELIZABETH TAYLOR

Looking Backward

I've been into a period of intensive soul-searching lately—partially because of writing these notes to you, partially because of your becoming fourteen and fifteen years old. Somehow, in my darkest moments, fourteen and fifteen seemed like the lights at the end of the tunnel, as if getting you to those ages would mean I had won my epic battle with the world. So today you, Bronwyn, are fifteen years of age. Twelve days from now, you, Cee Cee, will turn fourteen—you cannot in your wildest dreams imagine what that means to me.

Astrologically, fourteen- and twenty-eight-year cycles are said to mark the passage of Saturn, the celestial taskmaster. According to those who believe in such things, growth and evolution of the soul are the hard-won gifts he bestows. Somehow, sitting here today, writing in my creaky rocker reminiscent of the one in which I used to sing you both to sleep, I seem acutely sensitive to the possibility of such a cosmic cycle.

Fourteen years ago I left North Carolina, one of you tucked firmly under each arm. An ending and a beginning. A rite of passage. Never since that moment have I been without you both, still, in my mind's eye, each metaphysically tucked snugly beneath an arm, despite the fact that you are mostly women now.

It seems to me an appropriate time for musing on the passage of those years, the lessons learned, the growth marked like your height on the doorframe of my spirit. Just for the record, I'd like to tell you a few things today.

Despite the fact that I may be tarred and feathered by an angry mob of working mothers for this statement, I think you both would have been better off if I hadn't had to work when you were tiny. I know all the good parts about mothers working; how their children grow up fast and independently; how they learn to cope with everything and anything; how they become self-sufficient. All good, useful tools. Nonetheless, I think the demands on you were too great, the rewards too late in coming. It was unfair for you to have to worry about house-keepers' incompetence, or their possible cruelty. Unfair for you to have to worry about money, unfair for you to have to be patient about the nights I worked to support us, unfair not to have had me there when you came home from school bubbling over with thoughts to share. I know, of course, that all these items on my "unfair" list were probably good reality training, but in my heart of hearts I would have wished for you a kinder and a softer reality.

Many mothers, like me, have no choice but to work. They, like me, are comforted, I suspect, by all the modern verbiage about how children are better off with a fulfilled mother who works, than with an angry and frustrated mother who stays home against her will to mind her young. And yet, surely, it is only common sense to think that best of all for a child would be a mother who stays home and finds fulfillment taking extra-loving care of her children.

Without pretending to have the answers to what is to become of a woman's job and career while she stays home to mind her baby for a year or two, I still believe that for the child you love, it would be the better way.

My other reverie has to do with age. People are having their children when they are older now than in any other generation. While there's a lot to be said for the maturity and self-knowledge they will bring to the process of parenthood, still I believe there was a lot to be said for the stamina, vitality and youthful spirit that I brought to the task at twenty-three and twenty-four. I was looking at a snapshot in the family album today, taken when you were eighteen months and thirty months old, sitting on my very young lap, playing with my long loose hair. I was riveted by the realization of what a young girl I was then; what a fresh and tender facade for you to relate to. If the truth be known, I've liked our growing up together.

I think you've done a remarkable job of growing up so far—such a tough undertaking these days. I can't tell you how glad I am that having watched you arrive at your fourteenth and fifteenth birthdays, I find that the light I was looking forward to at the end of that tunnel is really quite dazzling. Now that we're out in the sunshine, I'm really looking forward to what the future promises for us all.

It was a hardship for me because you worked when I was small. I don't think mothers should work when children are little, because the kids really suffer from it.

Cee Cee,   age 14

I think it's great for women to work outside the home. I think it's good for the woman, and I think it gives the kids a sense of independence. If your mother's home twenty-four hours a day, you're not going to learn maturity early. You always worked when I was little, and I thought that was fine, because I had the whole house to myself and I felt very grown-up and independent.

Bronwyn,   age 15

I think kids should have parents who love them, and as long as your parents show you that they love you, then it's okay if they work.

Gigi,   age 15

The biggest problem I had with you working was when I got to be ten or eleven and we still had a housekeeper, because you didn't think I was old enough to stay by myself. That made me so mad, but my younger sister always said, "Mommy, you can't go out unless we have a babysitter," so I was stuck with it.

Bronwyn,   age 15

I know that being a woman in business is busy and demanding and I know that you've had to support us, Mom, and that's why you work so hard. I'm proud of your doing well in business. We're not poor and we're not rich—but we're in the middle, and you got us that way, and I'm really proud of that because I think it's very hard for women to get to be very successful in business.

Cee Cee,   age 14

> *May the Force be with you.*
> OBI BEN KENOBI,
> to the Jedai Knights

Envoy

My dear, dear daughters. There's so much I'd like to tell you about that I expect I may keep on writing as things occur to me, forever. Nonetheless, I've come to the last page, for now.

I love you so. If I were to try to spell out what I hope will be yours in the years to come (and if it could be put into words, a very difficult and inadequate medium where things of the spirit are concerned), it would go something like this:

With all my heart I wish you a life filled to the brim with adventure, contentment, contrast, constructiveness, fearlessness, common sense, happiness, laughter and love. I wish you knowledge, experience, daring and dreams. I wish you a strong and sturdy sense of yourselves, trust in your own instincts, and enjoyment of the special pleasures of being a woman. I wish you a husband whom you love truly, who loves you truly in return. And, finally, I wish you children who will bring to you what you have given me—a lifetime of learning, of sharing, of expansion and of love.